Praise for the Book

'Deftly and with great vividness, Manu S. Pillai takes us through 400 years of roiling history and returns the Deccan to the centre of our attention – where it belongs.' **Sunil Khilnani**

'Minutely researched and yet instantly accessible . . . *Rebel Sultans* will bring the fascinating history of the medieval Deccan to a whole new generation of readers.' **William Dalrymple**

'With enviable elan and ease this book recreates the history of the Deccan in the late medieval and early modern times. It is a marvellous achievement and will stoke future scholarship on the area and era.' **Rudrangshu Mukherjee**

'In this lively study, Manu S. Pillai does a superb job of re-orienting the narrative of late medieval and early modern South Asia towards the Deccan.' **Muzaffar Alam**

'In *Rebel Sultans*, the Deccan is presented in seven engaging chapters, each focused on a pivotal moment, character or symbol, that together trace the dynamic history of the region and convey its unique flavour.' **Navina Najat Haidar**

'One of India's finest young historians . . . Pillai unravels a forgotten chapter in our medieval past . . . A charming and contemporary history book.' *Times of India*

'Elegant and lucid . . . Pillai's book is significant not only because it is the first history of the Deccani Sultanates written for a general audience, but also because of the breadth of sources it integrates . . . an excellent contribution.' *Studies in History*

'Impressive . . . dazzling storytelling. Pillai has employed an extraordinarily powerful imagination and a prodigious talent with words to write a genuine thriller that is near impossible to shut before reaching the end.' *Indian Express*

'*Rebel Sultans* provides the much-needed bridge between the isolated world of academia and wider public audience . . . Writing in an eloquent and lucid style, Pillai holds his readers spellbound through a sweeping narration.' *The Hindu*

'One of India's finest young historians.' *Open*

'One of the brightest young writers in India today.' **DailyO**

'Engaging . . . *Rebel Sultans* is a remarkable, daring book.' *Hindustan Times*

'A fascinating book, with delectable minutiae in ~~practically~~ ~~e~~very page . . . Manu Pillai's volume tells us, succi~~nctly~~ . . . ~~turbu~~lent history of 500 years of the Deccan . . . [i~~

'Explores the rich tapestry of historical figures with nimble prose that in no way compromises on academic rigour; the result is an enjoyable, illuminating journey into the middle India of yore.' *Week*

'[A] fine book . . . [Pillai's] approach is nuanced . . . He is convincing when he is assertive . . . [this] is scholarship.' *Business Standard*

'Positively racy . . . a fast-paced greatest hits of the region's medieval roller-coaster ride.' **Scroll**

'For all its meticulous detail, *Rebel Sultans* is an enjoyable read.' *India Today*

'A historian of note.' *Mid Day*

'An engaging narrative, replete with riveting tales and compelling characters.' **SouthWord**

Rebel Sultans

The Deccan from Khilji to Shivaji

Manu S. Pillai

juggernaut

JUGGERNAUT BOOKS
C-I-128, First Floor, Sangam Vihar, Near Holi Chowk,
New Delhi 110080, India

First published in hardback by Juggernaut Books 2018
Published in paperback 2020

This book was made possible through a grant from the
Sandeep and Gitanjali Maini Foundation.

10 9 8 7 6 5 4 3 2 1

ISBN 9789353451066

Typeset in Adobe Caslon Pro by R. Ajith Kumar, Noida

Printed and bound at Thomson Press India Ltd

For Andyamichi

Contents

Chronology of the principal events mentioned in this book

1206: Founding of the Delhi Sultanate

1296: Alauddin Khilji's triumph over the Yadavas of Devagiri

1308: Second invasion of Devagiri by Malik Kafur

1310: Malik Kafur's triumph over the Kakatiyas of Warangal

1311: Malik Kafur's triumph over the Hoysalas of Dwarasamudra

1313: Annexation of Devagiri by Malik Kafur

1318: Rebellion of Prataparudra of Warangal quashed

1320: Rise of the Tughluq dynasty in Delhi

1321: Defeat of Sultanate forces at Warangal

1323: Prataparudra is defeated and Warangal is annexed

1325: Muhammad bin Tughluq becomes Sultan

1327: Daulatabad (formerly Devagiri) named capital of the Tughluqs

1335: Tughluqs resume ruling from Delhi

1336: Harihara I, son of Sangama, launches the Vijayanagar empire

1342: The last Hoysala sovereign is hanged in Madurai

1345: Amirs of the Deccan rebel against the Tughluqs

1346: Sangama brothers celebrate their conquests in the south

1347: Hasan Gangu crowned first Bahmani Sultan in Daulatabad

1347: Gulbarga becomes the Bahmani capital

1347: Sangama brothers first start using the title 'Sultan among Hindu Kings'

1351: Death of Muhammad bin Tughluq

1356: Death of Harihara I in Vijayanagar

1358: Death of Hasan Gangu

1363: Kapaya Nayaka presents the Bahmani Sultan the Turquoise Throne

1370: Vijayanagar annexes the short-lived Madurai Sultanate

1378: Bahmanis are defeated by Vijayanagar; a Sultan is murdered

1397: Firoz Shah Bahmani prevails at court and becomes Sultan

1406: Firoz Shah marries a Vijayanagar princess after a military victory

1418: Defeat of the Bahmanis by Vijayanagar

1422: Firoz Shah dies and Ahmad Shah becomes Sultan

1425: Devaraya II succeeds in Vijayanagar and opens an age of glory

1427: Bahmani Sultanate moves its capital to Bidar

1430: Vijayanagar absorbs large numbers of Muslim cavalrymen

1443: Assassination attempt against Devaraya II

1445: Abdur Razzak Samarqandi visits Vijayanagar as ambassador of the Persian Shah

1446: Death of Devaraya II; a slow crisis begins in Vijayanagar

1453: Mahmud Gawan arrives in the Deccan from Persia

1460: Arrival from Persia of the future Yusuf Adil Shah

1463: Mahmud Gawan becomes premier of the Bahmani Sultanate

1470: Sultan-Quli, the future Qutb Shah of Golconda, arrives in the Deccan

1472: Mahmud Gawan captures Goa

1481: Execution of Mahmud Gawan; decline of the Bahmanis begins, the Sultan politically emasculated

1485: Fall of the Sangama dynasty and rise of Saluva Narasimha in Vijayanagar

1489: Bidar comes under the Barid Shahs; the Bahmani Sultan made their puppet

1490: Nizam Shahi founded in Ahmadnagar

1490: Adil Shahi founded in Bijapur

1490: Imad Shahi founded in Berar

1502: The Adil Shah declares his state a Shia polity

1505: Tuluva dynasty (the Third dynasty) seizes power in Vijayanagar

1505: Vijayanagar proposes a marital alliance with the King of Portugal

1509: Krishnadeva becomes Raya of Vijayanagar and launches a second golden age

1510: The Adil Shah loses Goa to the Portuguese

1518: The Qutb Shah in Golconda becomes independent of the nominal sovereignty of the Bahmani Sultan

1520: Krishnadeva conquers Raichur from the Adil Shah

1523: Krishnadeva assumes the title of 'Restorer of Turkish Power'

1524: The Adil Shah and Nizam Shah seal a marital alliance but feud over territory

1526: Fall of the Delhi Sultanate and the rise of the Mughal empire in upper India

1527: The last Bahmani Sultan, Kalimullah, appeals to Mughal emperor Babur for help

1528: Kalimullah escapes Bidar and goes into exile in Ahmadnagar

1529: Krishnadeva dies in Vijayanagar; a period of crisis begins

1530: The Adil Shah resumes control of Raichur

1538: Kalimullah dies and the powerless Bahmani dynasty comes to an end

1542: Ramaraya becomes regent of Vijayanagar and centralizes power in himself

1543: Sultan Quli-Qutb Shah is assassinated; Jamshid becomes ruler; his brother Ibrahim goes into exile in Vijayanagar

1543: Miyan Ali of the Adil Shahi family goes under Portuguese protection

1545: Garcia da Orta comes to the Nizam Shah's court

1550: Jamshid dies and Ibrahim becomes the Qutb Shah in Golconda

1553: Husain Nizam Shah succeeds to the throne in Ahmadnagar

1555: Miyan Ali's attempt to seize the Adil Shahi throne with Portuguese aid fails

1558: Ali Adil Shah I comes to power in Bijapur and forms an alliance with Ramaraya of Vijayanagar against the Nizam Shahs

1561: Husain Nizam Shah sues for peace with Vijayanagar and the Adil Shah but resolves to fight again another day

1562: Ramaraya becomes de facto emperor in Vijayanagar

1564: The Qutb Shah, Adil Shah and Nizam Shah ally through marriage and form a league against Vijayanagar

1565: Vijayanagar is destroyed after the 'Battle of Talikota'; Ramaraya is killed

1570: The famous *Nujum al-Ulum* is produced at the Adil Shahi court

1571: Malik Ambar arrives as a slave in the Deccan

1574: The Nizam Shahs conquer Berar and the dynasty of the Imad Shahs ends

1580: Ali Adil Shah is succeeded by Ibrahim Adil Shah II; Chand Bibi becomes regent

1582: Chand Bibi retires to the Nizam Shahi court at Ahmadnagar

1588–91: Succession disputes and rivalries in Ahmadnagar; a Nizam Shah is assassinated

1589: The chronicler Ferishta arrives at the Adil Shahi court in Bijapur and writes his history

1591: Mughal Emperor Akbar turns his attention to the Deccan; a new Nizam Shah succeeds in Ahmadnagar

1591: The Qutb Shahs establish the city of Hyderabad outside Golconda

1595: The Nizam Shah dies and Ahmadnagar descends into factional chaos after the brief reign of a half-African Nizam Shahi prince

1595: Mughals lay siege to Ahmadnagar; Chand Bibi defends the city and terms are agreed

1596: Farrukh Beg, the painter, commences his thirteen-year stay at the Adil Shahi court

1597: Chand Bibi, with the Qutb Shah and Ibrahim Adil Shah II, fight the Mughals but the allies are defeated

1599: Chand Bibi is assassinated; Ahmadnagar falls into Mughal hands

1599: Ibrahim Adil Shah II establishes the city of Nauraspur

1600: Ibrahim Adil Shah II and the Qutb Shah send presents to Emperor Akbar

1600: Malik Ambar begins his resistance against the Mughals on behalf of a Nizam Shahi prince; his daughter is married to the new Nizam Shah

1603: Persian Shah seeks a marital alliance with the Qutb Shah in Golconda

1604: Ibrahim Adil Shah II meets jeweller Jacques de Coutre

1604: An Adil Shahi princess is given in marriage to Emperor Akbar's son

1605: Emperor Akbar dies and the reign of Jehangir begins in Agra

1610: Ibrahim Adil Shah II completes his *Kitab-i-Nauras;* the painter Cornelius Heda arrives in Bijapur

1610: Malik Ambar establishes his capital in Khirki (later named Aurangabad by Emperor Aurangzeb)

1616: Malik Ambar loses a major battle against the Mughals

1617: Ibrahim Adil Shah II comes to terms with the Mughals

1619: The Barid Shahi is destroyed and annexed by the Adil Shahi state

1624: Malik Ambar defeats the Mughals and regains his former prestige and power

1626: Death of Malik Ambar

1627: Death of Emperor Jehangir; Shahjahan succeeds to the Peacock Throne in Agra

1627: Ibrahim Adil Shah II dies in Bijapur

1630: A terrible famine ravages the Deccan; Shivaji Bhonsle is born to Shahji and Jijabai

1633: Malik Ambar's son surrenders what remains of the Nizam Shahi state to the Mughals

1636: The Adil Shah and Qutb Shah acknowledge the suzerainty of the Mughal emperor through two 'deeds'

1642: Shivaji is presented at the Adil Shahi court by his father

1643: Mir Muhammad Said emerges as the real power in the Qutb Shahi court and is appointed mir jumla (chief minister)

1647: Shivaji begins to expand his power from Pune and launches what will become the Maratha Swaraj, at the expense of the Adil Shahi state

1655: Mir jumla is dismissed by the Qutb Shah; the former seeks Mughal protection and brings Emperor Shahjahan's son Aurangzeb to Golconda; terms are agreed and a Golconda princess is married to Aurangzeb's son

1656: Aurangzeb lays siege to Bijapur and terms are negotiated with the Adil Shah; Bijapur loses territory to the Mughals

1658: Aurangzeb deposes his father and becomes Mughal emperor after a war of succession in the north

1659: Shivaji kills the Adil Shahi general sent to destroy him; Maratha power grows

1664: Shivaji sacks the Mughal port of Surat; war with the Mughals is escalated

1665: The Mughals, under Jai Singh, defeat Shivaji and terms are agreed

1666: The Mughals again lay siege to Bijapur but fail to take it

1666: Shivaji visits Agra but is placed under house arrest; he escapes

1670: Shivaji raids Surat again, swelling in power and wealth

1672: Abul Hasan, the last of the Qutb Shahs, comes to power in Golconda; real power is surrendered to a Brahmin minister, Madanna

1674: Golconda commences payment of protection money to the Marathas

1674: Shivaji crowns himself sovereign of the Maratha Swaraj

1679: Mughals return to Bijapur; terms are discussed and a princess is given in marriage to Emperor Aurangzeb's son

1680: Death of Shivaji and the succession of his son Sambhaji

1685: Madanna is assassinated in Golconda during a siege by the Mughals

1686: The Adil Shahi dynasty comes to an end and Bijapur falls to the Mughals

1687: The Qutb Shahi dynasty comes to an end and Golconda is annexed

1689: Sambhaji, king of the Marathas, is executed; Maratha resistance continues

1707: Emperor Aurangzeb dies; Mughal empire begins to decline

Introduction
Blood & Diamonds

Histories of the Deccan often begin with the story of Shivaji. But in this book Shivaji appears only at the end.

In 1630, when the Maratha noblewoman Jijabai brought forth the second of her two sons, little did she imagine that the boy would grow up to shatter forever the might of the Mughal empire. But the Deccan into which Shivaji arrived was already a fascinating place, populated by remarkable men and women who all claimed for themselves the esteem of posterity. In that very century, for instance, it had seen the daughter of an African slave become queen to a local potentate, cheerfully conspiring to murder a more favoured Persian wife. A few decades later, in another corner of the plateau, an ill-fated Brahmin minister curried favour with Aurangzeb, delivering to that emperor cartloads of mangoes, while plotting covertly to thwart His Majesty's imperial designs. The Deccan was that land where a Muslim prince warded off hysterical interventions by the orthodoxy when it was discovered that he exalted Hindu gods over the teachings of the Prophet. Saints and divines too solicited their share in this world of fortune, worshippers of Shiva descending every year upon a celebrated Muslim shrine. There were splendid palaces with golden thrones and forbidding fortresses with thunderous guns. Fine horses bred in Iraq trotted along the Deccan's roads, even as the region's elite succumbed to the sartorial fancies of their friends in Iran. Travellers from lands as diverse as Burma and France descended upon the Deccan's dusty plains, while its harems bewildered European doctors who encountered begums with skin as pale as their own. The Deccan, to the world, was uniquely Indian; to India, however, it was a mirror of the world.

It is this chapter in India's history that this book seeks to bring back to life. Too often the Deccan has been reduced to a mere battlefield in that titanic clash between Aurangzeb and Shivaji, everything else languishing in the shadow of their sensational vendetta. To be sure it is a story that must be told: It was in the Deccan, after all, that fearsome Aurangzeb – descendant of Genghis Khan and Timur the Lame – arrived as king, only to preside over the beginning of the end for the emperors of the Peacock Throne. It was here too that the Maratha Swaraj was born, its warriors springing forth in a volcanic burst of fury, flying their flag from Tanjore to Gwalior and from Bengal to Punjab. But the Deccan was remarkable even *before* the advent of the Marathas, witness to a saga launched long in advance of the first Mughal conquests in India. It was a different cast of Muslim kings who guided the Deccan's destiny in this era, rebels who broke from Delhi to seize lands where once reigned houses called Hoysala and Kakatiya. Together these Rebel Sultans birthed a whole new universe, a horizon both of breathtaking achievements and startling contradictions. And while they often fought and challenged one another, in the end they shaped a land that became the envy of the early modern world and the object of many an emperor's doomed desire. The Marathas and the Mughals are certainly important, then, but the splendours that tempted the latter, and the fire that propelled the former, emerged in a previous time, in a different context: that is the world into which we travel through this book, and that is the past we seek in the pages to follow.

The story of the Deccan has its roots deep in Indian history. The earliest chroniclers of the subcontinent paused at the river Narmada, giving the plateau across the water the Prakrit name 'Dakhina'. This in Sanskrit became 'Dakshina', eventually evolving into the now-familiar 'Deccan'.[1] In the first century CE, the mysterious *Periplus of the Erythraean Sea* named this triangular realm 'Dachinabades', the southern country, abundant in cotton and onyx, while the Chinese dreaded it in the fifth as Ta-Thsin, a 'precipitous' landscape where the 'roads [were] dangerous and difficult to find'.[2] In Emperor Ashoka's day, the Mauryas exercised a fragile suzerainty over these parts, but soon after his demise the Andhras of the Deccan threw off the northern yoke, swelling in power as the empire collapsed. In the fourth century, Samudragupta, king of Pataliputra, penetrated as far as Kanchi on the edge of the Tamil country, but was wise enough to accept pretended pledges of fealty over actually subduing these alien lands. For there could be no lasting triumph in the south, and no distant overlord prevailed forever – four hundred years after Samudragupta, the Rashtrakutas turned the tables of history, taking fire and steel into the very heart of the Gangetic belt.[3] Many were the twists and turns of time, but the Deccan remained unyielding in spirit and in its spine. To some it was a kingdom of tantalizing treasures and marvellous opportunity; to others, however, the Deccan became also something more sinister: the undoing of mighty kings, a graveyard of glorious empires.

To know India, then, we must know the Deccan. But to tell *all* its tales together is a daunting proposition – the land is rich, and a thousand pages would not suffice. The ambitions of the book you hold, therefore, are necessarily more modest. We begin in the age of the Sultans of Delhi, one of whom, Alauddin by name, marched to the south at the end of the thirteenth century, demolishing what lay accumulated from generations before. Heroic dynasties of whom we learn in ancient texts – Kakatiya, Yadava and Hoysala – were reduced to ashes, and the peninsula stood shaking at the crossroads of catastrophe. But from the ruins of that old world something new was created; something that endured for three and a half centuries, leaving an indelible mark on the destiny of the Indian people. It was from the ashes of that distant past, for example, that a band of brothers forged the kingdom of Vijayanagar, an empire painted as a bastion of Hindu resistance, when in fact it was something altogether more magnificent. The City of Victory, as we will see, was not a citadel of defensive orthodoxy but the seat of wondrous, brave innovation; its rulers wallowed not in a sea of religious resentments, but grasped keenly the attractions of an eclectic future. Men from the world over arrived in their capital, bringing old customs astride bold ideas: patterns seen in Persepolis were replicated in the mammoth pavilions of Vijayanagar, characters from Turkey and Arabia enshrined in its temple columns forever. The gaze of the Deccan's rulers may have rested upon an Indian landscape, but their minds beheld the astonishing vastness of the world beyond. By this they were enriched, invigorating also that greater narrative that is the story of India.

The Bahmani Sultanate that emerged from the clash between the Delhi Sultanate and ancient houses of the Deccan straddled the northern half of the plateau, growing also, like southern Vijayanagar, into an extraordinary place. But when that grand enterprise crumbled to dust, there were born five successor states, three of them destined for greatness. From Ahmadnagar ruled the Nizam Shahs, one of whom rained vengeance upon Vijayanagar in a battle unlike any other. In Bijapur emerged the Adil Shahs, thirsting for books and flirting with apostasy. And in Golconda, surrounded by earth bursting with gems, reigned the Qutb Shahs, their riches animating minds even in faraway America. Many are the stories that took shape around these courts: where there were treacherous eunuchs drawing princely blood, there were also servants of the state devoted to the country. While factions jostled for ascendance and gain, there were also warrior queens who embraced valour and led from the front. It was in the Deccan, at Goa, that the Portuguese established their principal post in India, reincarnating Muslim Alis into Christian Fernandos. Despite the gore in which it lay drenched, the Deccan created art too of striking originality – a portrait of the goddess of learning, Saraswati, for instance, unprecedented in its Islamic form, or of a Hindu yogini bearing influences from countries as distant as China. And, thus, between everything else that occurred in the heartless sweep of time, this land left upon history a mark that transcended the impetuous doings of imperfect men, touching those higher realms that revitalized an entire civilization. For this too, then, the Deccan must be recognized.

Death and damnation, of course, came to these dazzling kingdoms in the fullness of time, and friendless monuments are all that remain of them today. If you visit Golconda, for example, you will be greeted by a mountain of crumbling stone. Jean-Baptiste Tavernier saw a diamond worth half a million rupees in these parts,[4] while Jean de Thevenot claimed the Qutb Shah 'surpasse[d] all the Kings of the Indies in precious stones'.[5] Today the dungeons of Golconda are home only to colonies of bats, the graves of its former rulers awaiting vindication not in heaps of diamonds as much as mere coats of plaster and paint. But history is full of tragic tales – the real homage to the Deccan lies in learning from its exhilarating past. Free from prejudice, we discover, society can scale the heights of greatness. Divided and broken, on the other hand, doom is quick to ensnare. This was the curse of the Bahmanis and this too became the cancer which consumed our Rebel Sultans – united they could wreak destruction upon their common enemy in Vijayanagar in the south, but divided they fell, in the end, to the Mughals who were masters of the north. Their history is a mosaic of enduring wisdoms, a collective experience that is as much the Indian people's inheritance as those ruined edifices that amaze and astound. How we remember their lessons will vary, but remember them we must. For the Deccan was witness to the making of India, and the tribute India must pay is to remember and recall.

Life-size bronze images of Krishnadeva, Raya of Vijayanagar, with his two queens at the Venkateshvara temple in Tirupati, c. 1516

Prologue
The Emperor's Foot

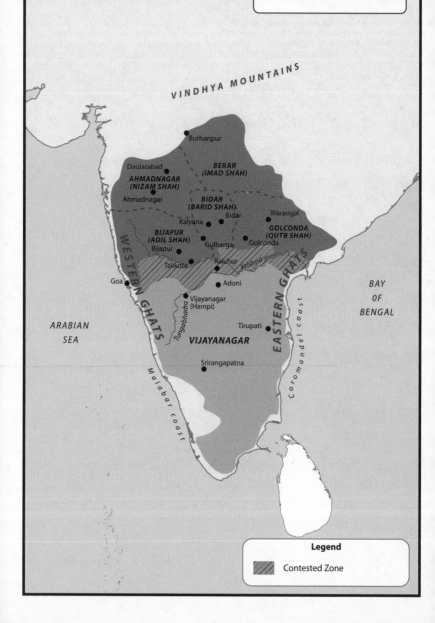

THE DECCAN IN 1520

VINDHYA MOUNTAINS

Burhanpur

Daulatabad
AHMADNAGAR
(NIZAM SHAH)
Ahmadnagar

BERAR
(IMAD SHAH)

BIDAR
(BARID SHAH)

Kalyana   Bidar

Warangal

BIJAPUR
(ADIL SHAH)
Bijapur

Gulbarga

GOLCONDA
(QUTB SHAH)
Golconda

Talikota   Raichur

Krishna

Goa

Adoni

ARABIAN
SEA

Vijayanagar
(Hampi)

Tungabhadra

Tirupati

BAY
OF
BENGAL

Coromandel coast

WESTERN GHATS

EASTERN GHATS

VIJAYANAGAR

Srirangapatna

Malabar coast

Legend

Contested Zone

On 19 May 1520, when Ismail Adil Shah, the ruler of Bijapur, hastily mounted his elephant to flee, he left behind much more than his princely honour writhing on the battlefield. Certain that victory would be quick, he had crossed the river Krishna with 18,000 cavalry, 120,000 infantry and not less than 150 elephants to wage war against the Raya of Vijayanagar, his hereditary rival to the south. These were, to be sure, stirring figures, but Ismail was well aware that his conventional military resources were several times *smaller* than the muscle and steel the legendary enemy king of Vijayanagar could marshal. What provided the Adil Shah a supreme air of assurance despite these circumstances, then, was not traditional parameters – it was his guns that would make all the difference. His calculation was correct, superficially speaking. But what he had forgotten to also calculate was the amount of time it would take his men to load and reload those very guns. In the end, their bovine slowness let him down, and when the Raya's 27,000 horsemen advanced like the wind to cut down the Adil Shah's horrified soldiers, hell showed itself on earth in an ocean of blood. It was narrowly that Ismail himself survived the carnage, and in his desperate retreat he left behind – on the wrong side of the river – almost 900 cannon, small and heavy, ready to be appropriated by the enemy he so gravely underestimated.[1]

The seed of the conflict between the Adil Shah and mighty Raya of Vijayanagar was as old as antiquity itself. Between the rivers Krishna and Tungabhadra lay the prized triangular district of Raichur, exquisitely fecund but also rich in iron and diamond deposits. In the days of yore, the Kakatiya and Hoysala dynasties had quarrelled over it, and the Chalukyas and Pallavas before them. And now, at the climax of the medieval age, the tract constantly attracted the covetous gaze of one or the other of the states that succeeded these ancient houses in the Deccan.[2] One of Vijayanagar's founders had held the district while the kingdom was still being forged – and on this rested their long-standing claim to Raichur.[3] In reality, though, for the most part the region had been under the control of the Muslim rulers of the northern Deccan, who viewed Raichur as an integral constituent of their own princely domains. In 1520 the doab happened to be in the infirm grasp of the Adil Shah who ruled from Bijapur,[4] till suddenly the Raya in the south, having conquered much of the peninsula and extended his rule nearly as far as the tip of the subcontinent, decided it was time to stake claim once again to Raichur fort, and to the valuable expanse of land that lay around it. And this for reasons of economics as much as sentiment.

Krishnadeva, the Raya of Vijayanagar, was a man who breathed magnificence. Poets heaped praise on him by the dozen, but the kingdom's Diamond Throne[5] was never meant to be his. To begin with, he was born to his father from an inferior wife, whereas his predecessor and half-brother emerged from a purer vessel.[6] When that brother was on his deathbed, the story goes, he made his minister promise to blind the ambitious Krishnadeva so that any threat to the royal prospects of his own children might be thwarted. The minister nodded at the disabled king, produced, it is said, goat's eyes as evidence of the deed being done and then proceeded to merrily install Krishnadeva on the throne anyway.[7] All rivals who lived were parcelled into a prison fortress far away, and soon Krishnadeva commenced his conquests (also finding time to compose half a dozen literary works on the side).[8] Perhaps having observed his own mother's plight, he elevated his beloved concubine, a dancer, to queenly status, married another princess and, after defeating the suzerain of Orissa, added his daughter also to the harem.[9] This latest wife, however, wasn't particularly pleased with being treated as a political compromise – the marriage was a failure both in terms of producing heirs as well as in her preference to keep as much distance from her royal husband as was possible.[10]

But domestic squabbles aside, Krishnadeva was a man destined for greatness, one subsequent text even painting him as an incarnation of Vishnu.[11] His flag flaunting the chakra and conch fluttered across campaigns in South India; as the Portuguese chronicler Faria y Sousa raved, when 'Crisnao Rao of Bisnaga' entered the field, his armies 'covered the plains and hills and stopped the flow of rivers'. Up to 700,000 men followed him, added to which was 'baggage in such quantities that courtesans alone numbered more than twenty thousand'.[12] Sanskrit inscriptions were more flamboyant. So overcome was the sun, we are told, by Krishnadeva's shining glory, that it sank 'into the western ocean as if quite unable to endure the distress of mind'.[13] The imperial vaults, meanwhile, were believed to shelter treasure worth more than a hundred crores, six crores of it in precious stones; their value a thousand times more in today's money.[14] Though his ancestral origins lay along the coast of Karnataka, the king donated more generously to temples in the Andhra and Tamil regions of his empire – starting in 1513 he visited Tirupati six times, showering the deity with riches, presenting also an arresting bronze image of himself with his two favourite queens. For all this, however, he was tormented by matters of succession. He had daughters (one of whom was a poet), and three sons. The first two died untimely deaths well before their illustrious father and the third was too young. So, in the end, Krishnadeva's heir would come from that very fortress where he had locked up those blue-blooded rivals he feared could challenge his power and state.

His dynastic travails notwithstanding, Krishnadeva remained the picture of gallantry. 'The king,' wrote traveller Domingos Paes, 'is of medium height and of fair complexion and good figure, rather fat than thin; he has on his face signs of smallpox . . . He is a great ruler and a man of much justice, but subject to sudden fits of rage'.[15] Every morning, reportedly, he drank a three-quarter pint of sesame oil, after which he 'anoints himself all over with the same oil; he covers his loins with a small cloth, and takes in his arms great weights made of earthenware, and then, taking a sword, he exercises himself with it till he has sweated out all the oil, and then he wrestles with one of his wrestlers'. After gymming so (and making a right royal display of it), 'he mounts a horse and gallops about the plain in one direction and another till dawn, for he does all this before daybreak'. When it was time to appear in court, he would throw on a tunic embroidered with 'many roses in gold', a brocade cap crowning his head 'like a Galician helmet'.[16] The only anomaly, as far as Paes could discern, was that the king was permanently barefoot. But seated on the Diamond Throne, surrounded by his ministers, Brahmins and robed eunuchs,[17] Krishnadeva was without doubt an impressive figure, one who certainly appeared capable of accomplishing any challenge he set himself, no matter how daunting.

All through the first decade of his reign, the Raya of Vijayanagar had carefully watched affairs north of the Tungabhadra. The whole of the northern Deccan – from the west coast to the east – had once been the dominion of the Bahmani Sultan, and from at least 1444, if not earlier, the Rayas had delivered sporadic tribute to this king, oscillating between willing submission and succumbing to military coercion.[18] By Krishnadeva's time, however, this traditional foe (and pretender 'overlord') was diminished into a hopeless nonentity. Emasculated and unable to resist the seditious designs of former governors like the Adil Shah, by the eve of the battle of Raichur in 1520, the titular Bahmani Sultan had been reduced to picking jewels out of his own crown and selling them for money – and this after denuding his throne of its gems.[19] His most powerful noblemen – the Nizam Shah, Qutb Shah, Adil Shah, and others – fought over the remains of the ailing state, carving out principalities for themselves though lip service was paid to the puppet Sultan and consolation offered by having coins still minted in his name. Beyond that, however, it was patent to everybody that the sun had set on the house of Bahmani; the last of them would, after Krishnadeva's lifetime, eventually escape his palace in disguise, board a boat to Mecca and disappear into perfect and indisputable oblivion.[20]

It was now, in 1520, discerning opportunity in the northern chaos, that Krishnadeva marched into Raichur and besieged the fort. The original structure was built by a Kakatiya general over two centuries before, with such massive slabs of granite that locals were convinced the walls could not be the creation of mortals. In the late 1460s the Bahmanis reinforced the inner citadel with strong outer walls, 'capitalizing on new engineering technology imported from north India and the Middle East', constructing a 'moat, numerous bastions, and imposing gates on the city's eastern and western ends'.[21] Fernao Nuniz, the Portuguese horse trader, noted that the walls of the fort were mounted with at least 200 heavy guns, and very many smaller ones, while thirty catapults were also available to the soldiers at Raichur to shoot large rocks at invaders.[22] The garrison itself was sizeable given the importance of the district to the Adil Shah – 8000 men were stationed inside, with 400 cavalry and twenty elephants, allowing for adequate manpower to reinforce the fort's impregnable walls. When Krishnadeva arrived, however, he came with nearly three times that many horsemen and over half a million infantry, instantly making known to the Adil Shah of Bijapur that if he didn't hasten to Raichur's defence in person, it would not remain in his hands for long.[23]

The pretext Krishnadeva furnished to invade Raichur was primarily, like most such pretexts, an innovative fabrication (if it was not manufactured in the fertile imagination of a chronicler, that is). A merchant who owed the government of Vijayanagar a certain sum of money was believed to be absconding in the Adil Shah's territory, and since the latter would not deliver him to the Raya, compensation would be forced.[24] Stranger causes had, in the past, led to war between the rulers of the northern and southern Deccan, conveniently shrouding more naked strategic calculations. In one instance, the Bahmani Sultan sent musicians who entertained him at court to his southern 'vassal', instructing him to settle their bill. When Vijayanagar refused to swallow the insult – and had the Bahmani envoy paraded on a donkey[25] – the two kings clashed.[26] In yet another instance a century earlier, a Raya of Vijayanagar heard of the beauty of a goldsmith's daughter in Raichur. When she refused to hop into his harem, he decided to send an army to seize her – the district also in the bargain. War was provoked once again on this admittedly spurious ground, with Vijayanagar comprehensively routed, compelled to shell out thirty-three lakh gold hons,[27] and the goldsmith's daughter taken not south but north into the harem of the Bahmani Sultan's son.[28] The son, as it happened, was later blinded and discarded, so the fate of the beauty from Raichur could not have been a very happy one, either way.[29]

In any case, in 1520, whether or not a merchant fleeing his creditor was involved, the Raya of Vijayanagar was himself now in Adil Shahi territory. Unfortunately for Krishnadeva, he did not possess artillery capable of smashing the sturdy walls of Raichur fort.[30] But ever resourceful, and with his mind perfectly equipped to seek simple answers to complicated problems, he deployed men with pickaxes and crowbars to start breaking through the walls in the most primitive fashion (with an additional duty to drag back corpses of all those who died from stones hurled by the defenders above).[31] The Adil Shah's men, meanwhile, had guns they could fire at the invaders, but these were mounted in so inflexible a manner that they could not be turned downwards to incinerate the crowbar-wielding workers – the former had all the technology, but were still not in a position to exploit it to their advantage.[32] Respite, however, arrived for a few days after three months of hacking and aimless shooting – hearing that the Adil Shah had crossed the river Krishna, the Raya lifted the siege and proceeded to meet his enemy. As Nuniz put it, 'Crisnarao, without even telling anyone, ordered to saddle a horse, and he rode at full speed' towards Ismail, halting only to collect some war horses from Portuguese traders on the road, even as his army scrambled to follow as quickly as they could.[33]

The battle on 19 May was a spectacular debacle for the Adil Shah of Bijapur. His guns were powerful and, early in the confrontation, Krishnadeva was adequately paranoid to remove his ring and ask a page to deliver it to his queens in case he died.[34] Guns, however, were but rarely used in the battlefields of the Deccan, and a tactical error by the Adil Shah's inexperienced forces opened a window of opportunity for the Raya's men – the gunners were in a single file, shooting all at once, so after an initial assault *all* of them were caught trying to reload, unable, then, to sustain pounding the enemy. Quickly the Raya's horses moved in and pushed the bulk of the Adil Shah's forces straight into the river they had just forded with such fanfare and certainty. To add insult to injury, the Vijayanagar soldiers then opened fire on the Adil Shah's drowning men, presumably with the very guns they had just abandoned, bringing matters to an especially disastrous finish – it was Krishnadeva who finally instructed his men to stand down, for enough blood had already reddened the flow.[35] The Persian chronicler Ferishta, sympathetic to the Adil Shah, would later blame the ignominy the latter endured on the fact that he was drunk – it was the alcohol that addled his senses and caused him to rush across the river to challenge Krishnadeva without thought.[36] And indeed, the story goes, Ismail vowed that he would not touch wine or succumb to vice till he restored not only Raichur to his dominions but also honour to his manhood.[37] More likely, however, it was foolish overconfidence that eroded the man's standing and brought upon him his most embarrassing defeat.

Having delivered more than a bloody nose to the Adil Shah, Krishnadeva now returned to Raichur fort with the remainder of his army, and a special mercenary force of twenty Portuguese snipers.[38] Before they knew it, the defenders were picked one by one off the fort walls, and on 14 June, when the commander of the garrison decided to stick his head out from one of the embrasures (openings in the fort walls) he was rewarded instantly with a shot through his head.[39] Morale died a painful death on the Adil Shahi side, and the next day the fort gates were unlocked, a flag of surrender raised. The garrison having bent the knee, Krishnadeva marched in and assumed formal charge of Raichur fort. All the historically disputed land that lay around it was now his, not to speak of the sheer prestige of once again being in possession of an ancestral domain that those before him had failed to recover. To commemorate his triumph, a northern gateway was added to the fort with a 'large inner courtyard whose upper walls contain narrative sculptural panels depicting scenes from the Mahabharata, the Ramayana' and other Hindu traditions. This, evidently, was intended as a 'deliberate attempt to stamp a distinctively Vijayanagar aesthetic onto this frontier site' that for so long had languished in the hands of the enemy.[40]

The Adil Shah, meanwhile, after a convalescence that involved licking the wounds to his pride and person, eventually dispatched an envoy to Vijayanagar to treat with the Raya. Not only did Ismail seek the return of Raichur to him, he also wanted all the guns and artillery that had been captured in the wake of his inglorious defeat to be couriered back. What followed was 'an extraordinary round of diplomacy', quite without parallel in the history of the Deccan.[41] Krishnadeva, savouring his delicious victory which 'was known all over India, and also in other regions of the interior',[42] kept Ismail's ambassador waiting for weeks before condescending to grant him an audience. When at last the Bijapuri envoy had the ear of the king, he directed towards it a sequence of strongly worded accusations – that it was Vijayanagar that broke the peace by invading the Adil Shah's territory, that the latter 'does not know why thou hast left thy kingdom and made such a war on him'. Moreover, while the annexation of Raichur might be 'pleasing to thyself', it was, clearly, an 'evil' proceeding, devoid of all justice and propriety.[43] Raichur belonged by law to the Adil Shah, concluded the messenger, and Vijayanagar had trespassed on its august neighbour's rightful possessions as much as it had battered his dignity.

Krishnadeva did not answer immediately. Having bestowed the usual honours on the ambassador he dismissed the man for the day, and waited till the next morning to summon him into court again. He would be happy, the Raya declared, to grant all of Ismail's wishes and to restore everything to him, 'provided', however, that 'the Ydallcao [Adil Shah] would come and kiss his foot'.[44] The insult was explicit, its severity not lost on anybody. It was also an indication that while Krishnadeva, owing to his own mixed origins, was generally sympathetic to the plight of the weak, he was also capable of 'an equal arrogance and insolence' towards those he counted as enemies.[45] But the envoy conveyed Krishnadeva's special message to his master regardless, and awaited his response. When it came, Ismail expressed that while he was 'of full mind joyfully to do that which the King wishes', as a sovereign ruler, he could not enter the territory of another prince.[46] In other words, kissing the Raya's foot was not the problem; the difficulty was of a technical and legal nature in entering foreign territory to do so. Perhaps the Adil Shah didn't know how else to respond.

Enjoying his moment of glory and the undignified quandary in which the Adil Shah was placed, Krishnadeva proposed, in that case, to himself call on Ismail and present his royal foot so the needful could be done. And without bothering to wait for a reply, the Raya and his armies proceeded to the frontier, and there, not finding a prostrate Ismail with lips in readiness to perform, decided to travel a few steps further, straight to the Adil Shahi capital of Bijapur. Embarrassed and with no intention absolutely of kissing any part of the triumphant invader's body, Ismail fled his palace. Naturally, it was Krishnadeva who had the last laugh. Having made his point and demonstrated to the world that the Adil Shah was a mouse before his might, the Raya returned to Vijayanagar. The capital he departed, famed as 'the best city' in all the south, meanwhile, 'was left almost in ruins'.[47] Incidentally, it was not his final visit to the northern Deccan – in 1523, some years before the last of the Bahmani Sultans absconded from India, Krishnadeva would call again on the upstart rulers like the Adil Shah who had impoverished their titular king. Defeating them, he would crown the last of the Bahmanis himself, confirming the latter (in theory) as monarch in the north, by his own royal command.

It was a strange twist in the saga of the Deccan. Once, not long ago, the Vijayanagar kings had been compelled to pay tribute to the Bahmanis; now they had been reincarnated as kingmakers to restore what honour was left to that aged Muslim dynasty. The wheels of time had turned their overlords into a void, while the star of the reluctant 'vassals' seemed destined to rise forever. Among the numerous titles

Krishnadeva flaunted that day, one more was added – one that was especially sensational and yet remains perhaps the least known of his countless honours. The Raya of Vijayanagar, it was announced to all, was now also the Yavana Rajya Sthapana Acharya – the Hindu monarch who re-established the kingdom of the Turks.[48]

I

Sons of Fury
The Birth of the Bahmani Sultanate

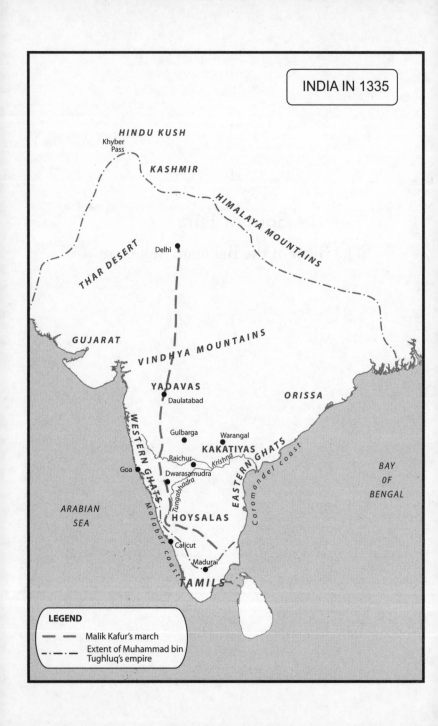

INDIA IN 1335

HINDU KUSH

Khyber
Pass

KASHMIR

HIMALAYA MOUNTAINS

THAR DESERT

Delhi

GUJARAT

VINDHYA MOUNTAINS

YADAVAS

Daulatabad

ORISSA

Gulbarga   Warangal

KAKATIYAS

Raichur

WESTERN GHATS

Krishna

EASTERN GHATS

Goa

Dwarasamudra

Tungabhadra

Coromandel coast

BAY
OF
BENGAL

ARABIAN
SEA

HOYSALAS

Malabar coast

Calicut

Madurai

TAMILS

LEGEND

— — —   Malik Kafur's march

—··—··—   Extent of Muhammad bin
           Tughluq's empire

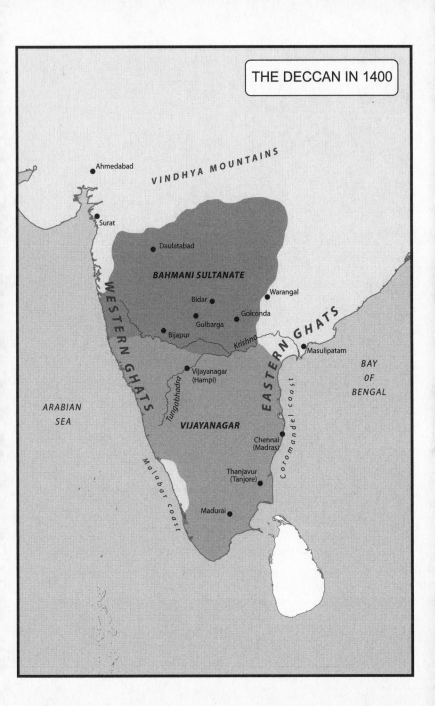

THE DECCAN IN 1400

Ahmedabad

VINDHYA MOUNTAINS

Surat

Daulatabad

BAHMANI SULTANATE

Bidar

Warangal

Gulbarga

Golconda

Bijapur

Krishna

WESTERN GHATS

EASTERN GHATS

Masulipatam

Vijayanagar
(Hampi)

Tungabhadra

BAY
OF
BENGAL

ARABIAN
SEA

VIJAYANAGAR

Coromandel coast

Chennai
(Madras)

Thanjavur
(Tanjore)

Malabar coast

Madurai

Long before Vijayanagar was celebrated as the City of Victory, it was the capital of the Yadava kings of the Deccan that poets eulogized in verse and song as the abode of the gods. In reality, of course, Devagiri was the abode not so much of the divine as much as of some exceedingly wealthy monarchs, talk of whose riches reached the ears of a Muslim prince far away in the north of India. It was he who changed forever the history of the south, and it was also this warrior-prince who opened a chapter in the story of India that many interpret as a totalizing clash of civilizations and a feud between two antagonistic religions and their cultures. The truth, of course, is a little more complicated.

Islam, tradition claims, had arrived on the Malabar coast during the lifetime of the Prophet himself, touching the Deccan at any rate by the tenth century thereafter. The process was peaceful, with traders serving as worthy ambassadors for the faith,[1] while some came seeking sanctuary from persecution in their own homelands.[2] In the Rashtrakuta kingdom, wrote the traveller Al Masudi, for instance, they were 'honoured and protected' and took to 'wearing the same dresses and having their beards grown in the same manner' as Hindus of the region.[3] Islam's inauguration in the *north*, however, launched an age of conquest and violence – as Al Biruni wrote with typical flourish in the eleventh century: invaders from the west 'utterly ruined the prosperity of the country' and 'the Hindus became like atoms of dust scattered in all directions'.[4] But in due course the foreigners settled down, and their rule culminated in 1206 in the constitution of what is called the Delhi Sultanate.

India fascinated these Turkic newcomers, and soon they obtained a sense of the cultural magnificence of the land they now called home, invigorated also by a comprehension of the extraordinary wealth of the country. Ghiyasuddin Balban, the ninth Sultan, for instance, never set foot in the south. Yet he felt impelled to have his power flaunted in a classical idiom of hyperbole to a very *Indian* audience: a Sanskrit inscription from his reign proclaims how, when

> he issued forth on a military expedition . . . the Gaudas abdicated their glory; the Andhras, through fear, besought the shelter of the caves; the Keralas forsook their pleasures; the Karnatas hid themselves in defiles; the Maharashtras gave their places; the Gujaras resigned their vigour; and the Latas dwarfed themselves into Kiratas.[5]

And all this when the Keralas and Karnatas had, in all likelihood, no clue who Balban was or what exactly about his expeditions was so earth shattering. Furthermore, the Sultan, who claimed to be Allah's shadow, is also portrayed as Vishnu's representative among mortals, so that with the 'earth being now supported by this sovereign', the lord 'taking Laksmi on his breast and relinquishing all worries, sleeps in peace on the ocean of milk'.[6] Indeed, as late as the eighteenth century, the Brahmin Peshwas in the Deccan would also, in the *Parasaramacarita*, refer to this 'king of the Yavanas' as one who 'protected this earth with [such] justice' that all the peoples of India 'accepted these (Muslims) as their own'.[7] This is not to say that the early encounters were amicable – Muslims injected new technologies in arms and cavalry warfare and an unfamiliar conception of power into the subcontinent, and no battle was ever a painless communion. But for the patchwork of principalities, full of countless diversities, spread across the land in an already violent age, the addition of yet another series of political elements was not particularly unusual – or deserving of exceptional hatred. The strategic landscape swiftly acknowledged these new contenders, and India's leaders adapted to changed circumstances, as they had before and would again many times in the future. Where some fell, others emerged.

When Balban's dynasty was violently extinguished in a 1290 coup, the decidedly fierce Khiljis came to power in Delhi. With much of the north already under their command, the nephew of the new Sultan decided it was time to travel south, and Devagiri was the first capital Alauddin besieged. Though legend suggests he left court to get as far away as he could from a 'nagging wife and overbearing mother-in-law',[8] there is little doubt that the glitter of Devagiri's wealth offered a special motivation for Alauddin's enterprise. After all, he did think of himself as a formidable conqueror, eventually flaunting the title of Sikandar Sani, or Alexander II.[9] And as the historian Abdul Malik Isami records, with a forgivable touch of poetic excess, 'Every house [in Devagiri] possessed diamonds and was full of silver and gold . . . In every street gold could be found in unlimited quantities . . . Very attractive types of cloth were found; and where else can be had such variety of cloth except at Devagiri?'[10] Simply put, the Yadavas presided over an extremely prosperous kingdom, and the riches they had accumulated over generations excited the avarice of our ambitious northern general. With the north plundered and tamed, it was only natural that the eyes of the conqueror turned their gaze towards lands that were yet untouched, paving the way also for Alauddin's own future career.

The Deccan, as Ferishta explains, was home to three peoples at the time: 'the Marhat, the Kanhar and the Tiling' (all of them, he claimed, descendants of the biblical Noah from a grandson conveniently called Dekhun).[11] The Yadavas were lords of the Marathi lands, while the Kakatiyas in Warangal ruled over Telugu domains. Karnataka was held by the Hoysalas from their seat in Dwarasamudra – and, predictably, all three houses made it their business to feud over some backwater or the other for as long as could be remembered. They had not, however, anticipated invaders from the north, although the Yadavas were vaguely conscious of the rise of powerful Turks in the distant horizon. Just as Balban claimed that the south quaked in fear at the very thought of his name, Ramachandra Yadava had also, with breathtaking humility, compared himself in 1278 to the mythological 'Great Boar in succoring the earth from the oppressions of the Turukas', decades before he actually encountered a single Turk.[12] And as it happened, when eventually his forces came face-to-face with Alauddin's men, the Yadava crown was more than a little alarmed by the fate that awaited its celebrated line of kings, and the seismic changes that refashioned the very course of the Deccan's future.

Alauddin and his 8000 cavalry met practically no resistance on their way to Devagiri in 1296, except at a single point where a chieftain, assisted by two nameless Maratha women (who 'fought like lionesses'), unsuccessfully stood in the way. In Devagiri itself, the Yadava king shut the fort and decided to wait out the siege, not least because the bulk of his men were deployed with his son near the Hoysala frontier. The strategy was promising. As a later chronicler observed, this was 'one of the best fortresses' in the country, 'the only way to it being so narrow that but one horse, or one camel, can [pass] at a time'.[13] But since an invasion from the north was the last thing Ramachandra expected, no provisions had been stocked, and a week was all it took for the prospect of starvation to persuade him to contemplate peace. His heir, meanwhile, sped back to save the capital, and nearly succeeded in repelling the invaders – that is, until Alauddin manufactured a rumour that 20,000 fresh cavalry were on their way to reinforce his onslaught. He had 1000 horsemen raise such a whirl of dust in the distance that the Yadavas believed this inspired canard.[14] And so it was that a ghost army behind a blur of earth and wind brought Devagiri to its knees. Such quantities of treasure were heaped before Alauddin in the aftermath that six decades later portions of it were believed to still be found untouched in the imperial treasury.[15] As Amir Khusro, the poet, wrote, 'Were I to attempt to recount the plunder of jewels and gold, no measure or balance would suffice . . . Camels and mules were laden with rubies and diamonds . . . and the most experienced jewelers were unable even to guess their value'.[16]

In what appears to have been customary at such junctures, and would remain a pattern in the Deccan, Alauddin also received a trophy from Devagiri in the form of a Yadava princess. And as was equally conventional, there was to be no happy ending for this lady: in 1316 a half-brother of Alauddin's would blind her son and have her put to death during a contest for Delhi's throne.[17] Alauddin had also seized the queen of Gujarat, and it was from that kingdom that the enslaved eunuch Hazardinari ('1000 coins', after his initial price) was acquired. Destined to go down in history as Malik Kafur, this man was Alauddin's most dreaded general – and his controversial lover. As Barani, the Islamic theorist, remarked with profound but predictable disapproval, Alauddin fell 'deeply and madly in love' with Kafur, and, over time, 'entrusted the responsibility of the government and the control of the servants to this useless, ungrateful, ingratiate sodomite'. 'Intoxicated' by power but also partly due to the envy the Sultan's affections aroused, Kafur too, in the end, met a savage end around the time the Yadava princess was murdered.[18] He had tried to play kingmaker after Alauddin's death, till his interlocutors in this dangerous game decided to simply cut him to pieces and speed things up in a direction of their own choosing.

For now, however, our 'sodomite' found his life's purpose in subjugating the Deccan for his master beloved. In 1296, after counting the Yadava treasure and demanding annual tribute, Alauddin returned to Delhi to, consecutively, murder his naive uncle, appropriate the throne and attend to other pressing military concerns – such as decisively defeating the Mongols, who had made it almost a custom to periodically assault north-west India. Such was the rout Alauddin inflicted on the marauders that 'all fancy for coming to Hindustan was washed clean out of their breasts'.[19] Meanwhile Ramachandra's son, conscious of the Sultan's northern preoccupations, persuaded his father to cease the transfer of gold to Delhi. A fair amount of time elapsed, but in 1308 the bells of Devagiri rang again in warning when Malik Kafur arrived at the head of what the *Smritisthala* declares a 'Khilji Avalanche'.[20] The Yadavas were defeated, and this time

Ramachandra was couriered to Delhi for half a year to cool his heels and soak up lessons in obedience. When Kafur proposed to go to Warangal to destroy the Kakatiyas thereafter, the chastened Yadavas even offered assistance, lending the general a company of sturdy Maratha fighters to show the way to that city.[21] By 1313, however, the Yadava king was dead and his unbending son sat on the throne. Devagiri stood up for the last time to Delhi, and on this occasion they were permanently crushed. The slave-turned-'sodomite' was appointed viceroy, and coins were minted in Alauddin's name. The first of the old kingdoms of the Deccan was hereafter only a southern province of the Delhi Sultanate.

The turn of the Kakatiyas and their Telugu kingdom in the east came next.[22] When, in 1310, Malik Kafur first breached the walls of Warangal, its ruler Prataparudra had sued for peace; in return, he was spared. As Isami records, the Sultan's instructions were that Kafur must shake Warangal 'to its foundations', but 'should the Rai of Telingana submit and present wealth in money and elephants, you should reinstate him under my sovereignty and restore his dominion; you should give him a robe studded with jewels and promise him a parasol on my behalf'.[23] That is precisely what was done, with the Islamic khilat (robe of honour, signifying both the favour of a superior and fealty to him) entering southern court culture for the first time, and the more familiar umbrella of state sent from Delhi for the vassal king to dutifully place himself under.[24] In 1318 Prataparudra tried to wriggle out into the sun, only to be punished for his attempt. Once again, he parted with mountains of gold, but this time he had to ascend 'the eighteen steps leading up to the parapets of the citadel's stone wall'. And there, 'standing on top of the ramparts, in full view of both his fellow Telugu warriors and the invading northerners, the king turned his face in the direction of the imperial capital of Delhi. Bowing slowly, he kissed the rampart's surface in a gesture of humble submission.'[25]

It must have stung Prataparudra to play the feudatory, even though the northerners were admittedly superior in military technology and in numbers. After all, he was a man of singular kingly credentials, and a beloved ruler. This was a region where Kakatiya inscriptions reveal remarkable social mobility in the medieval era, with nearly a third of inscriptional evidence showing fathers and sons holding different occupations, free from rigid compulsions of caste and birth. Kakatiya dynasts, unlike most Indian ruling houses that fabricated genealogies from the sun, moon or legendary heroes of their choosing, themselves claimed no exalted origins; 'with only one exception, [they] embraced *sudra* status'. They were devoted sons of the soil and in close contact with their people, for whose benefit thousands of tanks were constructed to irrigate the land during their heyday. After Prataparudra took his seat on their Lion Throne (inheriting it from his maternal grandmother), he instituted policies to foster an even greater ethic of egalitarianism: as Richard Eaton states, 45 per cent of his noblemen came from humble origins and only 12 per cent had inherited their status at court by the conventional logic of blood.[26] Prataparudra was a good man and a sympathetic prince. But, unfortunately, at this cusp of history, as a new age dawned and an old one folded, he too was not destined to endure.

Yet Prataparudra could be forgiven, given his admirable record, for trying again in 1320 to throw off allegiance to the emperor in Delhi.[27] The year was significant, for in the north too changes were afoot, and all in the Deccan sought to exploit it. Alauddin had died, and a new dynasty was in place by the turn of the decade. In 1321, having consolidated their grip over the capital, the future Sultan Muhammad bin Tughluq came to Warangal on behalf of his father, the usurper, to flatten Prataparudra's house once and for all. On his maiden attempt he failed and had to retreat. But while Warangal celebrated and assumed the chapter conclusively closed, in 1323 the Tughluqs returned with 63,000 mounted archers to besiege the fortress once again. In the catastrophe this unleashed for Prataparudra, the Lion Throne fell, his family temple was razed (a mosque replacing it) and he himself was imprisoned and escorted under strict guard to Delhi. Fearful, perhaps, of what awaited him there, this last (and very good) king of the Kakatiyas evidently killed himself on the banks of the Narmada, extinguishing forever the flame of his dynasty.[28] Another page in history was, thus, turned.

All that remained of the old order now was the raj of the Hoysalas in Dwarasamudra. The collapse of this principality came soon after Muhammad bin Tughluq's accession to the throne in the following decade. A cousin of his challenged the succession and broke into rebellion against the Sultan. When his uprising was put down, the Hoysala ruler Ballala III provided the rebel sanctuary, inviting through this kindness the wrath of Delhi on to his realms – this after his capital had once already been sacked beyond recognition in 1311. The imperial armies hammered at the Hoysalas' doors, and in the end the recalcitrant cousin was led away in shackles to his gory fate. According to the Moroccan traveller Ibn Batuta, the 'Sultan ordered the prisoner . . . to be skinned alive, and as his skin was torn off, his flesh was cooked with rice. Some was sent to his children and his wife, and the remainder was put into a great dish and given to the elephants to eat.' The elephants we know, reassuringly, refused to touch this ghastly offering, but the wail of the poor widow can only be imagined. Her husband's skin was 'stuffed with straw' and 'exhibited through the country' as a lesson for all who might harbour romantic notions about resisting the Sultan in the name of their own glory or to satisfy their own ambitions.[29]

The Hoysalas retained independence, in a certain fashion, for some time after this, but Dwarasamudra was lost. In the end, the chaos of their age consumed this last echo of the ancien régime too – like the rebel he once harboured, in 1342 the final Hoysala king was also captured, and after an initial period of good treatment (during which time, it is said, as much money as could be extracted was squeezed out of his court), he was flayed, his body hung outside a fort in the Tamil country for all the world to see.[30] The people who did this to him, though, were not acting for Muhammad bin Tughluq, now known, evidently, as 'Lord of the Skins of Kings'.[31] They were a rebel faction that established a short-lived Sultanate in Madurai. After all, the collapse of the three great houses of the Deccan had left behind an enormous political vacuum, notionally occupied by the Tughluqs, and many were those, Hindu as well as Muslim, seeking to turn the tide in their own favour. Some succeeded while most failed with disastrous consequences. But in the end, the ashes of the old birthed a whole new era in the history of the land. From this bloody mess that was now the Deccan emerged shortly the states of Vijayanagar, its founders sons of the soil, and Bahmani, whose architects were immigrants from the north. And it was in their image that the country would flourish for three centuries hereafter, embattled as much as enriched by the legacies they forged.

~

Although the arrival of Muslim warriors from the north had shattered the way things were in the Deccan, its people soon absorbed the newcomers and paved the way for fresh beginnings. Part of this was due to Muhammad bin Tughluq's failures. His empire had spread as far as the Tamil coast, but in the process, it had grown altogether unwieldy – a pattern recurrent in the Deccan's history. Existing structures of power and old institutions were destroyed in the fire of war, while the men brought in to design new ones proved as incapable as they were disloyal. The man in Madurai, for instance, declared his independence – Ibn Batuta married a daughter of his – and so too in other provinces did Muhammad face tumultuous disorder.[32] Every governor he sent to the Deccan was a little too readily tempted to rebel, and it wasn't always possible to make an example of each man by throwing parts of him into biryani. The Sultan then announced a new plan: he would not make the mistake of those ancient emperors who had tried to hold the south from their faraway seats in the north. Instead, he himself would go to the Deccan to control the empire from this more central seat. In 1327 the entire capital, and virtually everybody in it, was transplanted to Devagiri, now reincarnated as Daulatabad, water from the holy river Ganga delivered after a forty-day journey to ritually sanctify this new citadel of power.[33] For all the auspicious Hindu rites, however, this decision was to go down, sadly, as one of the most foolish commands Muhammad issued in his otherwise remarkable life and reign.

Though sensible in theory, the venture was doomed from the start. Under the Sultans before him, Delhi had transformed itself from a regional town into a glamorous international centre, rivalling, as Barani claimed, Baghdad and Cairo. Now, 'without carefully looking into the advantages and disadvantages on every side', Muhammad inflicted great damage on that city and its economic and cultural life. 'All was destroyed' and so 'complete was the ruin that not a cat or dog was left' to enliven the abandoned capital.[34] Families were bribed to travel all the way, and if they refused, swords were gently drawn to motivate them. Many fell on the road. Ibn Batuta even tells a wild story about a blind man who refused to leave. He was then dragged all the way till, upon arrival, it was discovered that 'his limbs dropping off by the way, only one of his legs' actually reached the new city![35] Those who succeeded in making it to Daulatabad with all their limbs intact didn't quite feel at home in alien territory either, yearning to return to the

Daulatabad fort

familiar surroundings of the north. In less than a decade, Muhammad discovered that he had committed a monumental blunder, and large numbers of people packed their bags yet again to return to the road, this time in the opposite direction. Some, however, were told to stay back to govern the region – and little did the Sultan imagine at the time that these very amirs (nobles) would one day 'break up the unity of the Empire . . . and establish the independence of the Deccan'.[36]

Soon after the emperor's homecoming to the north, those left behind – of Turkic as well as Indian descent – began to flex their muscles. Muhammad knew that 'it was the scions of the old nobility, whom he had sent from Delhi to the distant parts of his dominions in order to keep those far-flung corners in check, who were proving to be the chief culprits'.[37] It was also an open secret that several high notables of the empire, who were creatures of the aborted Khilji dynasty, harboured hostility for their new Tughluq rulers. The emperor's method of countering their influence, though, proved another sample in disastrous policymaking: the Sultan thought he could harvest a new aristocracy that would, out of gratitude, stay loyal to him and enjoy his trust, unlike those sympathizers of the deposed Khiljis. Barani's contempt for these new favourites of the emperor found resonance among many others at the time, for they included, reportedly, sons of distillers, singers, cooks, weavers, barbers, and others whom class and custom denied any pretensions of nobility (making a fine contrast in attitudes with Prataparudra's disbanded egalitarian court, for example).[38] When, in 1345, therefore, Muhammad recalled his old guard governor on grounds of fiscal bungling and entrusted Daulatabad to four freshly minted amirs, a final, furious rebellion broke out in the Deccan.[39] And before the end of it, there would emerge in the south a new king, chosen almost by lottery, who launched with him a sparkling new dynasty.

Muhammad never succeeded in quashing the rebellion, and after his death some years later, in 1351, his successor was 'too much engrossed in his own domestic commotions' to care.[40] The year 1345 became, then, the 'last year imperial coins were minted anywhere in the Deccan'.[41] It also didn't help the Sultan's cause that Hindu rajahs of the south, 'also suffering from the tyranny' of the emperor in Delhi, 'rejoiced at the revolt . . . in which some joined, while others more circumspect, only privately encouraged it', assisting the rebels 'with money and supplies'.[42] The amirs first elected a distinguished nobleman as their leader, and he was crowned in Daulatabad. But during the inevitable military contests that followed against the imperial forces, it soon became obvious that the real leader of the Deccan was a man called Hasan Gangu.[43] And after two years, the previous nominee graciously vacated his silver throne to allow the young commander to park himself upon it. On 3 August 1347, a date declared auspicious by Daulatabad's Hindu stargazers, Hasan Gangu was proclaimed Abul Muzaffar Alauddin Bahman Shah, first king of the Bahmani Sultanate.[44] For all who were involved in his enthronement, the outcome was glorious: money and favour were dispensed with befitting munificence. The only man to suffer, however, was he who had just volunteered to give up the crown – not too long afterwards, the newly installed Sultan had him executed in open court, just so that he could begin his reign with a completely clean slate, washing off the past with the blood that oozed from his predecessor.[45]

The Sultan's original name was an unusual one, and stories circulated that he inherited the second part of it from a one-time Brahmin benefactor whose favourite servant he was. One version suggests that while Hasan was formally a Muslim, in 'reality he was perhaps half a Mussulman and a half a Hindu'. This was not implausible, for Muhammad bin Tughluq and his father too were believed to be sons of Hindu mothers. But in Hasan's case, some thought he saw in Islam primarily 'a stepping-stone to his ambition', and that the name Bahmani betrayed his original loyalties.[46] This was all most likely apocryphal, however, for the actual circumstances seem to suggest that he was of Persian extraction.[47] His uncle was a courtier under the Khiljis, killed in battle against the Mongols when Hasan was a child,[48] and Hasan himself with his brothers had long served the Sultanate, after growing up in Multan.[49] In 1339 they led a resounding flop of a rebellion against the Tughluqs, and for their pains were exiled to an Afghan outpost. But six years later, when the Deccan announced its secession from the empire, the brothers returned and lent their swords with unusual vigour in carving up the south. The best among them was then rewarded with its crown for his exemplary service, and that is how Hasan Gangu transformed himself into the first of the Bahmani Sultans.[50]

Perhaps to honour the Hindu chieftains who supported him, and to distinguish the new state in the Deccan from its hated parent in Delhi, the Sultan became one of the earliest Muslim kings in India to declare that 'no *jiziah* should be levied from non-Muslims in lieu of military service', a policy most famously associated with the Mughal emperor Akbar who ruled many generations later.[51] Though they would all be vanquished in good time for reasons of realpolitik, a number of prominent local Hindu princes were invited to the Bahmani court which was established at Gulbarga. In 1352, endearingly, the Sultan even opened his eyes to the glories of Buddhist and Jain traditions by

Gulbarga fort

Dinodia Photos / Alamy Stock Photo

visiting the Ellora caves, taking with him a scholar to interpret all that he saw there in its ancient frescoes and carvings.[52] Local traditions, in fact, had by now come to terms with the immigrants, though the process did not have altogether cheerful beginnings: the Karimuddin Mosque in Bijapur, constructed between 1310 and 1320, has been appreciated for its architecture that closely weds different styles, resembling 'a Hindu temple more than anything Islamic'.[53] While Hindu influences were certainly absorbed and admired, at *this* stage the mosque appeared like a temple only because it was 'built entirely of robbed temple columns and beams' and reassembled (by Hindu workmen) into a place of worship for their Muslim overlord, whose name they inscribed in Kannada.[54]

So too, to a renowned Sufi saint of Daulatabad, the king donated 200 pounds of gold and 400 of silver to obtain his blessings and approval for the state. Indeed, a connection was even concocted with

Karimuddin Mosque. Henry Cousens, c. 1885

Nizamuddin Auliya, the 'spiritual patriarch' of the Tughluqs in Delhi. A story, spun much later no doubt to legitimize the Bahmanis, has a young Hasan Gangu calling on the saint at his shrine. Muhammad bin Tughluq was departing when Hasan arrived, and the Sufi is said to have prophesized: 'One sultan has left my door; another is waiting there.'[55] In other words, the rise of the Bahmanis – in reality, a purely political act of subversion against the northern empire – was preordained by the Almighty. To further cement their dynastic claims, in 1360 Hasan's wife travelled to Mecca, and from there established correspondence with the Abbasid Caliph in Egypt. From this supreme moral authority (in theory) of all Muslims of the world, the queen received the all-important formal assent for the Bahmanis to commence having their names mentioned at Friday prayers in the mosques in their domain (i.e. in the khutbah) and to mint currency with their own distinctive emblems[56] (though, ironically, it was mainly Vijayanagar's currency – or as Ferishta calls it, 'infidel coinage' – that actually happened to service Bahmani realms).[57]

With that the warrant of the Bahmanis to reign over the northern Deccan was formally established in the eyes of their peers and contemporaries. And three years later, when the Sultan defeated a local Hindu rajah, they received from him a magnificent present to embody, quite befittingly, their soaring power and splendour. It was a richly carved throne, three yards long and two yards broad, made of ebony, and covered beautifully 'with an enamel of turquoise hue'. Each Sultan thereafter improved its appearance, ornaments and gems added to such a degree that by the end, 'there was nothing visible except precious stones'.[58] Eighteen kings were to sit on the Turquoise Throne of the Bahmani Sultanate, and above them was fixed a canopy crowned, ironically, with a ruby presented by the Raya of Vijayanagar.[59] And, in good ways as well as bad, with strength but also tragic flaws, they would govern the destinies of millions of Indians for the next 170 years, leaving their imprint on the land that is the Deccan.[60]

II

The Turquoise Throne
Inside the Bahmani Kingdom

THE BAHMANI DYNASTY

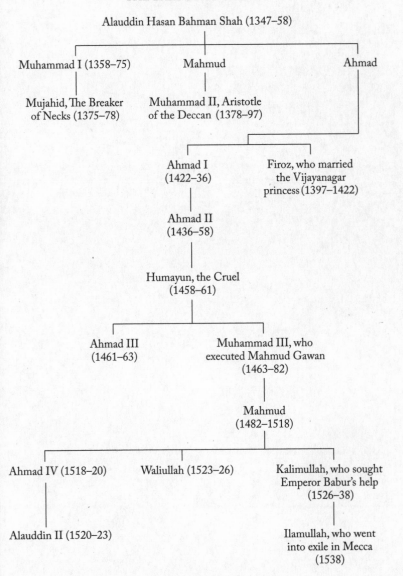

Alauddin Hasan Bahman Shah (1347–58)

Muhammad I (1358–75)

Mujahid, The Breaker of Necks (1375–78)

Mahmud

Muhammad II, Aristotle of the Deccan (1378–97)

Ahmad

Ahmad I (1422–36)

Firoz, who married the Vijayanagar princess (1397–1422)

Ahmad II (1436–58)

Humayun, the Cruel (1458–61)

Ahmad III (1461–63)

Muhammad III, who executed Mahmud Gawan (1463–82)

Mahmud (1482–1518)

Ahmad IV (1518–20)

Waliullah (1523–26)

Kalimullah, who sought Emperor Babur's help (1526–38)

Alauddin II (1520–23)

Ilamullah, who went into exile in Mecca (1538)

The Bahmanis, like most royal houses of their time, occupied a world of power, greed and the most intense internecine rivalries. Jealousies swirled all around them, poisoning bonds of blood and fidelity, brothers fighting brothers, suspicion breeding hatred. Cognizant of this, before he died in 1358, the first Sultan counselled his offspring to stand united, lest quarrelling drag their newly obtained state down an irreversible spiral of peril. And in those early days, things were, in a manner of speaking, orderly. Muhammad Shah Bahmani, who succeeded Hasan Gangu, set out first to consolidate his grip on power. He adopted protocols at court, invested the crown with ceremonious dignity and empowered a bureaucracy to administer daily affairs in his territories. The man was also an unafraid fighter, simultaneously establishing gunpowder factories to make the fullest use of firepower.[1] When Kapaya Nayaka – the leader of a confederacy of Telugu warriors, who two decades before had expelled Delhi's governors from the Kakatiyas' domains and replaced them as the principal force there – joined Vijayanagar to snatch Raichur from Muhammad Shah, the latter defeated him, chasing him 'as far as the gates of Warangal'.[2] In addition to the Turquoise Throne, the Nayaka remitted gold, his best elephants and, more significantly, the impregnable fortress of Golconda.[3] There began the eastward expansion of the Bahmanis, concluding only when their forces beheld the Bay of Bengal.

Muhammad Shah was succeeded by a son of astonishing physical proportions, but his was a short-lived reign. All of twenty years old,

Mujahid Shah invaded Vijayanagar, 'having heard great praises of the beauty of the city',[4] but also because his demand that the Raya hand over a fort was received with a snort.[5] When the boy-king arrived, he found that his enemy had vacated the capital, choosing to unleash guerrillas from a secret seat in the forest. The episode ended with the Sultan compelled to cross the Tungabhadra back into his lands, having gained little while surrendering a good proportion of his pride. At least one story adds that he returned also with a curse upon his head – while in Vijayanagar, he destroyed a temple to Hanuman and 'personally mutilated the stone face' of the deity. A dying Brahmin damned him thus: 'For this act thou wilt die ere thou reachest thy kingdom.'[6] Excusing the Brahmin's Shakespearean cry, the fact was that the young Sultan *did* perish shortly thereafter. And whether or not this had anything to do with a curse, karma was certainly involved. As a boy of fourteen, the Sultan had enjoyed wrestling and satisfied his vanity once by cracking a grown man's neck.[7] Now, in 1378, after his shambolic campaign in Vijayanagar, a plot was hatched to rid the kingdom of its king. On 16 April 1378, Mujahid Shah was murdered – and among the guilty was his betel-leaf bearer, son of the very man whose neck he had not long ago so proudly broken.[8]

Another grandson of Hasan's from his second son was installed on the throne. But an imperious granddaughter did not quite acquiesce to this selection, and in the same year had him stabbed while he prayed at the great mosque in Gulbarga. Even as her people took charge of the royal treasury, the dead man's nine-year-old son was blinded, and this line of Hasan's descendants was politically emasculated forever – under Islamic law, a blind man was ineligible to rule.[9] A seemingly more pliant Sultan now placed himself on the Turquoise Throne, having purchased all the necessary loyalties. This man, Muhammad II, was a well-meaning soul and in the nineteen years that he occupied the seat of power, he avoided political confrontations of all kinds, not least on account of a devastating famine that drew much of his royal attention. As the *Bahman Namah* tells of this 'Aristotle of the Deccan', 'The young king gained control of the world by his wealth / And held aloft the royal umbrella over his head / For many years he enjoyed a successful and prosperous life / And sat on the throne of the kingdom free from strife.'[10] One of his first deeds was to inaugurate a madrasa to educate the poor at the court's expense, and a number of other benevolent acts were to follow – a train of 10,000 bullocks regularly went out to markets beyond his realm to bring grain to moderate the impact of the famine, for example.[11] But his most sensational endeavour appeared when this patron of the arts invited the celebrated Persian poet Hafiz to emigrate to India. Hafiz was willing, and travelled to Hormuz to board his ship. But a furious storm soon after he embarked weakened his resolve – the poet turned back, and conveyed an ode of regret in his place.[12] For having tried, nevertheless, the admiring Sultan sent Hafiz a thousand pieces of gold from across the sea.[13]

This invitation extended to Hafiz was not an unusual one. The Bahmanis were placed in an awkward geopolitical space, with the Delhi Sultanate to their north sealing access by land to Persia and Central Asia. It was from here that the northern rulers recruited

The Great Mosque of Gulbarga. Deen Dayal, c. 1880

military talent and slaves, obtaining a steady stream of immigrants who came to India to make their careers – and, frequently, even to anoint themselves kings. Exposed to 'the flowering of the Persian Renaissance . . . a vibrant literary and cultural movement . . . these refugees [also] brought with them the entire spectrum of cosmopolitan Persian culture, which soon took root in North India'.[14] To access this pool of potential, then, the Bahmanis turned to the Arabian Sea, one of them in particular making unparalleled efforts to attract the best of the Islamic world into his kingdom. His ascent to the throne was convoluted – after the elderly, peace-loving Sultan Muhammad II died in 1397, a son of his succeeded him. Unlike the two-decade-long raj of his father, this man survived durbar intrigues for a matter of weeks. One evening, accepting the invitation of a perfidious courtier who promised him the embraces of his daughter, the Sultan permitted his host to ply him with wine. And when in a stupor after hours had thus passed, a slave pinned him down, while the nobleman replaced his own goblet with a knife.[15] The Sultan who went seeking ecstasy, returned minus his eyes.

Another son of the late Muhammad II, born, however, from a manumitted slave, was raised to the throne by the disloyal courtier, with the lady in question acquiring for herself the fancy title of Malika-i-Jahan.[16] For her and her creator, though, glory was short-lived. The blinded ex-king's brothers-in-law, also descendants of Hasan, rescued him now, and eventually orchestrated a coup – the courtier who maimed his royal guest died painfully, and the dowager queen, who barely had time to savour her new-found position, was exiled to Mecca with her dethroned progeny.[17] And so it was that Firoz Shah, the older of the brothers-in-law, ascended the Turquoise Throne as its eighth ruler in fifty years.

This monarch was something of an unusual creature for his time. Possessed of extraordinary intellectual capacities, he was a polyglot who knew Persian, Arabic and Turkish, as well as Telugu, Marathi, Gujarati and Bengali.[18] He composed poetry under the names Firozi and Uruji, and read the Hebrew Bible. Furthermore, he 'was fond of

natural philosophy. On Saturdays, Mondays, and Thursdays he used
to hear lectures on Botany, Geology, and Logic.' Three days a week
he even took classes himself for an assortment of high-born students,
'and if time did not permit him to teach in the day, he would make it
up by instructing students in the night'.[19] Brahmins were appointed
to high administrative positions in his government, Hindu chiefs
absorbed as amirs of the state, and courtly architecture too evolved
to reflect the multi-ethnic, pluralistic society over which he was lord
and king.[20] The position of the Bahmanis having been secured, they
sought now to build bridges with the original people of the land, and
Firoz Shah, with his broad mind and long reign, was unusually gifted
at doing precisely this.

If this was all already somewhat uncommon, Firoz Shah is also
believed to have been a man with a prodigious sexual appetite.[21] His
Sunni religious piety, however, got in the way, till he was instructed
by a sympathetic adviser that he could work around this by following
the Shia custom of the temporary *mutah* marriage.[22] The consequence
was that, in addition to Muslim wives, his harem featured Jewish and
Christian consorts, and early in his reign, after he defeated the ruler
of Kherla, in present-day Madhya Pradesh, he sealed their peace by
accepting a Gond princess in marriage (along, of course, with a dowry
of '40 elephants, 5 maunds of gold, and 50 maunds of silver', with each
maund roughly weighing 15 kg).[23] The Sultan's nephew too, in due
course, married the Hindu daughter of the Rajah of Sangameshwar,
calling his wife, memorably, Zeba Chehra (Beautiful Face), and
favouring her to such an excessive degree that his first wife's father had
to invade the kingdom to remind the prince of his commitments to his
own offspring.[24] Nothing, however, could surpass Firoz Shah's harem,
which came to include women from Russia, China, Afghanistan and
Central Asia,[25] and it was rumoured that he conversed, in bits and
pieces at any rate, with each of them in her own tongue.[26] Most of
these unorthodox unions were perhaps already in place by the time
he came to the throne, for when Firoz Shah succeeded as Sultan,
he was a middle-aged man.[27] Despite his years, however, his most

celebrated conjugal conquest was yet to be made, and it was war against Vijayanagar that delivered him his most important wife.

It was in Firoz Shah's time that the Raya of Vijayanagar decided to bring into his own custody the goldsmith's daughter from Raichur who appears in our Prologue.[28] When news reached the Bahmani capital of a large Vijayanagar army having invaded the kingdom, Firoz Shah himself led his men into battle, eventually carrying his flag and sword into enemy territory across the Tungabhadra. At this turn of events, the Raya had no alternative but to sue for peace; in addition to a very significant fort that the Sultan had captured on his way there,[29] the indemnity was to include a million hons of gold, 'five maunds of pearls, fifty elephants' and – interestingly, in a reflection of Firoz Shah's cultural preoccupations – 2000 slaves, male and female, all of them 'accomplished in the arts of reading, writing, music, and dancing'.[30] The most significant present, however, was the royal bride Firoz Shah would also take back with him from Vijayanagar – the first time a Muslim ruler from the northern Deccan married a Hindu princess from its south.[31] It was certainly unusual for the Rayas to give a daughter to a man beyond the pale of their caste and religion, but the king, 'out of necessity, complied' and a most magnificent wedding was put up in Vijayanagar, despite the political hatred that marked the relationship of the parties involved.[32]

The celebrations lasted forty days. The Sultan established a splendid camp at Hospet and the road to Vijayanagar was 'lined with shops and booths, in which the jugglers, drolls, dancers, and mimics of Carnatic displayed their feats and skill to amuse passengers'. On behalf of the bridegroom, his senior noblemen were escorted to the Raya's court, carrying the necessary ceremonial presents for the prospective father-in-law. A week later, after they were provided entertainments of a high order, they returned with the princess of Vijayanagar. As had been negotiated, Firoz Shah and his new wife then called on the Raya, who came out of the city gate to receive them with due pomp. 'The two princes rode on horseback together, between ranks of beautiful boys and girls who waved plates of gold [filled with incense] and silver flowers over their heads as they advanced.' When they reached one of the great gateways of the capital, the Hindu father-in-law and Muslim son-in-law 'ascended a splendid palanquin, set with valuable jewels, in which they were carried together to the apartments prepared for the reception of the bride and bridegroom'. For three days Firoz Shah feasted in Vijayanagar as the Raya's guest, after which, loaded with 'richer presents than before given', he took his leave.[33] Or this, at least, is the account we get from our only source who describes this episode.

On the way back, it is said that the Raya escorted his daughter and the Bahmani Sultan for about four miles outside of the capital, turning away thereafter to return to his palace. This upset Firoz Shah – he expected, as per his own standards of protocol and as a recently victorious monarch, his father-in-law to escort them *all the way* to his camp in Hospet, and then to enjoy Bahmani hospitality. Turning to a nobleman, he is said to have remarked (in what is proof that kingly arrogance in general, despite accomplishments of other varieties, was quick to flare) that 'he would one day have his revenge for the affront offered him by such neglect'. When these words were conveyed eventually to the Raya, he too made 'insolent remarks' in return, so that 'notwithstanding the connection of family', the hatred between their kingdoms 'was not calmed'.[34] Mutual hostility remained as pronounced as it had always been, with only the Raya's imperial pockets significantly lighter after the wedding accounts were drawn up, his daughter now parked in a place far from the land in which she was born, and presumably never saw again.

Destined to go down in history for his empire of wives (and, interestingly, as the first Sultan to design for himself a proper crown[35]), Firoz Shah also utilized his years in power to make the most determined effort yet to transform the Bahmani Sultanate into one of the more sophisticated seats of art and culture in the East. Among the first steps he took to fulfil this was to encourage a 'continuous influx of foreigners from . . . overseas' into his country, ranging from Persians, Iraqis, and even Hadrami Sayyids (descendants of the Prophet) from Yemen.[36] Indeed, every year he 'sent ships from his kingdom's two principal western seaports, [Dabhol] and Chaul, to the Persian Gulf to recruit talented men of letters, administrators, soldiers, and artisans'.[37] These vessels left the west coast empty but always returned with large numbers of foreigners to serve the Bahmani state and adopt India as their home. Beyond enriching the land with a wider pool of talent, this policy also provided the Sultans allies of their own faith to cement control over a tumultuous geography where they too were originally immigrants.[38]

In other words, contingencies of politics conspired with the provision of opportunity to help transform the Deccan into a seat of international cosmopolitanism. On the one hand, it sheltered the monarch for the time being, surrounding him with Muslims he could trust, not least because his patronage offered them futures vastly better than what was available in their own homelands. As one scholar notes, since these newcomers arrived 'to seek their fortune at Gulbarga, they proved more hard working and industrious than their counterparts', i.e. the old nobility from Delhi that had played a role in installing Hasan Gangu as king, and naturally felt more confident to question royal authority and protect their individual interests.[39] On the other, the influx of motivated young men from Islamic networks also helped design the cultural identity of a royal line of recent vintage. The Deccan's past, so far, was defined by its Hindu lords and by their great temples and splendid jewels – now it was part of a web that stretched not only from Cairo to Delhi but deep into the heart of India, turning dusty Gulbarga into an important node on the global map. Where the best of Indian traditions had met, the Deccan was now also ready to absorb the arts and traditions of lands as distant as Iraq and Persia. In due course, in fact, with the coming of the Europeans, white men too would make their mark in the Deccan – a sixteenth-century cavalry commander called Firangi Khan, originally Sancho Pires, was of Portuguese origin,[40] while the 1638 commander of Bijapur fort, Niamat Khan, was born in Rome.[41] No longer was the Deccan perceived through an Indian lens alone – it was fast becoming a land of fortune, noted in

the courts and palaces of the wider world for its splendour as well as
its alluring offer of a grander future.

This did not mean, however, that Firoz Shah was at all divorced from
local culture or the talents of his Hindu subjects, for he entrusted the
everyday administration of his Sultanate to larger and larger numbers
of scholarly Brahmins and local chiefs – it was the higher military
posts that were retained primarily for Muslims, in a not entirely fair
but strategically rational system. The arrival, in his southern bride's
dowry, of 2000 Vijayanagar artists introduced a pronounced Carnatic
element as well into Firoz Shah's tastes, and his evolving creativity
found expression in the city he designed, a few hours outside Gulbarga,
called Firozabad. Here, 'like Akbar's Fatehpur Sikri', a new urban
settlement bloomed, 'adorned with shops, wide streets, a citadel that
opened out onto the Bhima River, sumptuous apartments for the king's
harem and servants, and a mosque double the size of Gulbarga's royal
mosque'.[42] Even in that old town, in fact, architecture reflected the
Sultan's embrace of Indian traditions, most splendidly captured in the

Firoz Shah's tomb

Dinodia Photos / Corbis Documentary / Getty Images

tomb Firoz Shah constructed for his own eventual use. In addition to influences from Delhi's Qutb Minar, as one scholar notes, 'We see here the Perso-Bahmani arch supported by Hindu jambs on either side of the doorways, [while] the brackets supporting the *chajja* remind one of the brackets in the Hindu temples of the Deccan.'[43]

In emerging, quite deliberately, as a patron of art and architecture, Firoz Shah's effort was to emulate the man who had conquered the imagination of the Islamic world – in addition, that is, to the territories he overwhelmed. Timur the Lame, founder of the Timurid empire in Persia and Central Asia, sacked Delhi at the turn of the fourteenth century, and partly for diplomatic reasons (so he would not be tempted to turn south and also sack the Deccan), Firoz Shah sent 'ambassadors and gifts to Timur's court, begging to be counted among the Central Asian's dependents'. They spent six enjoyable months at the Timurid court, following which 'Timur graciously offered [the Sultan] sovereignty over Malwa and Gujarat—even though neither sovereign had ever conquered these regions—and addressing him as his son (*farzand*), sent the Bahmani king a belt, a gilded sword, four royal robes (*qaba*), a Turkish slave, and four splendid horses'.[44] This exchange also marked the consolidation of that long-standing Bahmani preoccupation with all things Persian, a trend their successor states also pursued, awed more by faraway Iran than the powerful Mughal empire that would soon flower in their own neighbourhood, and which would one day seek to swallow the Deccan whole.[45] Besides, cultivating a powerful ally at a safe distance also helped balance the ambitions of enemies at home, and, as we shall see, a time would come when the Shah of Iran even spoke for the Deccan to his counterpart, the Mughal emperor.

Meanwhile, the disruption caused by Timur in the north also meant that poets, artists and a train of other creative professionals ventured south seeking patronage of a standard that Firoz Shah was wholly delighted to provide. Indeed, even the octogenarian sheikh Gisu Daraz, 'the spiritual successor to India's most distinguished Sufi order and a scholar of formidable repute', accepted the Sultan's invitation to settle

Timur the Lame

A seventeenth-century Sufi saint

in Gulbarga.[46] As it happened, though, Firoz Shah would regret the warmth he showed him. The Sultan, himself a learned man, found the sheikh 'deficient in the external sciences' such as 'rhetoric [and] geometry' and made his assessment known.[47] The Sufi retaliated by favouring Firoz Shah's brother, Ahmad, and soon wafted through the air at court a most sinister chill. Matters grew worse on account of Firoz Shah's military woes. While in 1407 the Sultan enjoyed a stunning triumph over his age-old foe in Vijayanagar, obtaining territory and a daughter, subsequent efforts were listless – the Raya ceased the payment of tribute, and between 1418 and 1420 the Bahmanis were locked in a fruitless but expensive conflict with him. On one occasion, southern troops even subjected Firoz Shah's men to a violent chase, 'destroying a number of mosques on the way',[48] and unleashing a 'great slaughter of the Muhammadans'.[49] In the end the Sultan retained Raichur, but no longer was there about Firoz Shah that air of strength and masculine vigour that had marked his earlier days.

It was succession, however, that muddied the royal waters in Gulbarga. Firoz Shah desired his son to take the throne after him, but it was open knowledge that Gisu Daraz, who was held by his most fervent followers as superior even to the Prophet,[50] favoured Ahmad and *his* lineal heir.[51] An attempt by the Sultan to capture his brother and blind him failed – an army then marched to put Ahmad in chains. But luck as well as a spot of clever thinking came to his rescue. The prince knew he was outnumbered in terms of men, so when he had his cavalry lined up on the battlefield, he added to it lines of bullocks at the back, with armed soldiers on them, contriving the image of a much larger force than he actually could field. The ruse succeeded in demoralizing Firoz Shah's troops, and after a brief encounter, Ahmad and his faction carried the battle.[52] Aged as well as declining in spirit by this time in 1422, the Sultan invited his victorious brother to his bedside and accepted him as heir – his own son was blinded and packed off to spend his days in Firozabad, presumably with his goldsmith wife from Raichur.[53] Ten days thereafter Firoz Shah was in the grave – possibly suffocated to death[54] – followed by Gisu Daraz as well. The ninth of the Bahmani Sultans, and one of the Sultanate's most important rulers, now sat upon the Turquoise Throne.[55]

Ahmad Shah was wise and capable, but also forgivably cynical. While Gisu Daraz's support aided his rise to power, he cleverly refused to patronize local saints who might acquire so much ascendancy as to threaten the crown. Instead, spiritual figures were imported from Persia, and a grandson of Shah Nimatullah Walli, founder of the Nimatullahi order of Sufis, was married to one of the Sultan's daughters.[56] Ahmad Shah also brought in a body of 3000 archers 'from Iraq, Khurasan, Transoxania, Turkey, and Arabia',[57] and very quickly put them to good use. By 1425 a bloody war against the Telugu warlords in the east was begun, and sustained till, in his son's reign, the tract capitulated fully to the Bahmanis. But Ahmad Shah's principal victories were, as expected, against Vijayanagar, and soon after his accession, in 1423 the Sultan decided to avenge the humiliations his brother had suffered at the hands of the Rayas. Riding beyond the Tungabhadra with 40,000 cavalry and 200,000 infantry, this became one of the bloodiest meetings of the two states. Once again, the Raya elected to fight from the forests; Ahmad Shah, meanwhile, 'committed many atrocities' against shrines essential to the king's prestige, sending four idols to be placed in Gisu Daraz's tomb 'as a good omen'.[58] He 'laid waste the country, broke the idols in [yet more] temples, and destroyed,' we are told, 'the colleges of Brahmins'.[59]

This particular campaign also saw two unusually curious situations when the kings of both states nearly fell into the hands of their adversaries, if Ferishta is to be believed. In the first case, a group of Bahmani generals, with a relatively smaller force, crossed into Vijayanagar territory and came across a sugarcane field during a surprise attack. 'A body of the Mussulmans,' Ferishta writes, 'entered the garden for plunder', unaware that an oblivious Raya himself was camping there. The king, when he realized what was transpiring, fled in a panic 'almost naked into the sugarcane plantation' to hide, only to run into a group of enemy soldiers. Given his state of déshabillé, the latter assumed he was nobody in particular, and 'having loaded [the king of

Vijayanagar] with a bundle of canes, obliged him to run with it before them' as their donkey. The Raya, 'rejoiced at being undiscovered, held his peace, and took up the burden readily'. His moment of release came after intelligence arrived that Ahmad Shah had scattered Vijayanagar's forces. Guessing that 'more valuable plunder than sugarcane' would soon be available, the soldiers made haste and left their cane-bearing porter behind. The Raya, breathing a sigh of relief, at last made his way back to his own people, ending an adventure that could easily have been his last.[60] Or so goes the tale.

If this comical episode humiliated Vijayanagar's king, Ahmad Shah too had his share of strange experiences. Like all Sultans, he travelled with an entourage, and between battles there was always time for recreation. One day the king felt like a hunt and rode out with only his bodyguards. Before they realized it, they had strayed far away from the Bahmani camp, and wandered a little too close for comfort to an area teeming with Vijayanagar soldiers. Chased by a band, the Sultan had to ungallantly conceal himself inside a barn – his companions were cut down, but before the enemy could capture Ahmad Shah himself, a much larger force of his own men swept in to his rescue.[61] In the larger scheme of things, meanwhile, matters began to favour the Bahmanis. The Raya (now safe in his camp) sued for peace and agreed to dispatch to the Sultan elephants laden with the arrears of tribute that had provoked the war, his submission also marked by his heir leading the procession. Ahmad Shah received the Vijayanagar prince with the necessary pomp, presented him rich robes of honour, horses, elephants, greyhounds, 'and three falcons'. The prince accompanied the Sultan as far as the river Krishna before returning to his capital, and the feud was suspended for a while.[62] The Bahmanis' honour was restored, while Vijayanagar awaited another opportunity to strike.

While contingencies of battle involved the demolishing of temples in enemy territory in order to delegitimize the authority of the kings who patronized and were duty-bound to protect these shrines,[63] it should be noted that Ahmad Shah was no unrestrained iconoclast. And this despite tales that whenever he successfully slaughtered 20,000

Hindus in a campaign, he celebrated with a special feast.[64] On the contrary, he is remembered almost as a saint to this day in the Deccan, honoured by legions of non-Muslims. The urs (anniversary) of his death is counted not on the basis of the Hijri calendar but according to the Hindu lunar almanac, 'on the twentieth of the . . . month in which the Holi festival is celebrated'. Ceremonies associated with the commemoration are presided over not by a Muslim priest or even a Sufi saint but by the *jangam* (spiritual preceptor) of the Shiva-worshipping Lingayats of Madhyal. They, with hundreds of devotees (the Hindus considering Ahmad Shah a reincarnation of the twelfth-century Lingayat mystic Allama Prabhu[65]), arrive at the Sultan's tomb, where the *jangam* 'enters the sepulcher every day of the Urs with orchestra and all the emblems of royalty, blows the conch, crushes open coconuts according to the accepted Hindu fashion, and makes an offering of flowers' at the royal grave. In costume, however, the *jangam* appears like a Muslim, in flowing robes with a cap on his head.[66] None of this

Ahmad Shah Bahmani's tomb

Wikimedia Commons

is ironic – Ahmad Shah's son, for instance, was close to the Hindu saint
Narasimha Saraswati, and the *Gurucharitra* lauds this prince for his
benevolence, adding that it was 'a great augury for the kingdom that
the raja is a devotee of Brahmins'. That Muslim clerics disapproved
was another matter, and there were orthodox Hindu elements too that
were 'distressed that their brethren should discuss the sacred Vedas
. . . with a person who, though king' was of 'no caste', i.e. equal to an
outcaste by reason of his Islamic faith.[67]

It was also Ahmad Shah who constructed a new capital for the
Bahmanis, inaugurating an evolved Deccani style of architecture that
combined the 'elegance of Iran, the sensuality of South India, and
even the occasional influence from Europe'.[68] Gulbarga, he thought
understandably, was full of ghosts of the past – stabbings, blindings,
murder, and worse. In a quest for a more auspicious setting, Ahmad
Shah moved his establishment to Bidar, held since antiquity by great
lines like the Chalukyas, Yadavas and Kakatiyas, so that just as the
Tughluqs in Delhi transported Ashokan pillars to their capital in
an effort to draw parallels in greatness, the Bahmanis too sought
the legitimacy that came from occupying an ancient, historic city. It
also helped that Bidar was more centrally located in an expanding
conquest state, composed of Marathi-, Telugu- and Kannada-speaking
districts.[69] The results, at any rate, were encouraging: 'If we compare
the Gulbarga period of Bahmani rule with the Bidar period,' we are
told, 'we can immediately perceive a vast change in the spirit of the
Sultanate. The period of the Bidar Sultanate' became 'one of internal
peace. Intrigues there no doubt were . . . But it is remarkable that
after the blood-thirsty atmosphere which Ahmad left at Gulbarga
. . . we find that there is not a single case of regicide' until the collapse
of the dynasty in the next century. 'In fact it was during this period
that the right of primogeniture became firmly established' among
the Bahmanis, a custom that would never quite appeal to Mughals in
the north who derived power from settling matters by blows on the
battlefield.[70]

So, it was in Bidar that the Sultan celebrated the wedding of his son with Zainab, princess of the northern principality of Khandesh, with much 'music, incense and wine'.[71] And in a few decades, the Russian traveller Afanasy Nikitin would describe the city as 'the chief town of the whole of Mahommedan Hindostan'.[72] It certainly had, he agreed, snakes fourteen feet long in the streets every now and then, and the people 'all are black and wicked, and the women all harlots, or witches, or thieves and cheats' who were permanently attempting to 'destroy their masters with poison'.[73] But, on the whole, Bidar was a remarkable city. 'The palace is very wonderful,' he declared. 'Everything in it is carved or gilded, and, even to the smallest stone, is cut and ornamented with gold most wonderfully.'[74] In Ahmad Shah's time, then, the Bahmanis firmly imprinted on the Deccan their dynastic mark, and if Gulbarga was placed by Firoz Shah on the international map, Bidar only raised the bar and established new standards.

By the time the Sultan died, though, all was not perfect and untroubled in the Sultanate despite his general success and the wealth manifest in his new capital. On the contrary, seeds of structural dissension that eventually broke the very spine of the Bahmanis had already sprouted. The state, with its rich ports and large segments of its income derived through trade, was naturally exposed to a wider universe. Stallions from Persia, Arabia and Iraq were sold near Bidar by the thousands, for instance, and while the cotton of the Deccan had long ago earned a reputation abroad, in 'Bahmani times the silk industry [also] . . . became thoroughly globalized: silk procured in cocoon stage from China was brought to Konkan, where it was reeled, dyed, and woven before being exported to Middle Eastern markets. Similarly,' we learn, 'the technique for velvet production, though imported from Central Asia, [also] became indigenized in this region.'[75] Goods from the Deccan travelled across the world, and this was a most agreeable state of affairs for the kingdom's inhabitants who basked in the glory of its economic success. Indeed, such was the dignity ascribed to commerce as a vocation that the most senior minister at the Sultan's durbar held a title that was translated, befittingly, as 'Prince of Merchants'.[76]

What was less agreeable, however, was the degree to which the Deccan was allowed to become a magnet for international adventurers, who saw in the land a vast arena of opportunity and profit. Part of it was also due to a general outflow of Iranians eastwards: men from Persia served even in the Burmese court in Arakan, while in the seventeenth century the Thai king Narai of Ayutthaya was so impressed with Persian culture that he took to 'eating mutton cooked in the Iranian style . . . wearing Iranian-style clothes', eschewing only the foreign turban 'because of its excessive weight'.[77] In the Deccan, however, this Persian influx brought about the emergence of two rival factions at court: the Dakhnis, descended from those early Muslim immigrants from northern India who were of Turkic or local (converted) origins,[78] and the Afaqis, or 'Westerners', who had crossed the seas to win success under Bahmani patronage. (Hindu lords were lower down in the hierarchy to matter as far as court intrigues were concerned.) Ahmad Shah, like his brother, tended to vest considerable trust in the Westerners, and senior positions at court often went to Persian immigrants: three Bahmani princesses were married to Westerners, the military instructor of the royal sons was an Afaqi, and even the architects who designed Firozabad and Bidar were students of Persian aesthetics (which they married to Hindu influences).[79] As late as the 1470s, during the aforementioned Afanasy Nikitin's visit, he noted how 'Khorassanians [i.e. Persians] rule the country'[80] and that the 'rulers and the nobles in the land . . . are all Khorassanians'.[81] Indeed, even Ferishta was the son of an immigrant who came to make a career for himself in the Deccan.[82]

The Dakhnis, naturally therefore, nursed a grievance that despite having served the Sultanate since its early infancy, and despite having been integral to its founding, what was meted out to them was second-grade treatment. The issue, unfortunately, was 'inherently unsolvable,' and fated to destroy the kingdom:

On the one hand, the court was obliged to patronize the descendants of those north Indian settlers who had migrated to the Deccan in the fourteenth century and who, rebelling against Delhi, had launched the dynasty. But, on the other hand, in order to obtain the talent and prestige associated with the Timurid power-state [as the Sultans aspired, and] thereby to get on the big chessboard of global politics, the court wished to recruit immigrants from the Persian or Persianized world . . . If the [Dakhnis] manifested a colonial idea, namely a society composed of transplanted settler-founders . . . the Westerners represented a cultural idea: a refined style of comportment, an eminent tradition of statecraft, a prestigious language. Since each class was legitimate in its own way, neither could be dislodged; nor could one totally dominate the other.[83]

Then there was also the matter of sectarian feuds. Persianized and in awe of all that was emerging in Islamic lands abroad, the Bahmani Sultans had grown inclined towards Shia thought, which, in orthodox eyes, was nothing less than a betrayal of the original Sunni faith of the Dakhnis. For instance, Ahmad Shah's mausoleum was conspicuous for its Shia-inspired calligraphy and decorative style,[84] and, even in his lifetime, the Sultan kept the Westerners closer to him than he did Dakhnis.[85] To Karbala, deemed by Shias to be as holy as Mecca, he sent much money in charity, and when a Shia holy man was insulted by a Dakhni courtier, the Sultan 'had the culprit trampled to death by a mad elephant' despite the seniority of the foul-mouthed victim.[86] Language too contributed to the gulf: where the Westerners 'tenaciously cultivated the Persian language and despised the Marathi and Kannada vernaculars', the Dakhnis 'developed their own dialect [also called Dakhni], with little regard for the purity of Persian'.[87] By the time of Ahmad Shah's successor's reign, which commenced in 1436, differences reached a head. The Sultan commanded that, when attending court, Westerners should stand to his right side, and Dakhnis to his left – another indication of second-class status for the latter, for the left side was traditionally seen as inferior.[88] For the twenty-two years that this prince ruled, hatred continued to brew, each party trying to undermine the other, till the malaise spread like a cancer throughout the higher echelons of the Sultanate and its institutions.[89]

The man who, in the midst of this looming crisis, made an effort to bridge the distance between the factions was a 'Prince of Merchants' by the name of Mahmud Gawan. And as it happened, this wise statesman offered the Bahmani Sultanate its final era of prosperity, even as the dynasty itself tottered with intrigue and dissension. In 1458, for instance, soon after Ahmad Shah's son went to the grave, a set of nobles planted Hasan, a younger son of the deceased, on the Turquoise Throne. It was assumed that the older son with the stronger claim was done for, and a mob of people (with the tacit approval of the new Sultan) gathered outside his palace, preparing to plunder it. But the man inside, Humayun by name, was not one to be daunted, nor the kind who gave up without a fight – a prominent sheikh who commanded much respect was planted by Humayun's side, his presence injecting sobriety and shame into the rabid crowd. Then, with less than a hundred loyalists by his side, Humayun walked from his residence to the durbar, where he 'marched to the throne room of the palace, slapped Hasan on the face, unseated him and himself ascended the throne'.[90]

If only matters had ended as simply as that. Hasan escaped – in disguise after hiding with a barber – and moving out of the capital, launched a rebellion. When it was put down, he fled towards Vijayanagar to seek the Raya's aid, but was captured and in 1460 presented to his brother. Humayun, whose enduring weakness was his furious temper, 'had Hasan thrown before tigers, ordered some of his adherents to be cast into cauldrons full of boiling water and oil, and released mad elephants and other wild beasts to prey upon the unfortunate victims'.[91] So after all, Bidar too was tainted by the spilling of royal blood. It appears that many Westerners were implicated in the plot, and the places they vacated (not painlessly) in the aftermath were filled through the promotion of powerful Dakhnis. But if this faction assumed that a golden age had dawned with a sympathetic monarch in power, their hopes were quashed. A year later, perhaps at the instigation of disaffected Westerners, the Sultan (painted by now as Humayun the Cruel) was stabbed to death by a maidservant as he lay in bed, meeting an end that inspired more pity than rousing glory.[92] A son of his was raised thereafter to the throne, but he died two years later, following which another boy of ten was installed in his place. He would grow up to be scholarly and capable but the vortex of intrigue, in the end, consumed him too and rang the Bahmanis' death knell.

A Council of Regency was constituted to govern the state on behalf of the ten-year-old boy-king, featuring a nobleman called Khwaja-i Jahan Turk, Mahmud Gawan and the queen mother, Humayun's widow. The first of these was murdered in the presence of the boy-king after he made a silly attempt to dominate the Council and, worse, insulted the dowager. And so it was that Mahmud Gawan emerged at the forefront. This gentleman originally arrived in the Deccan as a Persian trader, landing at the port of Dabhol in 1453 with a cargo of 'silken fabrics, Turkish and Ethiopian slaves, pearls, jewels, and Arabian horses'.[93] Educated in Cairo and Damascus, he was knowledgeable and, shortly after his arrival in Bidar, made a strong impression on the Sultan. At first he was created a junior nobleman at court, but his matchless networks abroad, of an intellectual as well as commercial nature, promoted him into a particularly attractive asset for the crown – he could deliver the Bahmanis the best warhorses that were to be had overseas, even as he corresponded personally with the Ottoman Sultan and the king of Egypt.[94] When Humayun came to power after slapping his rival off the throne, he declared therefore: 'We are on the threshold of a new epoch . . . and I cannot do better than follow the advice of one who should be clothed with the outward attributes of truth and good faith and who should inwardly be free from vices and vanity.'[95] That person was Mahmud Gawan, and he was to serve as the king's minister.

Humayun's widow, Nargis, too vested her trust in Gawan, and in 1472 she granted him the privilege of seeing her face-to-face, out of purdah, for his wisdom and loyalty had earned him the status of a 'brother'.[96] And under his stewardship, as the poet Jami exclaimed, the Bahmanis became 'the envy of Rum [i.e. Europe] itself'.[97] It was not hollow flattery, for the 'premiership of Mahmud Gawan saw the Bahmani Sultanate attain a height unequalled in the whole of its history'.[98] It was Gawan, for instance, who established the Bidar Madrasa in 1472, a magnificent architectural structure (now in ruins, alas), endowed with an excellent library embracing 3000 volumes for the benefit of the heaps of scholars who came to study there.[99] 'Apart from the purely cultural aspects of his office, the frontiers of the kingdom were [also] made secure by the effective occupation of the Konkan territory as far south as Goa, and the annexation of the Godavari–Krishna doab in the east, while expeditions were led to the very heart of Orissa and the Coromandel littoral as far as Kanchi. For the first time the frontiers of the Bahmani realm extended from sea to sea.'[100] The Sultan too was maintained in great pomp: on festive occasions, he came out with elephants, a thousand horses with gold trappings, himself 'riding on a gold saddle', wearing 'a habit embroidered with sapphires, and on his headdress a large diamond'. His suit of armour was made of gold, inlaid with gems, while his brother

Dinodia Photos / Alamy Stock Photo

Bidar Madrasa

rode on 'a golden bed, the canopy of which [was] covered with velvet and ornamented with precious stones'.[101]

Naturally, all it took was a little time for others at court, like 'wounded vipers, writhing in the torment of jealousy', to resent Gawan's success.[102] The man was aware of this: 'Their treasuries', he declared, 'are full of sinfully earned money, just as their hearts are full of greed, ignorance and envy . . . the feelings of these men are such that out of sheer malice they would kill each other and make me the object of all wrongs which it is in their power to perpetrate'.[103] Hatred for him came from both factions in the Sultanate, not only because he tried to be as fair as possible in farming out official posts and titles, but also on account of his efforts to strengthen the monarchy by eroding the autonomy of the nobility. He shrank the size of *jagirs* and estates (and in conjunction, the military power) granted to nobles on both sides. The revenue system was modernized to break entrenched networks of corruption, and no governor was permitted to hold more than a single fort. Over time more and more land was classed as property of the crown, allowing the Sultan's government to directly oversee significant real estate and revenue without a crippling sense of dependence on noblemen, whose moods and agendas swung one violent way now and another next.[104] This strengthened the Sultanate but lost its minister all his friends.

By 1481 Gawan's star was on the decline as he became a victim of his own success. The Sultan, now a fully grown man, seemed to have inherited his father's temper, even as the moderating influence of the queen mother vanished with her death. A few Dakhni nobles, after plying Gawan's seal-bearer with alcohol, obtained the minister's stamp on a blank document, on to which was subsequently inscribed a pointedly seditious letter to King Purushottam of Orissa. 'Although I have been brought up on the salt of my royal master,' the letter read dramatically, 'if you swear over all that you hold sacred . . . that you would agree to partition the Deccan between you and myself, I would promise to help you to the best of my ability.'[105] This forgery was presented to the Sultan, who, drunk on power as much as on imported wine, summoned Gawan for an explanation. The latter declared his innocence, but the king knew only wrath – in the heat of the moment, he sentenced his minister to die. 'The death of an old man like me is, indeed, of little moment,' said Gawan prophetically to his sovereign. 'But to Your Majesty, it will be the loss of an empire and the ruin of your character.'[106] Kneeling in the direction of Mecca, Gawan bared his neck, and on 5 April 1481, this exemplary statesman of the Sultanate was executed by a slave, 'not by one stroke but by successive strokes till he was dead'.[107]

When he realized what an obscene blunder he had committed, the Sultan was full of belated horror. But of course, it was in vain. Very quickly he lost all interest in matters of state, and lacking a seasoned captain like Gawan to steer the ship of state, the whole vessel lost its bearings. The king sojourned in Firozabad where he channelled all his energies into 'drowning himself in drink and pleasure'. Finally, summoning his son, a boy of twelve, he entrusted the destinies of the dynasty and the Bahmani kingdom to this ill-fated adolescent. Even the Sultan could feel the shadow of ruin approach. As the schism between the Dakhnis and the Westerners grew wider and shriller by the month, the king ruminated, 'If they do not obey me, who reigned gloriously for many years, and conquered nations with my sword, how will they submit to a child?'[108] But without making the slightest effort to ensure a more certain future for his son, precisely one year after he committed the sin of murdering Gawan, in 1482 the Sultan also collapsed in a heap and was soon turned to dust.

This was the beginning of the end. The boy-king would grow up and live for many years. But he was less sovereign and more a shuttlecock in the hands of powerful noblemen of his realm. The court itself granulated, as one by one its leaders and generals retired to their estates to plot their own ambitions: it was open season in the Bahmani state, and the fittest alone could survive. Before a decade had passed, the Sultan's realms were carved up. Two Westerners and three Dakhnis stood at the forefront, not to rescue the Bahmanis but to feast over their remains. One drew power from his armies that were strong;

the other kept the Sultan on a leash, and exploited the legitimacy his name offered. The first half of the saga that began when Hasan Gangu proclaimed himself king in the Deccan wound painfully to a close – seven generations had passed, and the Turquoise Throne had no legs. Its occupant, hopeless in dismay, watched gloomily as all around him the kingdom his ancestors had built shattered into pieces, and a great churn unleashed new tussles for power and a terrible game of conquest.

III

Hindu Sultans

The Three Dynasties of Vijayanagar

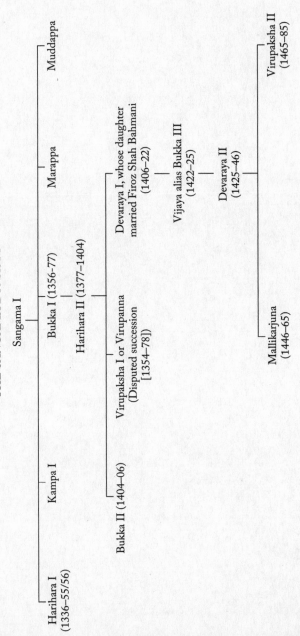

THE SANGAMA DYNASTY

Sangama I

Harihara I (1336–55/56)

Kampa I

Bukka I (1356–77)

Marappa

Muddappa

Harihara II (1377–1404)

Bukka II (1404–06)

Virupaksha I or Virupanna
(Disputed succession
[1354–78])

Devaraya I, whose daughter
married Firoz Shah Bahmani
(1406–22)

Vijaya alias Bukka III
(1422–25)

Devaraya II
(1425–46)

Mallikarjuna
(1446–65)

Virupaksha II
(1465–85)

Sometime at the beginning of his long and eventful reign, the Vijayanagar emperor Devaraya II (r. 1425–46) summoned a council of all his principal advisers and high nobility. And to this gathering he expressed wonder at how, despite his country being 'in extent, population, and revenue' vastly superior to the dominions of the Bahmani Sultans, his predecessors were 'reduced to pay them tribute'. Some with foolish beliefs declared that Muslims possessed a divine mandate 'for thirty thousand years' to dominate the universe, while others, with more rational instincts, pointed out that the strength of the Bahmanis came from their horses and mounted archers. 'Dew Ray [Devaraya] upon this,' we are informed, 'gave orders to enlist Mussulmans in his service, allotting them estates, and erecting a mosque for their use in Beejanuggar. He also commanded that no one should molest them in the exercise of their religion, and moreover, he ordered a Koran to be placed before his throne on a rich desk, so that the faithful might perform the ceremony of obeisance in his presence without sinning against their laws.'[1] And so the story goes that Muslims came into the service of the Hindu empire of Vijayanagar, with remains of their buildings and burial grounds still visible among the ruins of that city – one pillared pavilion, for long thought to have been a rest house, proved to be a mosque minus minarets and domes, known to inhabitants of the city not as a masjid but as just another *dharamsalai*.[2]

Ferishta, who narrates this tale, generally tends to flatter Islamic kings in his writings, and there is a hint of conceit in his suggestion of an inherent superiority in Muslim horsemen. But there is yet truth to this account for Devaraya II did indeed enlist a large body of 'Turkish' mercenaries into his service – an inscription from 1430 tells of 10,000 cavalry the king absorbed,[3] while Ferishta himself reports an initial induction of 2000 men.[4] None of this, however, was unprecedented. Three hundred years earlier, the Hoysalas had employed Muslims in their armies, though these came from settlements on the coast and were most likely of Arab descent unlike subsequent Turkish and Persian émigrés.[5] Devaraya II also had commercial dealings with Muslims, and made efforts to nurture the ports on the west coast and monitor the import of warhorses from overseas.[6] Bhatkal, for example, was home to a large community of Muslim traders, and when decades later a hot-headed successor of Devaraya II decided to massacre a good portion of them for serving the wrong buyer, the settlement escaped to Goa. Mahmud Gawan, then, swiftly swept up both Goa and these persecuted merchants to ensure an undisturbed source of mounts to his own Sultanate.[7] In the next century, even Krishnadeva perpetually fretted over a reliable supply of horses, making a sensational financial offer to the Portuguese if they promised him exclusive rights over their imports. Not oblivious to how fabulously profitable the traffic was, the latter shrewdly declined and kept their options, as well as coin boxes, open.[8]

Muslims who served the Rayas of Vijayanagar were granted senior administrative posts, though, like the Bahmanis where arrangements worked in the reverse, the majority of military ranks were divided among Kannada, Telugu and Tamil nobles with Hindu roots.[9] One later regent of Vijayanagar, himself having served a northern Sultan in his early career, permitted his Muslim subordinates to even consume beef, despite protests from Brahmins at court.[10] Admittedly, it was during his rule that the empire collapsed, but the fact was that in the Deccan, north and south, the elite 'enjoyed considerable mobility, moving from patron to patron according to changes in political winds', and not on the basis of what religion they pretended to uphold[11] – a state of affairs quite at odds with the enduring picture of Vijayanagar as a Hindu bulwark against Islamic bigotry. When the invaders from Delhi first came to pillage, plunder, rape and destroy, the typical narrative goes, their misdeeds 'set ablaze the latent energy of the Hindu Dharma'. The 'smouldering forces of Hinduism' united to defend their own, finding political expression in the ascent of Vijayanagar,[12] whose founders were pledged to 'the liberation of the Hindus from the Muhammadan yoke'.[13] Robert Sewell, who gave life to this fallacy, considered the kingdom 'a solid wall of opposition' that 'saved' Hindu culture from 'ruin', 'devastation', and indeed, comprehensive 'annihilation'.[14]

The rendition is certainly heady and has held appeal for decades, but the more accurate position is less sentimental. To begin with, the figures provided by Muslim chroniclers are often suspect. As one scholar states, if Ferishta's claims on the masses of Hindus killed by the Bahmani Sultans during their wars were taken literally, 'there would hardly be a Hindu left in the Deccan'.[15] In the early 1360s when the two states clashed, 'a half million' Hindus are said to have been put to death,[16] which, if true, would have converted Vijayanagar into a graveyard while it was still in the cradle – which, we know, was not the case, given the heights the kingdom scaled. And most revealingly, Bukka, one of the founders of Vijayanagar, invited the Sultan of Delhi *back* to the south so they could together eat the Bahmanis for breakfast – hardly the mark of an implacable Hindu zealot whose pre-Islamic paradise was shattered by Muslim barbarians from Delhi.[17] Like Ferishta, Bukka's chroniclers too were prone to exaggeration, celebrating him in overblown verse, as Krishna reborn 'to deliver the world when it was overpowered by Mlenchchas' (Muslims).[18] This when, in naked terms of strategy, he was more than agreeable to consorting with *mlechchas* for political ends. The fact, then, is that pronouncements made to flatter kings are not always a reflection of reality. Their world was not one of black and white, though religion did lend itself to the invention of grand narratives, regardless of which faith was under consideration, on either side of the political divide.[19]

So there is no irony in a record commemorating Bukka thus: 'When his sword began to dance on the battle-field, the faces of the

Turushkas shriveled up, Konkana Sankaparya was filled with fear, the Andhras ran into caves, the Gurjaras lost the use of their limbs on every road, the Kambojas' courage was broken, the Kalingas suffered defeat.'[20] Leaving aside how this is practically a mirror image of Sultan Balban's inscription from the previous century in faraway Delhi, here the king lists the Turks simply among all his other adversaries – the Muslim is not marked out for any pronounced hostility. So too a century and a half later, in other inscriptions eulogizing the past, the Sultans are listed merely among other dynasties such as the Hindu rulers of Orissa and the old Cholas of the Tamil country. 'In other words, Muslims are depicted as respected political rivals, just like other major Hindu powers of the peninsula.'[21] Among the oldest ruins visible today at Hampi, on the Great Platform in the Royal Centre of the city, there are various reliefs carved in stone, featuring not only Hindus but also Muslims – depicted with long noses, pointed caps and shoes with pointed ends – who are seen riding horses, bearing arms and even dancing for the Vijayanagar king. The Ramachandra temple nearby features stone carvings of Arabs leading horses, while

Dinodia Photos / Alamy Stock Photo

Panel depicting an Arab leading a horse in the Ramachandra temple

A column in the Vitthala temple showing a turbaned Muslim warrior

in the celebrated Vitthala temple there is a mandapa with a column that shows a 'turbaned Muslim warrior'.[22] The Hindus did not unite as one to challenge Muslims, nor, with their own feuds and internal dissensions, were the Muslims of the north a single consolidated block, baring fangs and victimizing Hindus en masse before supper. In fact, the Bahmanis forged several Hindu alliances – the Telugu Reddy and Velama chiefs stood with them at one time, and not with fellow Hindus in Vijayanagar,[23] and years later the suzerain of Orissa too allied with Bidar at the expense of the southern Rayas, despite their shared faith in the Hindu pantheon.[24] In due course, several more instances would arise when Muslims from the north sought Vijayanagar's aid for their wars, and a queen in Vijayanagar appealed to a Sultan to come to her rescue.[25]

This explains why literary sources incorporated Muslim rulers into familiar metaphors. The king of Orissa was Gajapati, or Lord of Elephants; the Bahmani Sultan was seen as Ashvapati, or Lord of Horses; and completing the circle was Narapati, or Lord of Men in Vijayanagar.[26] If all of the south towered in a 'patriotic national'[27] crusade against a monolithic blitz called Islam and its 'alien attack',[28] the founders of Vijayanagar would not have had to suppress 'widespread rebellions in Konkan and in the Tamil country', raised by *Hindu* chieftains in the early days of their empire.[29] To view the clashes of this age as a collision of religious identities is to ignore the fragmented era in which these confrontations occurred. And while it is romantic to proclaim that in founding Vijayanagar 'the Hindus of the south' were making a 'bid for freedom',[30] the actual careers of Vijayanagar's founders, one of whom, Harihara, is even said to have served the Delhi Sultanate, shows that plain realpolitik, often couched in a vocabulary of faith, was what actually motivated them. The first Rayas of Vijayanagar, in establishing a new kingdom, were not shielding Hinduism as much as taking 'advantage of a period of public commotion' to establish a state of their own and further their own dynastic interests, for reasons less poetic than many would prefer to believe.[31]

The origins of the five sons of Sangama who established the

Vijayanagar empire are unclear. Though at a later time they claimed descent from the mythological lunar race of the epics, in reality they were, in all likelihood, sons of the soil.[32] By the early fourteenth century, one after the other these brothers appear as chieftains in different parts of the tottering Hoysala kingdom, though one origin myth connects them not to Karnataka but to a Telugu lord destroyed by Delhi.[33] The brothers were carried off to the north where the Sultan either nodded as they willingly transferred allegiances to him,[34] or had them 'forcefully converted to Islam'.[35] If the conversion theory is correct (for it appears most prominently in local traditions), it might have been voluntary, for the brothers won the favour of Muhammad bin Tughluq who, with countless rebellions and betrayals on his imperial plate, tasked them with returning and taming the unruly south – he would hardly hand over such an important task to reluctant brothers who had been converted under duress.[36] It is now, in the 1330s, that the eldest of them, Harihara, appears in the Deccan as an amir of the Tughluq court (and it was in this capacity that the administration of Raichur was granted to him, later forming the basis for Vijayanagar's claim over that district).[37] But as 'soon as they touched their native soil, their national feeling was stirred up by the Hindu liberation movement', filled as they were with 'horror and disgust at the conduct of Muslim officials'.[38] Or so the yarn spins.

What seems to have happened is that as the Hoysala kingdom disintegrated, with its Hindu king (the very same who was flayed and hung) fighting a losing battle against Muslim warlords parked in Madurai, 'Harihara conquered . . . nearly the whole of the Hoysala territories' in coordination with his brothers, fanning out into various provinces of the dying state to pick up its pieces.[39] In other words, while an old Hindu dynasty perished, the brothers sought not so much to salvage it in the name of a common Hindu cause, but to launch a new line of their own, gaining from the chaos in the country. In February 1346, a year and a half before Hasan Gangu was declared Sultan of the Bahmani state, the five Sangama brothers met in Srirangam, an important centre of their Shaiva faith, to celebrate their 'coast-to-coast

conquests of the southern peninsula', by now also having discarded
their loyalty to Delhi.[40] In the wider context, thus, 'between 1339 and
1347, two families of obscure or humble origins, operating on opposite
sides of the Krishna River, led movements that radically redrew the
Deccan's political, and more importantly, conceptual map'.[41] The
Tughluqs had shattered the south and vanquished its old houses. And
from the doldrums emerged Vijayanagar and the Bahmani Sultanate
that, for reasons of economics cloaked in a language of religion, waged
war against one another till nothing but ashes remained.

That said, there was certainly a conception of 'us' and 'them' in
how the two sides viewed each other. For in 1347 one of the Sangama
brothers added to his titles (which included such inventive variants
as 'a great kite to terrify serpents' and 'terrifier of foreign kings'[42]) an
unprecedented honorific that had never been used in India before:
Hinduraya Suratrana, or Sultan among Hindu Kings. Five years later
another brother, governing a different part of this stitched-together
kingdom, took the same title, followed in 1354 by Harihara too naming
himself Sultan.[43] It was the first time Indian rulers applied the term
'Hindu' to distinguish themselves from Muslims of foreign origins –
in other words, a geographical term applied to Indians in general by
outsiders was now internalized. And in styling themselves Sultans,
these rulers were clearly marking their place in a wider world and a
changed geography where that term carried tremendous potency – to
be a Sultan was to be part of the new world that was being shaped.
Nor were the Sangamas alone in embracing the innovation: the Telugu
lord Kapaya Nayaka who presented the Bahmanis their Turquoise
Throne was Sultan of the Andhras, while a century and a half later,
another ruler in Vijayanagar exceeded them all by styling himself Gola
Suratrana, or Sultan of the World.[44] The concept of the Sultan seized
political imagination as a new order was born. 'In one form or another,
this title continued in use by . . . successors [of the Sangama brothers]
for at least another 250 years, through three changes in dynasty, until
as late as the opening years of the seventeenth century.'[45] And, at the
end of the day, in 'expelling Tughluq imperial might from the region,

leaders of both' the Vijayanagar and Bahmani kingdoms 'defiantly and successfully appropriated the conceptual basis of Delhi's authority—the title' of Sultan.[46] That one was Muslim and the other Hindu did not matter in this political sense, even though both parties knew their personal identities were dissimilar.[47]

The site the Sangamas chose for their capital lay along a bend of the Tungabhadra. It was a place with sacred associations, first with the river goddess Pampa (from which is derived its current name, Hampi) and then with a male deity called Virupaksha. Both were connected to Devi and Shiva of the Sanskritic mainstream, and the Sangamas adopted their worship.[48] The legend associated with the birth of the city, however, is a curious one. One day Harihara was hunting by the river when he witnessed a strange exchange: a hare, when chased by his hounds, instead of fleeing the other way, turned around and bit the dogs.[49] The king was mystified, and shortly thereafter he ran into the sage Vidyaranya, who advised him to construct a city on that very spot, promising that it would 'prove the strongest in the world'.[50] The story is a peculiar one to claim divine benediction for their chosen capital, but it is not unique: according to legend, Kandy in Sri Lanka was also founded after a prince encountered another hare of a courageous, dog-biting disposition.[51] That there were also a number of origin myths for the royal family itself – Kannada, Telugu, Hindu warriors, Muslim converts – is not necessarily an anomaly or a consequence of incorrect interpretations. Instead, it might simply be that 'these stories were composed by different authors to be communicated to very different audiences' to establish the credentials of a new house in a new realm, embracing peoples speaking a variety of languages and with diverse cults and cultures, all under a single imperial umbrella.[52]

Legitimacy for this enterprise was assembled over time. Where the Bahmanis claimed prophetic blessings from Nizamuddin Auliya and bowed to the Abbasid Caliph in Egypt, the Sangamas made up for their obscure origins and religious apostasy with links to Vidyaranya, who is believed to have converted them back to Hinduism. Other methods too were applied. Connections were established with the dead but indelible Hoysala dynasty – it was claimed that Harihara's daughter was married to a son of the hanged ruler of that line,[53] and that his nephew, who would succeed to the throne in due course as Harihara II, was married to a granddaughter of Ramachandra, the penultimate ruler of the Devagiri Yadavas.[54] A link to the Pandya dynasty in the Tamil country was similarly established – when in the 1370s Vijayanagar destroyed the Sultanate there and annexed its territories, the prince in command was aided by a mysterious woman who presented him, before his engagement with the enemy, 'the divine sword which had been the heir loom in the royal Pandyan family',[55]reminding him also that he is an incarnation of Vishnu.[56] The boar, which was the emblem of the lapsed Chalukya dynasty, was adopted as Vijayanagar's and the early architecture of the city imitated the pattern of Chalukyan capitals of yore.[57] So too when the Rayas began their expansions, they patronized richly the most important temples of the conquered provinces to win local approval and purchase the loyalties of local elites.[58] As the power of the Hindu Sultans grew thus, so did their bonds with every old (but defunct) house that public memory could recall and several significant places of worship, strengthening in the process their own legitimacy to reign as sovereigns.[59]

In the early period, Vijayanagar was governed through a system of parallel rule, with all the Sangama brothers in different provinces where they were practically autonomous. After Harihara's death in 1355–56, Bukka succeeded to the overlordship and reigned for more than twenty years, stabilizing the kingdom and adding territory to it. Temples that had fallen in the course of the Muslim invasions in earlier decades were restored, and with the incorporation of wealthy Tamil lands into the empire, Vijayanagar's prosperity became proverbial – in 1374 an embassy was even sent to China. While their legendary conflict with the Bahmanis concerned where the boundary between the states lay – and who, therefore, owned Raichur – where *religious* tensions did arise, it was not with Muslims. In 1368, on the contrary, Bukka, himself of Shaiva persuasion, had to settle a conflict between the Jains and the Vaishnavas. Summoning their chiefs to court, 'he taking the hand of the Jainas and placing it in the hand of the Sri-Vaishnavas of the eighteen [districts] including the *acharyas* of Srirangam, Tirupati, Kanchi . . . declared that there was no difference between the Vaishnava and the Jaina creeds'. He then confirmed the Jains in the enjoyment of all the privileges they possessed under previous regimes, and added that the Vaishnavas must marry the welfare of the Jains to their own, and that 'for as long as the sun and moon endure' the former must endeavour to protect the latter.[60] In Kanchi, at a later stage, when difficulties arose it was between Shaiva and Madhva Brahmins, and yet again a compromise was negotiated through the court.[61]

Bukka's son, Harihara II, forced changes in the basic structure of the state. Over the course of his reign, he ejected his cousins from control over the distant provinces of the empire, and appointed, much like the Mughal emperors, his own sons as viceroys in far-flung parts.[62] In due course, a system of shared sovereignty would emerge, known as nayamkara whereby chieftains called amaranayakas (*amara* derived from the Bahmani amir) were granted dominions to rule as subordinates of the crown in Vijayanagar.[63] But this did not mean transfers of power were particularly smoother, for when Harihara II died there followed a struggle for succession, so that in three years three kings ruled in Vijayanagar. According to a literary source, one of the contenders dealt with some of his 'envious' relations who tried to deny him his patrimony by killing 'the whole lot of them in their beds'.[64] But this is very likely an exaggeration, for though Vijayanagar would suffer an instance of parricide, in general those who were defeated were simply allowed to retire as governors. This was the fate of one of the other two claimants (who were Harihara II's sons from different queens) – he was defeated and ruled 'more or less independently' as a provincial lord for a decade thereafter, even as the victorious third son became the Raya of Vijayanagar.[65] It was this monarch whose daughter was married to Firoz Shah Bahmani in 1407, though another princess seems to have made a far less glamorous alliance when she took 'an officer of the Customs Department' as her husband.[66] Still, the royal

household was a most diverse setting, with one of the ruler's wives
following not any Hindu tradition but the Jain religion.[67]

Like all medieval kingdoms, Vijayanagar, which by now covered
140,000 square miles, was a decentralized state.[68] The districts
immediately adjoining the capital were governed directly by the Rayas
and the capital itself housed between 100,000 and 250,000 people.[69]
Indeed, by the end of Krishnadeva's reign this core of the empire would
be home to an estimated 480,000 people, 'making it second only to
Beijing in terms of population'.[70] Relations with the wider empire
were negotiated through feudatories, and subjects of the state could
challenge, sometimes violently, the imperial government. Less than
a century after the kingdom's founding, for example, 'communities of
cultivators and artisans of the Kaveri delta . . . rose up in widespread
rebellion against the oppressive taxes imposed' by the capital.
Vijayanagar, with its 'chronic inability to harmonize the agrarian
economy of the dry upland plateau with the commercialized economy
of the rich Tamil coast', granted the latter a degree of autonomy.[71]
Taxes too could be negotiated. We find, for instance, an artisan tax,
loom tax, marriage tax, oil-mill tax, and even 'egg duties' and cooking
tax.[72] Tamil weavers not only obtained benefits on account of their
importance to the economy, but were even granted superior status
with the use of palanquins and the right to blow the conch on ritual
occasions.[73] Decades later, barbers were granted certain exemptions,[74]
with the result that when the English East India Company tried to
drag the community back into the collector's net, they refused to pay
and told instead the story of how one of their forebears had given the
Raya of Vijayanagar such a wonderful shave that, delighted, he had
remitted taxes for perpetuity.[75]

By the period of the next emperor, the kingdom was firmly
entrenched in the south and was attracting the notice of the world.
Devaraya II 'was given much to letters and made many books and
(promulgated) ordinances in his land and kingdom'.[76] He obtained
tribute from the kings of Ceylon and exercised some form of distant
authority over the Malabar coast as well. At court he entertained not

only Sanskrit scholars and Hindu poets but even a Christian.[77] Abdur Razzak, a Persian ambassador, was bedazzled by Vijayanagar, 'whose inhabitants', he exclaimed, 'have no equals in the world'.[78] 'The country is for the most part well cultivated and fertile, and about three hundred good seaports belong to it. There are more than 1000 elephants, lofty as hills and gigantic as demons. The army consists of eleven lacs of men. In the whole of Hindustan, there is no Rai more absolute than' the ruler of Vijayanagar, he reported,[79] whose palace had 'numerous underground royal halls filled with molten gold'.[80] His capital 'is such that the pupil of the eye has never seen a place like it, and the ear of intelligence has never been informed that there existed anything equal to it in the world. It is built in such a manner that seven citadels and the same number of walls enclose each other.' Within were fields, parks, houses and bazaars. 'The jewelers sell publicly in the bazaars pearls, rubies, emeralds, and diamonds,' he added with wonder, before noting, with corresponding amusement, also how roses were sold everywhere. 'These people cannot live without roses, and they look upon them quite as necessary as food.'[81]

When Razzak personally beheld the emperor – an emperor who unexpectedly presented him a Chinese fan, along with the usual presents given to foreign ambassadors – he was impressed:

The prince was seated in a hall, surrounded by the most imposing attributes of state. Right and left of him stood a numerous crowd of men arranged in a circle. The king was dressed in a robe of green satin, around his neck he wore a collar, composed of pearls of beautiful water, and other splendid gems. He had an olive complexion, his frame was thin, and he was rather tall; on his cheeks might be seen a slight down, but there was no beard on his chin. The expression of his countenance was extremely pleasing.[82]

While Hindu elements derived from previous dynasties as well as Kannada, Tamil and Telugu influences pervaded the court, the Vijayanagar kings were not isolated from the wider Persianized

networks of their day, even though as non-Muslims they did not
attract Persian manpower in quite the way the Bahmanis did.
Persian culture was an arresting soft power asset, viewed across the
trading world as 'prestigious, cosmopolitan, and most important,
readily portable across ethnic frontiers' without narrow religious
connotations.[83] And as Vijayanagar's prosperity bloomed, it too
reflected foreign influences, perhaps even more sumptuously than
the Bahmanis. In matters of dress, for instance, early sculptures from
Hampi's fourteenth-century period show courtly attire as limited
mainly to dhotis, with the upper body left bare. This continued to
be the case in other parts of India into the fifteenth century as well
– Abdur Razzak remarked crustily that in neighbouring Malabar
'both king and beggar look like this' with 'loincloths tied from their
navels to their knees'.[84] The fifteenth-century monarch he surveyed in
Vijayanagar, however, was in a different league of sartorial refinement.
For by the age of Devaraya II, men wore shawls, scarves and caps,
which were succeeded, as evinced through surviving sculpture and
art, by 'close fitting, high-necked, full-sleeved shirts or jackets that
were usually buttoned down the front'. Similar innovations applied
to the dhoti, which was 'covered by broad girdles and waistbands,
the whole ranging from knee-length to ankle-length'.[85] In a custom
originally introduced in the south by Muslim invaders as we saw
after the defeat of Prataparudra of Warangal, the Rayas commenced
the practice of bestowing robes of honour on dignitaries, while men
as well as women took to wearing gem-embroidered conical caps,
inspired by fashions in lands to their west.[86]

Architecture too reflected a richness of influence from India and
overseas. Where in the early stages temples and buildings were typical
in their Deccani style, as Vijayanagar brought Tamil provinces within
its grasp, the imperial tastes of the Cholas, with exquisite carvings
and large temple gateways, were soaked up.[87] When Abdur Razzak
visited the dancing girls' quarters in the city, he saw along 'both sides
of the road . . . pictures of lions, leopards, tigers and other animals,
depicted with such verisimilitude that one would think that they are

alive'.[88] The centre of the city, where dwelt the king with his court, was full of Persian influence: 'domes, vaulted arches, parapets of merlons, corner finials, fine plasterwork, and so forth'. The multi-columned pavilion where Abdur Razzak studied Devaraya II was reminiscent of 'the throne hall and Apadana of Persepolis', and 'sculptural reliefs carved at the base of Vijayanagar's Great Platform depict processions of figures bearing tribute to the enthroned king', just as they do on the Apadana thousands of miles away.[89] This was not, however, a case of simply imitating a popular international style, for through all this was blended architecture 'derived from Hindu temple [traditions, including] stepped layouts, multi-tiered sculpted stone basements, curved eaves, stepped roofs, and plaster decorations', in a rich, eclectic mix that became the true highlight of Vijayanagar's imperial splendour.[90]

Devaraya II himself was most interested in the world beyond India, for when he met Abdur Razzak, many were the questions he asked about that envoy's sovereign – how many warhorses the Persian king

A detail from the Great Platform at Hampi

possessed, what his great nobles were like – besides also demanding information on cities like Herat and Shiraz; Hormuz was already known as 'Hurumanji'.[91] All this reveals Devaraya II's 'awareness of, and avid interest in' the very same Timurid court culture that so fascinated Firoz Shah, his brother-in-law across the river.[92] Part of this was also due to the nature of the political system over which Devaraya II presided. Earlier kingdoms under the Hoysalas and Kakatiyas largely governed regions speaking one dominant language, with a single cultural identity. Vijayanagar, however, like the Bahmani Sultanate, was a multiregional entity. Arabic and Persian linguistic influences melted into Kannada and Telugu, and urbanization was at an all-time high – from the recruitment of Muslim mercenaries to his tendency to reward military leaders over older elites, Devaraya II created a 'highly successful conquest state' where power, and not any religious ideas of Hindu supremacy that are so often said to have invigorated his ancestors, were enshrined in statecraft.[93] Indeed, when Vijayanagar's envoys were dispatched to Persia with Abdur Razzak, bearing rubies and other presents, these ambassadors of the Raya were also Muslims of Iranian origin.[94]

However, not all was smooth sailing at court. For even as Vijayanagar's might grew, loyalties were not always easy to sustain, and in the early 1440s there was a particularly violent plot to assassinate Devaraya II, hatched by a brother.[95] This man had constructed a new palace for himself where, in the name of a house-warming feast, large numbers of the emperor's senior nobility and confidants were invited to dine. While Abdur Razzak indicates that they were picked off one by one – for reasons of caste, not all could eat together and so each went inside at a different time from others at the gathering – by the end of the day, the palace descended into a 'place of carnage'.[96] 'Care had been taken,' we are told, 'to bring together all the drums, kettledrums, trumpets, and flutes that could be found in the city, and these instruments playing all at the same time, made a tremendous uproar' in which the cries of those being slaughtered were drowned. When many courtiers were thus liquidated, the brother proceeded to Devaraya II's own palace. 'The villain then entered into the king's presence, holding in his hand a dish covered with betel-nut, under which was concealed a brilliant poignard (a thin dagger). And addressing the monarch he said, deceptively, "The hall is ready and they only await your august presence."'[97]

It so happened that the Raya was not in the mood for a party and cited ill health. 'This unnatural brother, thus, losing the hope of enticing the king to his house, drew his poignard and struck him there—with several violent blows, so that the prince fell at the back of his throne. The traitor, thus believing that the king was dead' went out to the portico and announced: 'I have slain the king . . . and such and such amirs, Brahmins, and viziers; now I am king.'[98] In a much later account by Nuniz, Devaraya II is not struck, 'as he was a man who knew how to use both sword and dagger better than any one in his kingdom' and 'avoided by twists and turns of his body the thrusts aimed at him,' sustaining only a few injuries.[99] In the first version related by Razzak, the king, who is not actually dead, drags himself to another portico nearby and screams, 'I am alive. I am well and safe. Seize that wretch!'[100] In Nuniz's retelling, however, the king disarms and kills his murderous brother in his chambers, and 'this done, he ordered a horse to be saddled, and mounted it, and rode' out of the palace, with the head of the assassin in his hands in a macabre display.[101] Either way, the event did provoke trouble, for taking advantage of the confusion that erupted, the Bahmani Sultan crossed the border. At first Devaraya II had the upper hand, and Ferishta records how 'the Mussalmans experienced great difficulties'. But then, when the emperor's son himself fell in battle, the Raya halted and paid for peace.[102] Even Devaraya II could not fight at once both an external enemy and crisis at court.

The period after Devaraya II's eventual death in 1446 was not propitious for the state. His son and heir was weak, and not only did he face joint invasions by the Gajapati of Orissa and the Bahmani Sultan, he also lost much treasure and territory to these rulers.[103] And while his own inscriptions laud him as a great ruler and destroyer of

Turks, we learn that he died in 1465 'of a broken heart'.[104] Things did
not improve for Vijayanagar under the next Raya – it was he who put
to flight Muslim traders and lost Goa and other ports to the Bahmani
Sultanate – and it took a long time for his eventual successors to restore
order and regain the trust of merchants from abroad. Any hint of order
that remained was due to the deft handiwork of a general called Saluva
('the Hawk'[105]) Narasimha, who happened to be related to the royal
family.[106] When, for instance, the Bahmani Sultan plundered Kanchi
and its temple in 1481, before the treasure could all be carried away,
Narasimha intercepted his men and brought all the gold back where it
belonged.[107] In the end, however, the man would have a much larger
role to play, serving as a 'bridge into a new political phase' in the history
of Vijayanagar; a role more significant, and indeed treacherous, than
any of his numerous military successes or his efforts to keep the state
together in the face of a monarch given to vice and vacillation.[108]

That moment arrived in 1485 when the reign of Devaraya II's
grandson came to a particularly blood-curdling end after his own
son murdered him.[109] 'The parricide, however, refused to inherit the
throne out of moral fear and offered it to his younger brother.'[110] Since
by now royal blood had already been spilt on the Diamond Throne,
this younger brother decided to continue the tradition and put to
death the very man who offered him power in the first place.[111] Chaos
spread through the empire, and the new monarch did not appear to
be urgently interested in attending to the business of state. When
that generalissimo Narasimha returned, he was more engrossed in
other pursuits such as authoring a book of erotica, in which thirty-
two stanzas are devoted to the art of oral sex.[112] The consequence was
the dawn of a new age in the history of Vijayanagar. The last of the
inscriptions issued by the house of Sangama is dated 29 July 1485.
Fifteen months later, the records announce the advent of a new Raya:
Saluva Narasimha.[113] The final of the Sangama rulers, who seemed to
have no kingly talents (even if he had promising literary faculties), had
been deposed and the Diamond Throne was usurped by his general,
who thought himself far better suited for the purpose of sitting on it.[114]

In the end, though, Narasimha's Second dynasty also failed to endure. He died a few years after seizing the throne, entrusting his sons to the care of a trusted comrade. One of the two children was murdered, while the other was maintained as a puppet for nearly fifteen years. At the end of this, when his demands to be handed over real power began to irritate the regent, he too was shoved into the embrace of death. The regent's heirs launched the Third dynasty of Vijayanagar in 1505, which too was famously receptive to the world – in the same year, when a 'Brahmin' (priest) from Portugal called Frei Luis arrived at court, he was loaded with presents as well as a letter proposing a marital alliance between Vijayanagar and Portugal! The idea was that a Vijayanagar princess would proceed to Lisbon to become queen there, and a daughter of King Manuel of Portugal was to be sent to India, so that the 'two kings would be allied for the purpose of joint actions on land and sea' and 'the blood of the two royal houses would mingle'.[115] Nothing came of the idea – though it is tantalizing to imagine what Portuguese power at sea and Vijayanagar's greatness on land might have achieved – and real glory in the league of Devaraya II came to the Third dynasty four years later when the man we have already encountered by the name of Krishnadeva ascended to power.

It was he who put to flight enemies to the north, who thrilled in his mischievous title as restorer of the kingdom of Turks and who reasserted the prestige of the empire. And it was also he who, in demanding his royal foot be kissed by his enemy, unleashed events that two generations after his time precipitated a storm of political fury, engulfing Vijayanagar and taking it to its annihilation. Where once a great city stood, ruins would come to be, and as a traveller wrote dejectedly, the whole place was finally 'emptie' with nothing dwelling there 'but Tygres and other wild beasts'.[116]

IV

Rebel Sultans
The Five Mutinous Bahmani Governors and
the Fall of Vijayanagar

IV

THE DECCAN IN THE
17TH CENTURY

MUGHAL EMPIRE

Ahmedabad

Cambay

VINDHYA MOUNTAINS

Surat

Burhanpur

Daulatabad ● Aurangabad

Mumbai
(Bombay)

AHMADNAGAR
(NIZAM SHAH)

BIDAR
(BARID SHAH)

Warangal

Kalyana

Gulbarga ● Bidar
Hyderabad

Nauraspur

Golconda

GOLCONDA
(QUTB SHAH)

Bijapur

Firuzabad

Talikota

Raichur

Krishna

Masulipatam

Goa

BIJAPUR
(ADIL SHAH)

Adoni

Vijayanagar
(Hampi)

Tungabhadra

WESTERN GHATS

EASTERN GHATS

Coromandel coast

ARABIAN
SEA

BAY
OF
BENGAL

Chennai
(Madras)

Pondicherry

NAYAKA
STATES

Malabar coast

Legend

Approximate extent of
Mughal empire

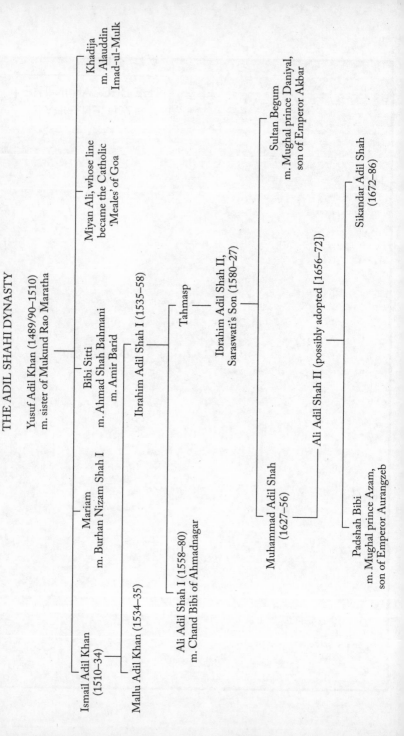

THE ADIL SHAHI DYNASTY

Yusuf Adil Khan (1489/90–1510)
m. sister of Mukund Rao Maratha

Ismail Adil Khan (1510–34)

Mariam
m. Burhan Nizam Shah I

Bibi Sitti
m. Ahmad Shah Bahmani
m. Amir Barid

Miyan Ali, whose line became the Catholic 'Meales' of Goa

Khadija
m. Alauddin Imad-ul-Mulk

Mallu Adil Khan (1534–35)

Ibrahim Adil Shah I (1535–58)

Tahmasp

Ali Adil Shah I (1558–80)
m. Chand Bibi of Ahmadnagar

Ibrahim Adil Shah II, Saraswati's Son (1580–27)

Muhammad Adil Shah (1627–56)

Ali Adil Shah II (possibly adopted [1656–72])

Sultan Begum
m. Mughal prince Daniyal, son of Emperor Akbar

Padshah Bibi
m. Mughal prince Azam, son of Emperor Aurangzeb

Sikandar Adil Shah (1672–86)

THE NIZAM SHAHI DYNASTY

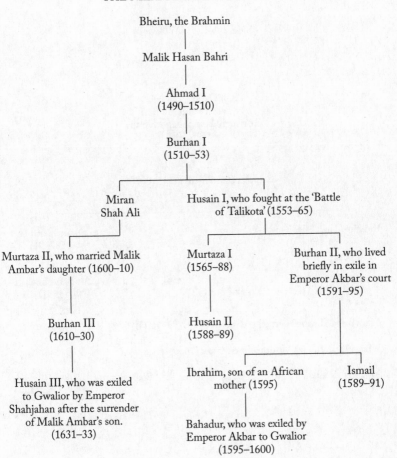

Bheiru, the Brahmin

Malik Hasan Bahri

Ahmad I
(1490–1510)

Burhan I
(1510–53)

Miran
Shah Ali

Husain I, who fought at the 'Battle
of Talikota' (1553–65)

Murtaza II, who married Malik
Ambar's daughter (1600–10)

Murtaza I
(1565–88)

Burhan II, who lived
briefly in exile in
Emperor Akbar's court
(1591–95)

Burhan III
(1610–30)

Husain II
(1588–89)

Husain III, who was exiled
to Gwalior by Emperor
Shahjahan after the surrender
of Malik Ambar's son.
(1631–33)

Ibrahim, son of an African
mother (1595)

Ismail
(1589–91)

Bahadur, who was exiled by
Emperor Akbar to Gwalior
(1595–1600)

THE BARIDI DYNASTY

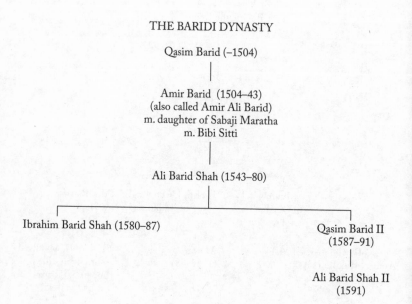

Qasim Barid (–1504)

Amir Barid (1504–43)
(also called Amir Ali Barid)
m. daughter of Sabaji Maratha
m. Bibi Sitti

Ali Barid Shah (1543–80)

Ibrahim Barid Shah (1580–87)

Qasim Barid II
(1587–91)

Ali Barid Shah II
(1591)

Amir Barid II, who usurped the throne (1591/92–1600)

Mizra Ali Barid, who usurped the throne (1600–09)

Amir Barid Shah, who lost his kingdom to the Adil Shahs forever (1609–19)

The League of Sultans that would rain death and destruction upon Vijayanagar was born out of the chaos engulfing the Bahmani state. In 1489, with Mahmud Gawan dead and lamented, and an adolescent on the teetering Turquoise Throne, the opportunity was ripe for a strongman to replace the decrepit dynasty with a new house. Unlike in Vijayanagar, however, where a single powerful alternative emerged during each shift of power, the Bahmani Sultanate had far too many men of ability and ambition, none of whom saw eye to eye, and whose failure to unite would ultimately invite damnation upon them all. For the time being, though, as a neutered Sultan watched from his palace in Bidar, the kingdom was carved up. He couldn't have done much in any case, for he was a prisoner already in the hands of one of the five lords who now defined the fate of the northern Deccan. In a few years, in fact, so absolute was the Sultan's resignation that when another faction sought to 'rescue' him, perfectly conscious that this merely meant accepting a new watchdog in place of the old, the man chose to carry on with his bath than come out and make a brave choice. In the end, when told off sternly for his indifference while blood flowed around him, he elected to stay with his existing jailor rather than risk going over to a new one, about whose temperament he could predict nothing.[1]

The custodian of the Sultan and the lands around Bidar came to be known as the Barid Shah, though like the others in the game, the actual sovereign style of Shah was only assumed tentatively some years later, in 1542, when no figurehead Bahmani remained to embarrass the claimant.[2] The man began life as simply Qasim Barid, a Turkish slave from Georgia who was imported by a nobleman and gifted to a previous Bahmani Sultan. He was, apparently, 'an expert in handwriting and also played well on musical instruments'[3] but the man's real talent appeared in military affairs soon after these recitals in the palace. When he put down a rebellion by a Maratha chieftain, the fallen Maratha lord's estates were granted to him by a very pleased monarch – and the dead man's daughter married Qasim's son and heir, infusing local blood into this Westerner house's foreign veins.[4] After Gawan, for a long time the Baridis succeeded in holding power as proxies for the minor Sultan, but with the death and eventual absconding of the last of the Bahmanis, they were reduced to frying smaller fish. They tried to win over Vijayanagar at a certain moment to further their interests against the other Shahs emerging in the neighbourhood, and in due course also attempted to persuade the Mughals to extend them protection. The plots did not succeed in the long run, however, and in 1619 the Barid Shah's tiny state was annexed by a rival line, bringing the dynasty to an end.

The rival line in question was that of Yusuf, the founder of the Sultanate of Bijapur, also a Westerner. A subsequent scion of his house would claim that Yusuf was nothing less than an Ottoman prince: a son of Sultan Murad II of Turkey who was rescued from a bloodthirsty brother seeking to put the boy to death. His mother, then, 'entrusted him to a merchant of Sava to be raised', and in due course, he stepped on to Bahmani shores, where he found his bearings as well as his destiny.[5] More likely, however, he arrived in the Deccan around 1460, among the legions of Westerners who came seeking a future here, and was of equally conventional Turkish or Persian extraction.[6] Furthermore, he too embraced local blood by marrying the sister of Mukund Rao, the Maratha Rajah of Idar.[7] Soon, Yusuf emerged as a confidant of Mahmud Gawan, who, in recognition of his 'capacity as a soldier and statesman', appointed him a governor.[8] Some even said he was 'adopted' by the slain minister, for after his death Yusuf, who held the title of 'Adil Khan' at the time, succeeded as one of the principal leaders of the Westerners at court during the whimper of a reign led by that adolescent Bahmani Sultan.[9] Most nobles of his faction would not even attend court unless Yusuf confirmed they could.[10]

When it became clear that Qasim Barid intended to keep the boy-king as his puppet and rule in his name, Yusuf was among the earliest to claim his share of territory where his successors later ruled as Adil Shahs. While he himself did not declare independence, he took some of the best districts in the Sultanate with Bijapur as his seat, and Raichur firmly in his grasp. Another contender, meanwhile, *did* proceed with the unthinkable and declared, from a newly established capital in Ahmadnagar, his sovereignty as the Nizam Shah – when an irate Qasim Barid demanded how there could be two Sultans in the same kingdom, and why this upstart had begun to use the white royal parasol, the latter replied that 'he was doing so only in order to keep off the sun' from his face.[11] It was defiance, sharp in its threatening sweetness, for there was little that could be done to prevent him. The Nizam Shah, interestingly, was from the Dakhni faction, and of Brahmin descent.[12] Some believed his father, son of one Bheiru, was captured from Vijayanagar, while others suggest his roots lay in Pathri in Marathwada, making him a native of the northern Deccan. Indeed, years later, when a rival seized the place, the then Nizam Shah reclaimed it by force and bestowed the fief on his 'Brahmin relations' as 'a charitable gift', confirming the Hindu antecedents of his Muslim line.[13]

In Berar in the north, meanwhile, another convert – and therefore also a Dakhni – was pleased to announce his own promotion from governor Imad-ul-Mulk to the dignity of Imad Shah. And in the east, from the formidable fortress of Golconda reigned the dynasty of the Qutb Shahs, the fifth of the Deccan's parvenu princes, whose diamond mines and textile wealth would deliver them riches in legendary quantities. These self-proclaimed princes too manufactured origin myths, but their rise was also noticed in neighbouring Vijayanagar with the kind of sharp interest that masquerades as disdain. As a Telugu text summed up generations later, it was through 'a fellow named Barid of Bidar' that the new order began to take shape. 'His hawk keeper,' the account sneers, 'came to be known as Nizam Shah, his water-pot bearer became known as Adil Shah, and the man who was in charge of keeping the dogs became known as Qutb-al-Mulk.' In theory, as far as the southern neighbour of the Bahmanis was concerned, these splinter Sultanates that now began to take form were all of lowly, mean origins, not worthy of any real dignity or kingly attention.[14] In reality, though, it was these upstarts who eventually plotted Vijayanagar's collapse and final demolition.

Meanwhile, for Qasim Barid, Yusuf was a particularly detestable enemy, not least because Bijapur, the latter's seat, was a province he himself coveted.[15] But Yusuf proved a sharp strategist who knew how to prevail. After 1490 he commenced the expansion of his kingdom, often thwarting rival designs but occasionally suffering due to the enemy in the capital. Seeking access to the sea, Yusuf simply wrote to the Bahmani governor of Goa 'demanding his presence at Bijapur'. When the governor answered this summons, it was a more than tacit recognition of Yusuf as his overlord – for so handing over Goa without a single sword raised, the governor was confirmed in his position.[16] With another provincial lord, however, who was Qasim Barid's creature, Yusuf resorted to arms and took by force several districts, including prestigious Gulbarga which was once the Bahmani capital.[17] Of the kingdom's original twelve provinces, Yusuf and the Nizam Shah of Ahmadnagar systematically swallowed up as many as they could, a clandestine pact in force between them that only the strongest of the Bahmani court deserved to claim sovereignty now that the Sultanate was in terminal decline.[18] And though Yusuf's heirs and the Nizam Shahs would fight battles of their own, at this time this Westerner and the Dakhni were prepared to join hands for mutually rewarding goals.[19]

What did, however, give Qasim Barid an excuse to seek Yusuf's destruction was when the latter went a step too far. By 1502 he was already having the khutbah read not in the name of the Bahmani Sultan but in his own, though rituals retained the Sunni flavour in keeping with the kingdom's formal religion. Now, however, emboldened by the rise of the Safavid dynasty in Persia that had made the Shia faith its official religion, Yusuf too planned to declare Bijapur a Shia state, governed hereafter by his own religious affiliations. His motives, incidentally, were never purely theological to begin with: by seeking to emulate Safavid Persia, Yusuf was attempting to strengthen his position among his rivals in the Deccan and win the friendship and protection of one of the greatest empires on earth – in 1519 the Safavids would bestow the title of 'Shah' formally on his house, legitimizing them as sovereigns in their own right.[20] A century later, one of Yusuf's successors would insist to 'the exalted' Shah Abbas I of Persia that he was but his 'humblest slave' whose Deccan territories 'are as much a part of the [Safavid] Empire as the provinces of Iraq, Fars, Khurasan, and Adharbaijan'. His forefathers, this Adil Shah declared, had merely been 'appointed to rule over these territories and protect them by His Majesty's ancestors' and his own innocent motivations were to serve 'on His Majesty's behalf and defend [his lands] from foreign aggression'.[21] Despite appearances, this was not undignified grovelling. For by this time the Deccan was indeed in need of protection from whatever quarter it might be provided, for the gaze of Delhi had turned once again towards the citadels of the south.

In 1502, though, Yusuf was warned that this was precisely the kind of impetuosity that might rouse Qasim Barid and the Sunni Nizam Shah of Ahmadnagar into a dangerous marriage of convenience, but he went ahead anyway with his proclamation.[22] Officially, this 'proved Yusuf's allegiance to two different rulers. He owed nominal political sovereignty to the Bahmani Sultan and religious allegiance to the Shah of Iran',[23] who was the only Shia emperor in the whole world, so powerful and splendid that the Mughals too were later often in his awe. Armed, thus, with the pretext of betrayal, Qasim Barid had the Sultan issue a call for all his other governor-princes to march against the heretic. The confederacy miscarried, then, only due to the Imad Shah of Berar's intervention – with a cool head, he enlightened those in the alliance that if Bijapur were to fall at the altar of Qasim Barid's ambitions, it would set a precedent and invite grave danger for the rest of them as well. Qasim Barid, he warned, exaggerated his Sunnism only to 'hide his sinister ambition of reducing the whole of the Deccan to his obedience'.[24] The Imad Shah gave Yusuf too an earful, reminding him of the cardinal rule that faith must always retreat before the more pragmatic demands of the balance of power. For the time being, then, Yusuf was 'compelled to re-instate Sunnism'.[25] But when two years later Qasim Barid died, Bijapur reverted to Shia veneration, only this time Yusuf distributed his largesse among the authorities who mattered to buy their assent, guaranteeing Sunni nobles that they were free to follow their own practices.[26]

Yusuf's fluctuation between Sunnism and Shiism provoked enduring repercussions for the future of Bijapur. Of the nine Adil Shahs who ruled from that city, five were Shia, and the kingdom swung half a dozen times between one variant of Islam and the other.[27] The consequences were twofold: on the one hand, Shia rulers tended to glorify the Persian emperor as their overlord and spiritual mentor, while Sunni Adil Shahs preferred the Ottomans as their role models. This naturally meant a repeated recalibration of their foreign policy. But on the other, more uncertain, hand, this instability also coloured local politics. Shia princes in Bijapur, for instance, made it a habit to be overgenerous to Westerners over the Dakhnis, with the exact opposite result every time a Sunni was in power. The curse that destroyed the peace of the Bahmanis was inherited by this successor state, and the 'alternation of Sunni and Shia doctrines with the change of rulers' shattered the loyalty of noblemen 'who were the virtual pillars of the kingdom'.[28] The Adil Shahs themselves erred by not rising above sectarianism, as they ought to have – one prince dismissed as many as 3000 Westerners from his service in a single flourish of autocratic fury, with the result that they moved en masse into the service of Vijayanagar and fought for its Hindu dynasty against their previous employer who had revealed himself a bigot.[29]

By the time Yusuf died in 1510, the Adil Shahi dynasty looked prepared for a long and eventful reign from Bijapur. There were losses –

the Portuguese, who had sailed into this dramatic Indian Ocean world at the turn of the century, seized Goa from under the nose of its governor, for instance. In an initial response during the monsoons in 1510, Yusuf led 6000 men on to the island of Tiswadi, the Portuguese's principal possession in Goa, and restored his power, reducing the stranded Portuguese to eating rats aboard their ships and cooking repulsive broths with whatever leather they could find.[30] But when Yusuf died later that year, the Europeans obtained a window to make a second attempt to secure the place; most of the garrison had left for Bijapur to pledge allegiance to Ismail Adil Shah, Yusuf's heir, and the Portuguese took Goa with yawning ease, never again surrendering it to an Indian power until the twentieth century. Victory, of course, was followed by 'ruthless pillage' and, while farmers and Brahmins were spared, 'it was an indiscriminate massacre. Many mosques where the citizens had taken refuge were burnt down', not to speak of Hindu temples.[31] In the end Bijapur came to terms with the foreigners – Goa was ceded to the Portuguese on the condition that the latter would not molest other ports down the coast that belonged to Bijapur and contributed richly to its revenues.[32]

The loss of Goa, however, invited a cascade of disasters – in 1520, for instance, Krishnadeva of Vijayanagar seized Raichur in the episode we have already witnessed featuring the Raya's royal foot. But if Bijapur was incapable of grappling with external pressures, it was also on account of internal conflict that poisoned the air at court. The young Ismail initially ruled under the regency of a nobleman. This grandee pitched his flag decidedly in the Dakhni camp and 'One of his first acts was to discontinue the Shiah form of Islam.' All and any opposition to his deeds was flattened firmly – this when Ismail himself was a Shia raised by a Persian aunt who held the faith in the highest regard. Westerners who had thrived during Yusuf's reign found themselves divested of their offices, which were now distributed among the regent's men. Worse still, the regent was discovered to be in bed with the Barid Shah, the latter guaranteeing him support if he were to overthrow Yusuf's family and take Bijapur for himself, and the former offering military aid in subduing the rebel 'king' of Ahmadnagar, the Nizam Shah. But while the pieces on the Deccan's chessboard were thus preparing to make maiden moves and rewrite its destiny, the women of the harem rose swiftly to the challenge: an old loyalist took up the cause of the ladies and, during an audience with the regent, stabbed him to death.[33] The matter was closed, and Bijapur again became a Shia state, with Westerners firmly in charge – Ismail himself spoke better Persian than he did Dakhni.[34]

In 1534 Ismail Adil Shah died (by this time, however, having retaken Raichur from Krishnadeva's heirs), and the next period saw a number of reversals for his family, besides a constant conflict with one or another of their neighbours. Ismail's sister Mariam, for instance, was married to the Nizam Shah of Ahmadnagar who expected the fort of Solapur and the expanse around it in her dowry; when it was made clear that this was too generous a wedding present, war broke out. Even though Ahmadnagar lost the opening round, Solapur festered like a wound between Ahmadnagar and Bijapur for generations, opening yet another front for perpetual hostility – in 1543, with Vijayanagar's aid, the Nizam Shah could finally wrest this object of his desire.[35] In the meantime, while Mariam suffered insults and her husband's hideous temper, in her maternal home in Bijapur, royal women involved the harem in every issue that mattered. Ismail's son, Mallu, for instance, proved not to be up to the mark, and so he was casually blinded at the instance of his own Maratha grandmother and replaced with a brother.[36] There could be no complacency, the ladies were aware, and where difficult dynastic choices emerged, they knew which one to take without sentiment complicating the way.[37]

This new ruler, Ibrahim, said not to be of wholly legitimate blood,[38] early in his reign had to face a most curious challenge for succession. An uncle of his – a younger son of Yusuf's by the name of Miyan Ali – began to attract interest from detractors at court as a potential alternative to the newly installed Adil Shah. Conscious that this might invite from his nephew the use of poison (or worse) to get rid of him, the uncle proposed to travel to Mecca, only to find himself robbed at sea and washed up back to India in 1541. After a two-year exile in Gujarat, he was eventually persuaded to join a faction of Bijapur rebels who promised to seat him on the throne with Portuguese aid. And so it was that Miyan Ali appears in Goan records, becoming what the scholar Sanjay Subrahmanyam calls a 'Muslim fly in the ointment' to these colonizers on the west coast.[39] Ibrahim at first sought to buy his uncle for 50,000 gold pieces from the Goans, sweetening the deal by giving them (to his abiding regret) lands adjoining Tiswadi, namely, Bardez and Salcette.[40] The Portuguese smilingly accepted the presents, and then just as happily reneged on their word, resulting in a great deal of acrimony and enduring suspicion in their subsequent relations with Bijapur.[41] Miyan Ali's destiny, meanwhile, was to languish forever in foreign custody; on one occasion, the Portuguese shipped him all the way to Malabar and back, but for years he resided in Goa, waiting for the stars to align in his favour.

Matters looked promising briefly in 1555, after over a decade of indecision, when a campaign against the Adil Shah was launched and the Portuguese started treating Miyan Ali formally as a 'Highness'. But this was all too good to be true – the military venture fizzled out and before he knew it, the Bijapuri aspirant was back in Goa, defeated and finally certain that he had no prospects of ever wearing the Adil Shahi crown. Two years later a Jesuit called Luis Frois described Miyan Ali as a 'Moor [Muslim] who is already of a certain age, prudent and experienced and . . . a great follower of Muhammad and well-versed in their scriptures and Quran'.[42] In 1557 the old man was to receive yet another blow, though, this time of a personal nature. His daughter had cultivated the acquaintance of a local Christian woman with whom she 'talked through the windows' of her room (and in more elegant settings, no doubt, when the woman came calling) about sweet nothings – such as, it turned out, the Bible.[43] That year the daughter expressed to her friend a desire to become Christian herself, even as her father was preoccupied with trying to marry her off to the Nizam Shah of Ahmadnagar or the Raya of Vijayanagar, if one of them would agree to an alliance. Unhappily for him, however, a secret plan was hatched, featuring senior officials of the Goan government, and one fine Sunday morning, a large group of dignitaries arrived at Miyan Ali's house to put into action their singularly undignified scheme.

As Frois writes, 'both the girl's mother and the other female relatives ... with great outcries and shouts [began] pulling harshly on her ... The Portuguese women grabbed hold of the girl from the other side, so that the struggle assumed such proportions that all their hair came undone.'[44] In the end the Goans won the battle for the Adil Shahi princess, who was immediately carried elsewhere (along with a loyal eunuch) and given 'a rich dress in Portuguese style'. On 15 August that year, she was relaunched into society as Dona Maria de Alem-Mar, going on to marry a brother of that friend who first conveyed to her the word of Christ. Even as Miyan Ali's distraught wife shaved her head, their daughter began her new life, paving the way for several others of the family to transfer their loyalties to the Catholic faith. The heirs of one of Miyan Ali's sons would, for instance, convert in due course, and though at the time of his own death in 1567 the old man was still defiantly Muslim, in only a few decades a number of his descendants fully transformed themselves, bearing names such as Dom Joao Meale and Dom Fernando Meale. There was, to them at any rate, little irony that their new surname was simply a corruption of the name of their tragic ancestor, the ill-fated Miyan Ali.[45]

While Ibrahim Adil Shah's rival thus met a depressing end in Goa, he himself too suffered in the palace in Bijapur. After inaugural successes in his career, the ruler found himself at the losing end of most battles. For instance, he was firmly in favour of the Dakhnis, and not only replaced Persian with Kannada and Marathi but also handed over Bijapur's revenue affairs to Hindus, which were all welcome moves.[46] As time passed, however, and he lost more than he gained, 'a sudden streak of inhuman cruelty' manifested itself in the prince. Part of it was his own doing, for as a Sunni he had thrown out senior Shia aristocrats from court. Then, in a two-month-long reign of madness, he put to death 'forty Hindu and seventy Muslim officials of rank', some of whose adherents, for this reason, transferred their allegiance to old Miyan Ali when he still had a chance. Seething with rage, Ibrahim Adil Shah died in 1558, without anybody to bring him even medical assistance – during the course of his illness he had made it a habit to have all physicians who failed to alleviate his pain trampled by elephants. The result was that there was a 'complete exodus of medical practitioners' from Bijapur, making it certain that the ruler's end was as inconvenient as it could be.[47] The man was so passionately hated that when the Shia faction returned to power in the next reign, the force of their self-assertion involved the employment of thousands of people specially 'to revile the first three Arab Caliphs (whom Shias do not accept) by publicly cursing their names in the court, through the streets, and in the bazaars'.[48] Clearly, in the Deccan, there was never a dull moment.

The hated man's successor, Ali Adil Shah, led a most interesting life and reigned over Bijapur at a critical moment in its history, when a final and decisive clash with Vijayanagar began to loom on the horizon – and his actions were catalytic to what lay ahead. To begin with, he ate not less than twelve eggs on a daily basis[49] and moved around with great pomp. With 80,000 cavalry and over 700 elephants, his military power was stout, even after he bullied the Dakhnis out of all significant posts in the kingdom – indeed, such was his prowess that even in faraway Malabar, in the kingdom of the Zamorin of Calicut, there was creative work being dedicated to Ali.[50] While his patronage of the arts pales in comparison to an illustrious successor, about whom we shall read soon,[51] he did continue the tradition of construction: As was once noted, the Adil Shahs of Bijapur in general 'were a race of builders and left more buildings of note than all the other Deccani kingdoms together'.[52] Theirs was 'essentially a Persian style profoundly modified by Hindu influence' – where in the north the Mughals, for instance, married the Rajput tradition into their own court architecture, in Bijapur it was the South Indian fashion with its 'distinctly baroque character, full curves, and rich jewelery' that came to dominate – though most of this evolved under Ali's successor.[53]

Under Ali Adil Shah himself, however, Bijapur's fortifications were

Ali Adil Shah of Bijapur

strengthened, and an outer wall was constructed around the citadel. In due course the British aristocrat Lord Napier beholding Bijapur's ruins was so moved as to compare it to nothing less than Istanbul and Samarkand.[54] To such building work, Ali Adil Shah also energetically added the cultivation of stronger trade links. Launching nearly 200 ships in the Arabian Sea and the Bay of Bengal, he went out of his way to establish bonds with the Persians as well as the Ottoman Sultan (besides selling them the Deccan's abundant cotton), keeping the interests of Bijapur foremost in his mind – something that led him to Vijayanagar's doors too, before he turned on them.[55]

~

If Ismail Adil Shah was offered Krishnadeva's foot in 1520, it was Ahmadnagar's Husain Nizam Shah's fate to suffer an equally humiliating insult at the behest of the ruler of Vijayanagar only four decades later. At least in the Adil Shah's case the royal foot was only *offered* for a kiss and there was no actual meeting between the two protagonists of that tale. Husain, however, must have been ill-starred, for he physically had to endure something which so punctured his sense of dignity that only viewing the severed head of the man who brought it all upon him could deliver him peace. Indeed, such was the force of Husain's hatred that he was able to put aside all his ancestral rivalries with Bijapur and other squabbling successors of the Bahmanis in the Deccan, so they could come together and wage one of history's most terrible battles against the man in the south, in whose hands their fates had come to perilously hang. Husain, in other words, was to become the principal factor that brought upon Vijayanagar its destruction, working, ironically, with his oldest enemy, the Adil Shah of Bijapur, to deliver this plan to fruition.

Husain's ancestors had never had pleasing careers, and this evil blighted his life too. His great-grandfather was one of the three masterminds embroiled in the infamous conspiracy that culminated with Mahmud Gawan's beheading. This treachery, after an initial promotion,[56] brought this Brahmin convert his just deserts a few years afterwards when he was assassinated. Enraged but also seeing opportunity in the crisis, the dead man's son, Ahmad, rebelled and proclaimed his independence in 1490 as the first of the Nizam Shahs, decimating the men Qasim Barid sent to chastise him – the prisoners captured during the skirmish were forced to ride buffaloes to send their employer in Bidar a lesson.[57] Indeed, so fearsome was Ahmad's temper that 'no officer of the Bahmuny government was willing to march against him',[58] and in the end Bidar had no alternative but to confirm the Nizam Shah in his possessions, under the nominal authority of the Bahmani Sultan. It was an authority he always flouted with pronounced enthusiasm, doing precisely as he pleased and taking every Bahmani district and province that caught his violent fancy. For all practical purposes he was sovereign, but the only thing that seemed to drive this first Nizam Shah was his insatiable fury.

The second Nizam Shah, Burhan, was seven years old when he succeeded in 1510 to his father's newly built throne, and reigned for forty-three whole years. 'So much attention was paid to [his] education' at first, we are told, 'that in his tenth year he read poetry with facility and proper emphasis, and wrote exceedingly well'.[59] But, as the prince Burhan came into his teens, his precocious interest in academics was replaced with a prodigious appetite for sex, featuring prominently a courtesan who introduced him to wine and its delights.[60] His regent, 'who was straining his nerves to safeguard the interests' of the state, resigned in disgust, and till 1520, when another minister of ability was found, chaos abounded in the kingdom while Burhan drank and slept.[61] The new regent had success in reforming the young ruler's conduct – in 1524, after Burhan's marriage to the Adil Shah's sister Mariam, the prince was made to renounce Sunnism and embrace the Shia tradition. But here again, luck did not shine upon the Nizam Shahs, for when in 1548 Burhan sought Safavid's assistance to resist Bijapur (at that time under a Sunni monarch), the Iranians ignored him – Bijapur was always favoured over Ahmadnagar, even when there was no friendly Shia on its throne.[62] The Nizam Shah's only consolation, perhaps, was that while Persian recognition did not arrive, the Persian Shah's personal doctor emigrated to his court and became a servant of the state of Ahmadnagar.[63]

Having moved on from wine and fornication, Burhan's enthusiasm was channelled into more constructive areas of interest such as the military and matters of government: it was to his court that the previously mentioned Sancho Pires, wanted for murder in Goa, escaped and became a favourite artilleryman and cavalry head by the name of Firangi Khan.[64] An Ottoman engineer of considerable ability called Muhammad bin Husain also arrived to serve the Nizam Shah, casting for him a famous fourteen-foot-long bronze gun by the name of Malik-i-Maidan, based on technology sourced from Hungary and so heavy that hundreds of oxen and elephants were needed to drag it into battle.[65] So too came the mango-loving physician Garcia da Orta, author of a celebrated work on India's medicinal plants, for whom the Nizam Shah became not only an exalted patient but also a source of refuge. Da Orta, whose Hebrew name was Avraham, was secretly a Sephardic Jew. When the Inquisition, which persecuted Jews and other 'heretics' in the name of the Catholic Church, was about to come to Portugal, da Orta had resigned his position at the University of Lisbon and come to Goa, which was safer. For years he lived in peace here, till tremors of the Inquisition began to be felt on the Indian coast as well – around 1545, the doctor left Goa for Ahmadnagar, even as his sister, who stayed back, was burned at the stake for being 'an impenitent Jewess'. Da Orta's own remains were eventually dragged out of the grave for posthumous punishment,[66] but his years in Ahmadnagar were peaceful – he taught the Nizam Shah's sons Portuguese, lamented the ruler's occasional foolishness when he gave much money to a man claiming to sell a 'unicorn's horn', interacted with local physicians, carried on his researches and presumably ate mangoes to his heart's content.[67]

When Husain Nizam Shah succeeded to power in 1553, his ancestors' bad luck continued to haunt him. To begin with, Husain had several brothers he needed to get out of the way, the only difficulty being that they had all cleverly put themselves beyond his reach.[68]

Then, there were battles to fight. In 1558, exploiting the death of the Adil Shah of Bijapur, Husain annexed some territory from the former's kingdom. The new Adil Shah, Ali, turned the tables by not only declaring war but also persuading Vijayanagar to join his campaign against the Nizam Shah. Husain was reminded that 'passion and obstinacy in the discussion of political questions' was a recipe for disaster, and that if he did not return the stolen territories, 'he should expect the march of an army into his dominions, which would lay it waste without mercy'.[69] Even as his court made every effort to convince him to avoid bloodshed and forfeit Solapur (this had been taken by Ahmadnagar in 1543), the man prepared for battle. A princess of Berar was obtained in marriage, sealing his own alliance with the Imad Shah in the forthcoming confrontation. When the time came, Husain's father-in-law sent a prominent general along with a strong army to aid him in his confrontation with the forces of Bijapur, Vijayanagar and the Qutb Shah of Golconda, who too threw his hat into the ring on the strongest side.[70] It was a formidable gathering. And from the onset it was clear to all that the most significant factor in the coalition was neither of the Muslim kings; it was the Hindu Sultan from the south who held the mightiest position in the field.

Like the princes of the northern Deccan, this man too had led a most colourful life. Many years earlier he was a military servant of the Golconda court,[71] but during the reign of the legendary Krishnadeva, he moved across the Tungabhadra and offered himself to that sovereign in Vijayanagar. Ramaraya, as this ambitious man was called, also had impressive family credentials to obtain in marriage one of Krishnadeva's daughters, an alliance that proved to be his stepping stone to unprecedented power in that state.[72] Not all historians are certain what to make of him – some have gone as far as to describe Ramaraya as 'devil incarnate' who 'drank the blood of lakhs of soldiers' when he, eventually, smashed his father-in-law's empire.[73] In any case, his path to power was not free of complications. Krishnadeva was succeeded by his brother, who in turn, while capable, was entirely in the hands of his wife's family.[74] But while Ramaraya accepted this new monarch at first, his mind was constantly alert to seizing power. One attempt at a coup was a disaster,[75] but when Krishnadeva's brother died and his wife's brothers began to plot against his successor, Ramaraya saw an opening again. The dowager queen, fearing for her son, offered the Adil Shah 'gold and rubies' to come to their rescue, but her brothers paid an even larger bribe of six lakh hons to keep away, before having the boy – and their sister – killed.[76]

Ramaraya now unearthed another child from the old royal family and in his name raised a successful rebellion. The boy was planted on the throne, while Ramaraya became his regent, enjoying, however, all the powers of a sovereign. From being titled, for instance, 'the right arm of Sadasiva' (i.e. the emperor),[77] he started styling himself in much grander ways, indeed even as Krishnadeva's successor.[78] When the boy-king grew up and demanded his powers, he was imprisoned, allowed hereafter to show himself only once a year to the masses – by 1562, even this was prohibited. What was most significant, however, was the change Ramaraya initiated in Vijayanagar's northern policy. The kingdom, in the past, 'never interfered [openly at any rate] in [the] internal affairs' of the Bahmanis' successor states.[79] But after 1542, with Ramaraya at the fore, he altered the policy altogether – it was with his Machiavellian assistance that the Nizam Shah took Solapur from the Adil Shah in 1543, embittering relations that were already frosty between those two states. At another time, he also supported rebellion in Golconda. With the splintering of the Bahmani kingdom into five smaller states, Ramaraya appears to have calculated that he could play them against each other for his own gain; a perfectly reasonable assessment till it proved to be precisely the thing that brought about his downfall.[80]

In 1558, with hostilities about to break out with Husain Nizam Shah, Ali Adil Shah – that lover of eggs for breakfast – personally rode to Vijayanagar seeking Ramaraya's assistance. Formally, his visit was a condolence call: the latter had just lost his son, and Ali's gesture was a touching one. The truth, however, was that when the Adil Shah sought Vijayanagar's aid, he was told he would have to ask for it in

Husain Nizam Shah as painted in the *Tarif-i-Husain Shahi*

person. The demand miffed him somewhat, since he was a sovereign ruler and Ramaraya officially a mere regent, but he went anyway.[81] The summit was a success worth his pains, for Ramaraya's wife symbolically adopted Ali as a replacement to the son she had just lost.[82] In 1559, therefore, Ramaraya travelled north with practically his entire army to assist the Adil Shah, and soon Husain found himself besieged inside Ahmadnagar fort, with 100,000 cavalry at his gates. He had no option but to flee, and things got very ugly over the course of the next few months. The excellent general lent to the Nizam Shah by the Imad Shah of Berar[83] terrorized the invaders, but the latter retaliated by wreaking havoc across Ahmadnagar – Ramaraya's men are even said to have 'demolished magnificent buildings and mosques' and 'insulted Muslim women'.[84] The Qutb Shah of Golconda, who half-heartedly joined Ramaraya, was uncomfortable enough to withdraw from the campaign at this juncture.[85]

It was 1561 by the time Ahmadnagar, forced to extremes by now, sued for peace. But Ali Adil Shah and Ramaraya, who had been cheerfully drawing up plans to partition the Nizam Shahi dominion between themselves, had no desire to make things easy for the hounded enemy. Peace was possible, it was announced by Ramaraya's ambassadors, but if Husain accepted, without a single qualification, three conditions: to hand over some prime real estate to Bijapur; to execute the general lent him by the Imad Shah; and finally, and most importantly, to personally bring himself to Ramaraya's camp and 'eat *pan* (betel nut) from his hand'.[86] It was clear to everybody that beyond the loss of territory, which princes often suffered in their lives in the regular course of events, the symbolism of accepting a treat from a triumphant enemy meant degradation of uncommon severity. However, Husain had no alternative but to agree to every condition, including putting to death the general who had shown only the most exemplary valour in his cause during the war. This being done, on the decided day, Husain Nizam Shah entered Ramaraya's tent to receive his betel nut.

The ruler of Vijayanagar rose from his seat and led him inside by the hand, perhaps in a gesture to make things a little easier for his

vanquished foe. But the latter, clearly still defiant and not prepared
to swallow his humiliation fully, horrified the gathering by proving
he had some fight left in his heart, if not in his armies: he asked for
a basin of water and washed his hands after Ramaraya had touched
them. The mood turned instantly chilly. And in everyone's hearing,
Ramaraya muttered to a companion: 'Were he not my guest, I would
have cut off his hands and hung them round his neck.'[87] The meeting
came to a sour conclusion on this note, but the peace held. Husain,
though, was not done. Indeed, such was his wrath that he barely
waited a year before plotting Ramaraya's downfall. Aware that the
Qutb Shah of Golconda had had mixed feelings about the conduct
of the Vijayanagar forces during the aforementioned war, Husain
opened negotiations with him, and an alliance through marriage was
agreed upon. It was decided that the two rulers would jointly besiege
Kalyana fort, which had been recently ceded by the Nizam Shah – and
to underline their defiance, the wedding ceremony of the Qutb Shah
with Husain's daughter, Jamal Bibi, was celebrated right 'beneath the
walls of that fort, just beyond the range of its cannon'.[88] But pointed as
this was in its intent, when it came to actual war, Husain continued to
hammer at his enemies with no luck – after untimely rains destroyed
his gunpowder and artillery strength, he was compelled to withdraw.[89]
Meanwhile, the Adil Shah of Bijapur obtained Ramaraya's personal
intervention for the second time, and Ahmadnagar's Nizam Shah was
forced to flee to a distant town to lick his wounds, while his kingdom
suffered. But Ramaraya, evidently, did not stop with basic plunder –
once again mosques appear to have been razed and civilian damage
inflicted.[90] And after this, most curiously, Vijayanagar's forces looted
not only some of the Qutb Shah's lands but even territories belonging
to their ally, the Adil Shah.[91]

Now, after so much blood had flown and such loss of property and
prestige had been suffered, all the princes of the northern Deccan
realized what precisely it was that was playing out before them.[92]
Many years earlier, when Qasim Barid had tried to form a confederacy
against the Adil Shah of Bijapur, it was the ruler of Berar who had

wisely counselled that they must never allow one man to gain such an ascendancy that he might threaten the balance of power existing between them as independent princes. Now, it was the Qutb Shah of Golconda who decided to remind his fellow rulers of that valid lesson.[93] The recent campaigns brought 'home to the mind of the Sultans of the Deccan, the undesirability of an alliance with the rulers of Vijayanagar and the crying need of suppressing its power and arrogance'. They were all now convinced 'of the community of their interests and of the necessity of joint action'.[94] More immediately, the Qutb Shah and Adil Shah were appalled by Ramaraya's haughty conduct, for after the conclusion of the recent campaign, he had taken from them too certain territories.[95] In only a matter of weeks it became clear that Vijayanagar now saw itself as supreme in the peninsula and that it recognized its strength to shove aside one state after another in the pursuit of its own strategic interests, not to speak of reinforcing Ramaraya's personal ambitions.

For the first, and indeed the last, time in the history of the land, in 1564 the successors of the Bahmani Sultanate came together in a league to destroy their common enemy, helped also by their common religion and exhortations from the Persian Shah that they cease fighting among one another.[96] This new alliance was fortified through marriage – Husain Nizam Shah was already father-in-law to the Qutb Shah of Golconda, and now he gave another daughter, the redoubtable future heroine, Chand Bibi, to Ali Adil Shah of Bijapur. The fort of Solapur, that so poisoned relations between their states for decades, was presented to Bijapur as the bride's dowry. Meanwhile, Ali Adil Shah's sister was married to Husain's son and heir, while another daughter was given to the Qutb Shah, tying the futures of all three dynasties more intimately together than ever in the past.[97] In December 1564, the combined forces – to which was added the Imad Shah of Berar's army – gathered at Talikota, and in January they crossed the Krishna to come face-to-face with Ramaraya's power, which had reclaimed for Vijayanagar the old and contested Raichur doab as well. It was the Adil Shah who officially issued the notice for war, and waiting for the northern invaders were 70,000 cavalry and as many as 900,000 infantry – practically the totality of Vijayanagar's military strength.[98] As one writer notes, 'Though arrogant, Ramaraya was not oblivious to the situation which was developing against him' and had 'long foreseen the contingency of a concerted attack on his capital'.[99] When the enemy arrived at the scene of their confrontation, the man in the south was ready for them.

After a number of initial exchanges, the final battle between the two forces began on 23 January 1565 at a place known as Bannihatti. 'Husain Nizam Shah took the centre, Ali Adil Shah was to his right, and Ibrahim Qutb Shah and Ali Barid Shah to his left', with their respective armies, the Imad Shah's forces playing a relatively minor role.[100] In the beginning it looked as though Vijayanagar would again prevail by sheer strength of numbers – just as, forty-five years earlier, Krishnadeva had defeated Ismail of Bijapur. At that time, Bijapur's forces had been too slow with their artillery; now, however, Husain made no such mistake.[101] 'Under [his] constant fire, the enemy could not come within an easy distance for a hand to hand fight with the invaders. This saved the centre, and ultimately the allies.'[102] Eventually the allies' cavalry charged into the heart of the defenders, and the battle arrived at its bloodiest stage while on the side secret negotiations were opened with Muslim captains in the Vijayanagar camp to betray their patron. What turned the tide for the princes of the north, however, was the fate of Ramaraya himself, who had confidently been moving around in an open litter to boost morale, and had declared to his soldiers that after he captured the northern princes, he would keep them in iron cages for the rest of their lives. (Except, of course, for Husain, in whose case what Ramaraya wanted was his head.[103])

There are several accounts about what followed. According to one version, Ramaraya's capture was an accident. 'One of the Nizam Shahi war-elephants had strayed beyond his line and come up with the palanquin which carried' Ramaraya. 'His bodyguard was panic-stricken and fled', while the man inside was seized. Watching this, 'the Vijayanagar army broke up like a herd of stampeding cattle' and fled. [104] Another version, however, states that the Nizam Shahi army cleverly stuffed their cannon with copper coins, firing them at the enemy, 'with the result that lakhs of heavy, flat expanding shot fell on the centre of the enemy lines, just where [Ramaraya] was sitting in his *shamiana*', doing greater damage than could be done with cannon balls[105] – where cannon balls were deadly, coins essentially acted as bullets, covering a larger area and wiping out, it is said, five thousand soldiers in a deadly blast of gunpowder.[106] The ruler of Vijayanagar is said to have died then and there, with his body later delivered to the allies. The enduring, and perhaps most dramatic, version, however, shows a vengeful Husain having the last laugh. Ramaraya, despite being an octogenarian, had come out on his horse, before falling due to a spear wound on the battlefield. He was carried into the presence of the Nizam Shah, 'who confronting his bitter adversary for the last time, ordered him beheaded on the spot, and his head stuffed with straw'.[107] It must have been sheer fury that kept Husain going for so long, for five months after the event, he too died, drinking himself to the grave.[108]

For Vijayanagar though, this was the climax. Ramaraya's brothers fled back to the city, where instead of preparing its defences, they simply collected the titular emperor and with 550 elephants laden with all the gold, diamonds and other treasure they could pack, the brothers escaped.[109] They would continue to rule from other cities and towns – one of them becoming king without a kingdom – but the city itself was destroyed.[110] In the capital, first there was confusion, for a contingency like this had never before arisen. But then, 'a panic seized the city. The truth became at last apparent. This was not a defeat merely, it was a cataclysm.' Those who could escape – primarily the rich with horses, elephants and carts – fled, and those who were unfortunate enough to trust in prayers and stay were murdered, violated or looted by hordes of robbers. When three days later the Shahs of the Deccan marched into Vijayanagar, orders were given for a comprehensive sack. Temples, palaces, houses, statues – everything was plundered. Fires were lit, and thousands were killed.[111] The plunder, Ferishta records, 'was so great that every private man in the allied army became rich in gold, jewels, arms, horses and slaves'.[112] And as the chronicler's father, who was a one-time tutor at the Nizam Shah's court, declared with almost unconcealed delight, 'What an excellent event the killing of [Ramaraya] was!'[113]

It was Robert Sewell who summarized the fate of Vijayanagar. 'Never perhaps in the history of the world,' he wrote, 'had such havoc been wrought and wrought so suddenly on so splendid a city; teeming with a wealthy and industrious population in the full plentitude of prosperity one day, and on the next seized, pillaged, and reduced to ruins amid scenes of savage massacre and horrors beggaring description.'[114] But that was what happened to Vijayanagar. A city that was one of the world's greatest was now reduced to rock and rubble. The princes of the Deccan had closed the story of Vijayanagar, unleashing destruction and pain.[115] But soon, once the ecstasy of this monumental victory wore off, they would turn around and resume their own battles, till in the end they too were reduced to nothing.

A Summary of Events So Far

The fall of Vijayanagar in 1565 was not the end of that kingdom. Beaten and heavily damaged, both in terms of prestige and power, successors of Ramaraya managed to retain authority for several decades. Eventually, however, splinter states broke off and, by the mid-seventeenth century, Vijayanagar was reduced from a potent political entity to a wistful memory. Much like the Adil Shahs, Nizam Shahs, Qutb Shahs and others who emerged in the northern Deccan, it was the subordinate amaranayaka lords of Vijayanagar who rebelled and established their own new autonomous states in the south. Where the Rebel Sultans destroyed the capital in 1565, those who once pledged allegiance to Vijayanagar did the rest, and now departed to pursue their own independence. The 'Battle of Talikota'*, then, might not have immediately vanquished Vijayanagar, but it certainly marked the end of an era.

The lessons for the Sultans in the northern Deccan from this episode should have been clear. It was the inability of the Deccan's ancient rulers – the Kakatiyas, Hoysalas and Yadavas – to join together against their common enemy that led to the fall of their order at the hands of the Khiljis and Tughluqs. When the Bahmani Sultanate emerged, its leaders too, ultimately, failed to rein in dissension, and in only a few

---

*Though popularly called 'Battle of Talikota', the actual engagement took place at a spot that appears as Rakkasa-Tangadi.

generations the kingdom was on its way to decline and disintegration. The Rebel Sultans who seceded from the Bahmanis continued this tradition by constantly feuding with one another. But Ramaraya's ambition reminded them, at last, that in the game they were playing, they were all destined to suffer as losers. Together, then, they rose against Ramaraya and demolished Vijayanagar for once and forever, achieving in a stroke something that even they, perhaps, could not have believed was entirely possible.

And yet, as always, it did not take long for the Rebel Sultans to descend again into the most trivial quarrels. As the chapters ahead will show, they achieved a great deal and opened a new age of kingly splendour. Great men and women emerged among them, and their courts reached the very pinnacle of prosperity and power. Their territories grew, as did their legitimacy to rule. But all through this they remained bitter and suspicious about their neighbours. Never again were they able to fully come together, and even when the greatest threat they ever knew – the sceptre of the imperial Mughals – raised itself on the horizon, the Deccan's kings failed to realize that if they did not rally for each other, what awaited them in the end was utter disaster. The following pages, then, continue the story of the Rebel Sultans and their power, but also tell that unknown to them, the dawn of the seventeenth century marked the beginning of the end.

V

Saraswati's Son
The Greatest Prince of Bijapur

THE IMAD SHAHI DYNASTY

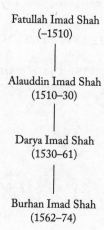

Fatullah Imad Shah
(–1510)

Alauddin Imad Shah
(1510–30)

Darya Imad Shah
(1530–61)

Burhan Imad Shah
(1562–74)

When in 1526, a Central Asian called Babur marched into Delhi and seized its throne, there appeared in the eyes of a sorry figure far away in the Deccan what seemed to be a glimmer of hope. Kalimullah had recently succeeded to the embarrassment that was the Bahmanis' Turquoise Throne, but generations before, when his ancestors were still feared, they had corresponded with Timur the Lame, seeking his favour and benediction. Now that Timur's descendant ruled in Delhi, this unfortunate scion of the Bahmanis made him an appeal of his own – if Babur would march to the Deccan and liberate him from the clutches of the Barid Shah, he would cede to the Mughal emperor the provinces of Berar and Daulatabad.[1] Babur, unfortunately, had other concerns, for he was informed, his memoirs show, that 'no independent authority' was left in the Bahmanis.[2] And so Kalimullah was left to his devices, till in 1528 he finally stole out of Bidar when his secret communique to the north was discovered, and took refuge in Bijapur.[3] But finding his host less than pleased with his royal presence, the homeless Sultan knocked next at the doors of Ahmadnagar. For ten years he lived at the Nizam Shah's palace, prohibited, however, from appearing at court – it was always awkward for a prince to claim sovereignty when living proof of his illegitimacy slept under the same roof.[4] When Kalimullah died in 1538, nobody saddled his son with the hollow title of Sultan, and the boy saved everybody any further awkwardness by simply going as far away as he could on a foreign ship.

But if Babur had been unwilling to pay the Deccan a visit, his

Babur, the first Mughal emperor

Emperor Akbar

grandson was more than anxious to make his acquaintance with the princes of the south. Emperor Akbar was of the conviction that 'a monarch should be ever intent on conquest', and the Deccan was ripe with prospects.[5] The Portuguese were also a thorn in his side, for the seas were entirely in their control now and they terrorized all ships that did not buy a licence from them to be left alone. In 1575, for instance, when Gulbadan Begum, Akbar's aunt and Babur's daughter, wished to go to Mecca, she was delayed for an entire year at the port of Surat with the Portuguese refusing her permission to sail – it took the grant of an entire city, Bulsar, to them before she was permitted to board her vessel.[6] Some years before, two Mughal ships and all their goods had been seized by these Europeans, and Akbar, who once referred to them as chickens (whose necks presumably required wringing), more than once promised retribution.[7] Then, of course, there was the matter of the Deccan's variety of riches. As one reporter sent south wrote, the land offered very good papayas and there was also an abundance of bananas there.[8] And so, from Akbar's generation, 'it became a cardinal goal of Mughal foreign policy to advance southward, destroy or weaken the Deccani kingdoms, and absorb their populations and wealth into the Mughal realm'.[9]

It did take the emperor a great deal of time to turn his attentions south, but once he had prevailed over every other direction, established order and a system of government, and confirmed his imperial credentials in the popular imagination, in 1591 he dispatched emissaries to the Deccan. It was an effort to prod its princes and test if they were amenable to quietly becoming vassals to the Mughal crown. In 1593 the ambassadors returned to report their response to Akbar's proposal: they were not.[10] Never mind, the emperor thought, for there were other instruments at the disposal of kings. As his associate and chronicler Abul Fazl remarked, construing the independence of the Deccan as disobedience of imperial might, the 'sole idea of [the] Shahinshah was to clear the territory of Ahmadnagar of the weeds and rubbish of rebellion, and then to prevail over Bijapur, Golkonda and Bidar'.[11] Daniyal, Akbar's son, was commanded to march with an army and employ the threat of war where cajolements and presents had so obviously failed.[12] The prince did as he was told, and besides the territory he would soon acquire for his illustrious father, he also obtained from the south a royal bride for himself. In these promising circumstances, little did anyone imagine that one day the Deccan, so desirable from afar, would prove the very undoing of the Mughal empire.

Daniyal's future father-in-law, incidentally, was a man Emperor Akbar would have been delighted to meet, for they had much in common both in terms of life experience as well as their outlook on matters of social importance. The man was Ibrahim Adil Shah II of Bijapur. Ibrahim II was a Sunni but when he died, such were the suspicions around his true loyalties that his epitaph served primarily as a reassurance to all concerned: 'No, Ibrahim in truth was not a Jew, neither a Christian; but he was a Muslim, and one pure of faith; certainly he was never of the idolators.'[13] The last line, as we will see, was insincere. This most fascinating of all the Adil Shahs of Bijapur had succeeded Ali Adil Shah and mounted the throne as a boy in 1580, two years before Akbar began his own experiments with faith and religious philosophy in the form of Din-i-Ilahi. The circumstances of Ibrahim II's installation, though, were awkward – his uncle, Ali, a key constituent of the league that destroyed Vijayanagar, was put to death in his chambers one evening by 'two handsome eunuchs who had for a long time excited his perverse attention'.[14] With his heir, Ibrahim II, aged only nine, Chand Bibi, the Nizam Shahi princess married to the deceased Ali as part of the alliances that were formed in 1564, now assumed the regency.

This dowager was an extraordinary figure, described as 'one of the greatest women that India has produced' – and who would one day rank among the staunchest warriors for the independence of the Deccan.[15] Notwithstanding her husband's glances at eunuchs, she seemed to have enjoyed a successful marriage with him. Portraits of her show her hawking, and she could play the sitar, paint as a pastime and reportedly speak five languages.[16] Evidently, she did not care very much for purdah and the established rules of feminine etiquette for, we are told, she frequently 'accompanied her husband in his campaigns and rode by his side to battle. During times of peace a large portion of the public affairs were entrusted to her, and she gave audiences and transacted business in open durbar. She was beloved by all, not only for her daring, but also for her justice and firmness.'[17] Unafraid she may well have been, daughter as she was to Husain Nizam Shah whose vengeance and anger proved one of the strongest motivations behind the fall of Vijayanagar. As regent now, however, Chand Bibi had to rely on others, and to aid her in her work, she appointed a trusted nobleman. This grandee, however, soon 'grew intoxicated with power' to the extent of being rude to the queen. Quickly, she 'turned her thoughts to his destruction'.[18] In the plot that inevitably resulted, the man ended up jumping over the walls of the fort into the swamp below. He was fished out, beheaded and replaced.

The officer that followed also rapidly proved himself a headache for Chand Bibi – when her brother, the Nizam Shah of Ahmadnagar, invaded Bijapur, the officer accused her of having conspired with him and betraying Ibrahim II's interests. Having obtained the adolescent Adil Shah's decree, the dowager was imprisoned.[19] Trouble, however, did not end there – seven months into Ibrahim II's reign, the court was dancing to the tunes of a *third* man. Chand Bibi was released at the behest of this new candidate, a Dakhni. Having thanked him for his kindness, she then decided to balance him out, resulting in more intrigues, more murders and the final triumph of a military commander who established himself as supreme at court for the next eight years, supplanting even Chand Bibi.[20] Aware that her standing was damaged, when a marriage was settled between Ibrahim II's sister and the Nizam Shah's son, the queen 'escorted' the princess to Ahmadnagar, preferring thereafter to spend her days mainly there.[21] The rest of her career, as we shall see, was to play out in the kingdom where she was born, and not in Bijapur where she first arrived as a bride.

Through these twists and conspiracies, meanwhile, Ibrahim II grew up and by 1590, approaching twenty, decided he had had enough of his regent. The boy certainly had resolve – when, for example, the Qutb Shah of Golconda seemed to dilly-dally on a proposal sent for the hand of his sister, Ibrahim II had an army dispatched to move things along. Predictably, they returned with the bride.[22] Ibrahim proved equally strong-willed in expelling his regent from his position of power. On a summer night that year, when his warden had decided, to his enduring regret, to devote his attention and energy 'to a beautiful virgin of the Deccan, whom he had long sought to gain', Ibrahim II escaped from his custody.[23] In the events that followed, the regency terminated abruptly, the old man in charge woke up to discover that he was, in fact, no longer in charge, and finally fled to Ahmadnagar. After years of living under others' thumbs, Ibrahim II was his own man now.[24] Two years later, he would persuade his former keeper to return, and when the old man made the mistake of accepting the offer, he was blinded and packed off to the very fort Chand Bibi once occupied as state prisoner.[25] So too was the fate of Ibrahim II's brother who was instigated to rebel by the Nizam Shah of Ahmadnagar – when he bought into the idea and got carried away with it, Ibrahim II made him pay with his life.[26]

But if Ibrahim II occupied a decidedly bloodthirsty world, where the survival of monarchs depended on not just the possession of strength but also its periodic demonstration through spectacular violence, he deserves credit for exerting himself simultaneously for the intellectual and cultural reinvigoration of his kingdom. His predecessor had already taken the first steps in this direction. Though not in Ibrahim II's league, Ali Adil Shah had interests outside of court intrigue, warfare and murderous eunuchs. Around 1560, for instance, he invited three Catholic priests to court for an exchange on religion.[27] He was instrumental in patronizing Mir Fathullah Shirazi, a scholar and mechanical engineer who invented a number of clever artillery machines, before Akbar snatched him after Ali's death for the interests of the Mughal empire.[28] Ali, who styled himself Adil Shah Sufi, was also 'somewhat of a freethinker' who 'took cartloads of books with him on tours and military campaigns'. Before he was killed, in 1570 he commissioned (or perhaps himself helped author) the *Nujum al-Ulum* (Stars of Sciences), 'written in Persian but replete with Dakhni Urdu', which 'drew on Indic, Islamic, Hellenic, and Turkic traditions to provide a comprehensive vision of medieval Deccani court culture. Blending astronomy, mysticism, and politics,' we are told, 'the text shows that despite the bitter class struggles between [Dakhnis] and Westerners or the sectarian strife between Sunnis and Shiahs, courtly knowledge in the Deccan could achieve a remarkably eclectic synthesis of Indic and Persianate cultural traditions.'[29]

This is no overstatement – the *Nujum*, with its 348 folios and 800-odd illustrations, features within it portraits of obscure Hindu deities such as the frightful Chalandhari, who dangles severed heads from her hands, quite in contrast to Subhapgi who 'nurses a baby while attendants hold a parasol over her, fan her with a fly whisk, and massage her feet, as if she were royalty'.[30] One of the illustrations even features eight angels who, however, are distinguished by their unusual heads – where the Hindu god Ganapati had an elephant head, these angels of the *Nujum* are cows above the neck. The style of painting stands out, for it has few discernible Persian elements and fits more easily into traditional temple art from South India – perhaps a Vijayanagar influence – so that 'goddesses wear flower garlands and oversized gold jewellery, including large disc-like earrings that are often as large as their heads. Most have ample breasts that contrast strongly with their small waists.'[31] Where on the one hand the *Nujum* cites authorities as diverse as Plato and Siraj al-Din al-Sakkaki, it also contains a translation of a Sanskrit work on Varshik astrology.[32] Chapter five of the *Nujum* is about horses while chapter sixteen classifies men and women on the basis of their 'modes of sitting'. And where chapter twenty-six offers mantras to destroy enemies, chapter fifty describes varieties of halwas and sherbets.[33] With its fascinating images, astrological expositions, magic and other outlandish contents, the (now largely missing) *Nujum* was added to the shelves of an already flourishing Adil Shahi library, the care of which was entrusted to a Brahmin, presiding over sixty men and in receipt of an annual salary of 1000 hons.[34]

Ibrahim Adil Shah II of Bijapur

Ibrahim II's aspirations, however, surpassed those of his predecessor. He was certainly full of surprises for his court, and not only because he coloured his nails red.[35] His regent had raised him Sunni, but many assumed he would revert to his uncle Ali's Shiism upon attaining majority. In anticipation of the act, a number of them fell over each other to convert and win the young Adil Shah's goodwill. To general horror, then, Ibrahim II announced his intention to continue as a Sunni, exploiting every occasion thereafter to make fun of the overenthusiastic noblemen who he joked were 'political Sheeas'.[36] What was even more surprising was his sympathy for Hinduism, for in the course of his nearly four-decade-long reign, we discover him endowing temples, affirming rights of Hindu pilgrims at popular shrines and more. As a young boy, he once came across Shiva-worshipping Nathpanthis and was profoundly influenced by his exchange with them.[37] In the copper coins he minted, Ibrahim II referred to himself as *Abla Bali* (Friend of the Weak) in Sanskrit.[38] Portuguese Jesuits, similarly, were permitted to establish missions in various parts of his kingdom – some of these institutions were still fully functional, holding the Adil Shah's farman, as late as 1866.[39] As a visitor remarked of Ibrahim II fourteen years after he had seized power, 'He is an amiable and peaceable prince—no tyrant, but a friend of foreigners, and of all neighbours that are at peace with him.'[40] If they broke the peace, of course, the gentleman prince was replaced by his other avatar where brothers could be killed and overpowering regents blinded.

But when he was in his gentler, constructive mood, Ibrahim II could charm the world.[41] A number of his farmans begin with an invocation of the Hindu goddess Saraswati.[42] It was, in fact, this unconcealed devotion to the deity that eventually convinced a section of his court that the Adil Shah, if he was not already secretly a practising Hindu, was flirting dangerously with apostasy – at one point, he renamed Bijapur (originally Vijaypur, the City of Victory) as Vidyapur (City of Learning).[43] In a poem Ibrahim II composed, he expresses ideas that to the conservative looked dangerously heterodox and antithetical to their brand of puritanical Islam. Thus, for instance, we have the prince declare:

There are different languages;
But there is one emotional appeal.
Be he a Brahmin or a Turk,
He is only fortunate on whom
The Goddess of Learning [Saraswati] smiles.
O Ibrahim, the world only seeks knowledge.
Serve and meditate upon with steadfast heart,
The power of words.[44]

When Ibrahim II composed his celebrated *Kitab-i-Nauras*, of 'fifty-nine devotional songs and seventeen couplets', what he offered the world besides the 'rich syncreticism of the period' was 'an engaging text that is, in parts, highly visual in its imagery and metaphor'. It refers to the world of politics as much as it does to his household, featuring characters such as Chand Bibi, not to speak of his pet elephant, Atash Khan. There are Hindu gods like Shiva and Parvati, alongside influences from the great Hindu epics.[45] 'Ibrahim's somewhat eclectic religiosity is expressed from the opening dedication, which brings together references to Islamic and Hindu divines.'[46] More beautifully, among the several paintings he commissioned, is one of Saraswati where she appears on a golden throne, with all her traditional instruments and symbols – the peacock, the conch, a veena, a lotus and so on. But the 'figure of Saraswati itself follows no known established pictorial model' – unlike her current representations or even old sculptures, Ibrahim's Saraswati is dressed in white robes, appearing more 'in the form of a royal Deccan princess' than in any immediately recognizable 'Hindu' style.[47] Equally striking, however, are the words that appear within the painting affirming the depth of the Adil Shah's devotion to this goddess: Ibrahim II is described as he 'whose father is guru Ganapati, and mother the pure Saraswati'.[48] Many of his other portraits too depict him surrounded by musical instruments, wearing the rudraksha beads associated with Hindu ascetics.[49] No wonder some at court were apoplectic.

While the Sultan's intellectual bent thus embraced Hindu traditions in all their richness, his policy had practical repercussions too. As a Sunni, Ibrahim II favoured the Dakhnis over the Westerners, which worked to the advantage of the upwardly mobile Maratha chiefs as well – to balance the influence of the Persians, the Dakhnis often worked in conjunction with the Hindus, who shared ethnic roots with them. In matters of court culture, etiquette and dress, however, all factions were equally besotted with Persian fashions, a tendency that would carry well into the times of the Maratha confederacy of the eighteenth century.[50] Following the fall of Vijayanagar during his uncle Ali's reign, large numbers of Hindu artists were set adrift, and Ibrahim II now opened his heart and his treasuries to support them in Bijapur.[51] Where Marathi Brahmins were powerful in the bureaucracy, Ibrahim II introduced Telugu and Kannadiga professionals into the fields of art, music and architecture.[52] The Adil Shah himself, a Mughal envoy was surprised to discover, preferred speaking Marathi in court,[53] and one of his harem favourites was a Maharashtrian dancer called Rambha.[54] It was also well known that Ibrahim II had an excellent grasp of Sanskrit, far superior than his grip over Persian, the language of his Westerner ancestors and of the imperial durbar in the north.[55] To the more orthodox, the Adil Shah's Dakhni preoccupations looked almost like a betrayal, when it is remembered that only some generations ago, his ancestor Ismail was an exact contrast in his conduct, exalting Persian, banishing Dakhni influences with a vehemence and even having his soldiers imitate Iranian patterns in their uniform and drills.[56]

But the flowering of local culture under Ibrahim II was not confined to the court alone. Under this Adil Shah, the city of Bijapur was completely transformed. Four decades earlier, one of Ali's visiting Catholic guests was appalled by the capital's condition, where most seemed to dwell in tattered tents in a state of resigned poverty. To a degree, this review was plain prejudice, for the same man also blames Muslims for being 'as numerous as insects'.[57] Improvements did,

Jami Masjid

however, begin soon after the 1565 battle in which Vijayanagar was destroyed – Bijapur doubled both its territory (including reclaiming Raichur) and income at Vijayanagar's expense, and riches plundered after the fall of Ramaraya's city were pumped into major urban development projects that reached fruition in Ibrahim II's reign.[8] It was at this time that the Jami Masjid, among the biggest mosques in the Deccan, was constructed, alongside parks, city walls and a whole series of public and private buildings. Water from the riverside village of Torvi was channelled into the capital, with underground tunnels at times plunging as deep as sixty feet below the ground in a remarkable manifestation of local engineering.[59]

In 1599 Ibrahim II commenced the construction of a sister town called Nauraspur, where 20,000 workmen hammered away to create the Adil Shah's dream capital.[60] So by the time the Mughal ambassador visited Bijapur, fourteen years into Ibrahim II's reign, he was able to record that the city was prosperous, with bazaars 'filled with rare goods, such as not seen or heard in any other town'. Cloth, jewellery, wine, food was all available in abundance. 'In one street were a thousand bands of people drinking, and dancers, lovers, and pleasure seekers assembled; none quarreled or disputed with another, and this state of things was perpetual. Perhaps no place in the wide world could present a more wonderful spectacle to the eye of the traveler.'[61] What is interesting is that the Mughal envoy, as representative of an enemy king, had no particular cause to flatter the Adil Shah of Bijapur with such splendid descriptions. And so, allowing even for a degree of hyperbole, we can take it on reasonable authority that Ibrahim II's reign was a prosperous one, with the benefits of his munificence touching his ordinary subjects – those in urban parts at least, if not the vast numbers living in the country.[62] And, to be sure, there was purpose to this flaunting of wealth, for in India, kings drew legitimacy by displaying power and flaunting their opulence – and in a state like Bijapur, originally a mere province of the Bahmani Sultanate, ritual legitimacy could be built in the eyes of the people and factions that mattered only with a great show of what had been achieved by these successor kings whose origins were less than royal.[63]

Among the creative professionals drawn to Bijapur in this golden age was a Dutchman called Cornelius Clausz Heda. Arriving in 1610 when he was already in his forties, this man found his life's real purpose in the Adil Shah's court, after decades of uninspiring plodding as a painter. He thought his native Holland too competitive and first went to Prague to try his luck there. Sadly, there was no luck to be had, till in 1605 Heda made his acquaintance with some members of an Iranian delegation. That year he left Europe with the Persians, and in a journey that took him via Spain and Portugal, he made it as far as East Africa, where suddenly the local Portuguese authorities accused him of being a Dutch spy – instead of the court of the Shah of Iran, Heda found himself soon in prison in Goa (which might explain why he described the Portuguese as 'shitheads unworthy of trust'). Eventually, however, he was absolved, and at last in 1610 he decided to come to Bijapur to try and obtain the patronage of the Adil Shah. Ibrahim II certainly impressed our Dutchman – he described the ruler as 'a good lover of all the liberal arts, very mild and kind-hearted, unlike other Moors [Muslims], and having also good judgment of all the arts' – while Heda too left a positive impression. So pleased was Ibrahim II with the foreigner that when he produced his first painting, he was instantly rewarded with 500 gold pieces. This may not have been because the work was of an uncommonly high order, but it was fashionable for opulent princes to collect exotic art as well as artists, and the Adil Shah was probably pleased to have acquired a European before even the Shah of Iran (who had to wait till 1617 for a firangi to arrive at his court with a brush).[64]

Art in general reached its apogee in the Deccan during Ibrahim II's reign. From 1596 till 1609, Bijapur hosted a celebrated Persian painter called Farrukh Beg, who had already spent some years at the Mughal court serving Akbar, and would later return to a delighted Emperor Jehangir after his stint in the south. Several are the portraits Beg did of his Bijapuri patron, in which his Persian roots, experience in Afghanistan and Mughal days all come into play – we see Ibrahim II with a smooth chin, hawking, just as we witness him atop Atash Khan, his elephant. In yet another painting, the prince plays a tanpura. These pictures are all in that typical style seen in miniatures of the time, but the arrival of Heda soon after Beg's departure introduced European Mannerist references also into Deccani art, blending these with Bijapuri components. A three-dimensional realism, the hallmark of post-Renaissance Western art, begins to appear in local works, whether they are clearly paintings inspired by Christian themes, such as one of the Virgin Mary, or of Deccani women, who appear in dresses that look markedly European in the flow of the drapery (besides, of course, the occasional hat-wearing white man who appears within these frames). In one painting, we see a woman in a rich red dress, pouring herself wine into a Chinese cup. Her headdress flaunts a single but striking long feather, and the scene is a mix of multiple influences, local as well as foreign. In paintings such as this, there is all at once 'a sense of play, of fantasy, of poetic allusion, and of internationalism'.[65] 'The poetic conduit', in fact, notes Deborah Hutton, is so strong even in paintings of the Adil Shah that they are 'perhaps better understood not as portraits of Ibrahim II but rather as visualizations of poetic *ideals* regarding Ibrahim II'.[66]

International influences arrived in other ways too in order to satisfy Bijapur's peculiar consumption of luxury goods. Some years before, in 1604 Bijapur received another European visitor in the form of Jacques de Coutre, a Flemish gem trader, who too was struck by the materialistic culture supported by Ibrahim II. At their first meeting, de Coutre saw the Adil Shah hold court outdoors, surrounded by 500 bejewelled women entertaining him with musical instruments – on this occasion, he sold the king three emeralds (the biggest, of 300 carats), while his son purchased an Arab horse.[67] When the merchant returned the next year, he found Ibrahim II enjoying wrestling matches in his palace, and then travelling to a stone theatre outside the capital to watch elephants tussle – when it was time for de Coutre to depart, the Adil Shah had him 'covered in perfumed water, a silk robe, and garlands of flowers'.[68] What the visitor disapproved of, however, was the hedonistic lifestyle of the Bijapuris. They were given to 'pomp and excessive spending', riding around in bejewelled palanquins with massive escorts of men and beasts. Some of the women wore earrings 'as big as the palm of the hand', their necks covered with pearls and other ornaments, including the special Bijapuri pendant called the *urbasi* – a kind of gem-studded disc that could also be strung together to form a bracelet.[69] On the whole, the place reeked of such excessive wealth that the visitor was not only overwhelmed but positively mortified by the casual ostentation of the city and its elite residents.

With unusual visitors and even more unusual activities blooming at the Adil Shahi court – it was here that the chronicler Ferishta spent years writing his history, which carried among other titles the name *Gulshan-i Ibrahimi* – it was not surprising that reaction from the orthodoxy awaited only round the bend. In the Adil Shah's case, interestingly, the backlash originated not from conservative clerics as much as from the Sufis. For instance, when one saint arrived in Bijapur, and learnt that the ruler was 'enamoured' of 'Hindu singing and playing', he insisted that Ibrahim II proactively cease surrounding himself with such ungodly influences. The latter, still young at the time, said, like young people do to evade tiresome old men, that he would try. When in 1596 the same Sufi was embroiled in a riot during a Shia festival, Ibrahim found an opportunity to get rid of him altogether. Some nobles conveyed to him, politely, that the 'piety' of the Sufi 'notwithstanding, the glory of the kingdom might be better served if he were absent' from it. Delighted, Ibrahim II packed the man off to Mecca, with a pension to moderate any bitterness.[70] Another saint's hagiography has large numbers of people seeking his aid to rescue the Adil Shah from the hands of a Hindu 'yogi' – in the story, the Sufi succeeds and not only does Ibrahim II return to the right path, but the yogi also converts to Islam. Regardless of the veracity (which is dubious) of the account, the picture is clear: the ruler was surrounded by enough non-Muslim influences to give cause for worry to influential parties in Bijapur.[71] Our Flemish jeweller even expressed moral horror. The Adil Shah was debauched, he claimed, for he maintained 900 concubines who 'served him carnally when he wished'.[72] In the end, though, Ibrahim II smoothly navigated such pressures or simply ignored them when that was more fitting to his dignity.

The decline of Persian cultural influence during his reign, however, was ironic, because this was the very same Adil Shah who wrote obsequious letters to the Shah of Iran, seeking his protection and favour. Some habits, of course, were ingrained in court culture – for instance, when a letter from abroad was received, ambassadors ordinarily handed it over to a nobleman, who then placed it in the ruler's hands. It was only with farmans from the Safavids (and later, the Mughals) that the Adil Shah himself 'condescended to accept the royal letter directly'.[73] In 1612 we see Ibrahim II seeking 'clarification' from Iran on matters of policy, promising he would 'act as directed', while earlier, when changes were under way at the Mughal court with corresponding tremors in their Deccan policy, the Adil Shah implored that 'His Majesty [of Persia] should not leave us undefended' and must 'unhesitatingly come forward'.[74] In what is not surprising, the

Shahs were sympathetic – after all, they had offered advisory services to the Sultans of the Deccan on the eve of the 'Battle of Talikota', instructing them to unite as one against Vijayanagar.[75] At one point, the Safavid ruler wrote to the Mughal emperor that the 'noble rulers of the Deccan' were his 'neighbours', to whom he must 'open the doors of mercy and favour' for the sake of Perso-Mughal 'concord, amity and friendship'. When in due course it appeared that the Mughals would annex all that belonged to these southern 'neighbours', the Shah even declared he would 'be happy to give up an equivalent or even larger territory' from his own empire if Delhi left the Deccan alone.[76] Given that the Mughals and Safavids were constantly quarrelling over who legitimately owned Kandahar and the Afghan mountain-lands, this was an unusually generous offer to make on behalf of the Deccan states which the Persian king had no hope of ever directly possessing.

The Shah was probably quite aware, though, that his offer would not be accepted, for the more his foreign court showed its keenness to protect the freedom of the Indian peninsula, the greater was Mughal resolve in subjecting the Deccan to its authority. Indeed, behind each of Ibrahim II's appeals to the Safavids was a patent nervousness born in the wake of the first Mughal diplomatic exchanges with him and his fellow rulers. But the charismatic Adil Shah needn't have worried, for Akbar's eyes coveted not so much his lands just now as much as those of his relations: it was the Nizam Shah of Ahmadnagar who was to suffer misfortune, and those around Ibrahim II knew that while resistance in Ahmadnagar continued, the Mughals could be kept at bay.

~

When the Nizam Shahs conquered Berar in 1574, the horizon showed no signs of the catastrophe that was to befall them shortly afterwards. For the time being, all they saw in Berar was great opportunity. Its rulers, the Imad Shahs, were perhaps the least inspiring of all the dynasties that rose from the ruins of the Bahmani Sultanate. The third of this line, 'in his long and chequered career', had 'repeatedly played the role of intermediary but never that of hero on the battlefield'.[77] As stated earlier, his daughter married Husain Nizam Shah, but his own death not too long afterwards unleashed chaos. With a usurper on the throne, in 1574 Ahmadnagar's armies easily engulfed the state, imprisoning not only the pretender but also the legitimate heir of the Imad Shahis – it is said that they were all, after some time, strangled to death.[78] But before Ahmadnagar had fully enjoyed the fruits of its acquisition, a perverse sense of justice prevailed when things came full circle. Murtaza Nizam Shah, Husain's heir, was murdered – interestingly, while in a steam bath[79] – and the culprit was his son.[80] To be fair, though, the father had first tried to have the son killed by setting his bedroom on fire.[81] Some said Murtaza was mad (especially when he threw treasure from the Vijayanagar loot also into a fire[82]) while others believed he was entirely in the hands of a minion slave boy who doubled as his lover.[83] Either way, the man lost his life, and Ahmadnagar its future.

It was into this dynastic nightmare that Chand Bibi arrived when she renounced her husband Ali Adil Shah's kingdom of Bijapur and returned to the land of her birth. 'She had hoped to find peace in her old home', one historian notes gloomily, 'but she found the home more convulsed with faction and more distracted' than the place she had left.[84] Realistically speaking, she might have hoped for opportunity rather than retirement, given her own interests in government. There was certainly precedent to encourage her, for between 1565 and 1571 it was her mother, Khunza Humayun, who held the reins in Ahmadnagar. But that period had ended in a debacle.[85] For Chand Bibi, it also didn't help that a sequence of murders had commenced with her arrival: Murtaza, of course, went to the grave, and the son who sent him there was also soon buried.[86] A boy of sixteen, he had thrown 'himself headlong into a life of sensual debauchery. Reeling with intoxication he would ride through the streets of the city, accompanied by his drunken associates, trampling innocent persons to death and indulging in excesses of the most heinous character.'[87] There were not many who felt sorry when he was brought down just as quickly as he had been raised as king, by his own court and nobles.

But if this was already one tragic case of a father and son destroying one another, one more example was about to unveil itself. For the nobles put on the throne Murtaza's nephew. The step incensed the new prince's father, who some years ago had himself tried to claim power, only to fail and go into exile in Emperor Akbar's capital. He now plotted to supplant his son as the Nizam Shah. Oblivious to this, within Ahmadnagar the court went around in circles with its own complicated feuds. While the Westerners primarily approved of the new ruler, most of the Dakhnis opposed him. But with no candidate left after the head of Murtaza's son, whom they championed, appeared on a spear,[88] the Dakhnis accepted the ruler grudgingly. Before doing so, however, to gain a point in this continual contest of one-upmanship, they ordered a massacre of Westerners, 'of every rank and occupation . . . and for plundering and burning their dwellings. The soldiers and their followers being [at] once let loose, put to death indiscriminately the nobles, masters, servants, the merchants, pilgrims' and anybody else they could find who might belong to the wrong party. 'Their houses were set on fire. The heads of those lately exalted to the sky were brought low and trampled in the dust, while the very females who from modesty concealed their faces from sun and moon were dragged by the hair into the assemblages of the [drunk].'[89]

In May 1591, after three years of disorder in Ahmadnagar, Akbar's protégé, the Nizam Shah's father, returned to the city and promptly unseated his son. Where the Dakhnis had imposed their own faith and posted their people, the Shia faith was restored, favour once again shining on what remained of the Westerners. The Mughals hoped that the new Nizam Shah would demonstrate gratitude to the emperor by accepting vassal status. But they were dejected when he showed no such desire.[90] Where Akbar had wanted his name read in the khutbah, when a *khatib* (prayer leader) at court actually attempted to do so, 'it is reported that he (rather than the sheep or goat traditionally used for the purpose) was slaughtered by the Persians present, and before the eyes of . . . [the] Nizam Shah himself'.[91] As the emperor's chronicler remarked bitterly, 'When [the Nizam Shah] prevailed over [his own son], he should have increased his devotion and gratitude, and been an example of obedience to other rulers in that quarter. The wine of success [however] robbed him of his senses, and he forgot the varied favours he had received from [Akbar]. In his evil fortune, he set himself to oppress the weak, and considered that his profit consisted in the injury of others.'[92] In any case, the supposedly ungrateful Nizam Shah died in 1594–95, and yet another round of succession struggles broke out in Ahmadnagar. Only now, the Mughals did not wait, and their armies arrived in the Deccan to convey the full force of imperial might to the Nizam Shahis and their brother princes of the south. The beginning of the end was in sight.

In this hour of crisis, it was Chand Bibi who made a final effort to rally Ahmadnagar's nobility around the cause of the throne (regardless, in theory, of who sat on it) and to persuade them to put aside their differences. However, the idea was not easily sold. The queen had as her candidate for the succession a grandson of the ungrateful Nizam Shah, while two other factions offered nominees of their own with real or imagined connections to the royal family.[93] Coming to terms with them eventually, she 'sought their cooperation, made administrative arrangements, and with the consent of her nobles proclaimed' her protégé as the Nizam Shah.[94] But soon Ahmadnagar was surrounded. 'Her Highness the Bilqis of the Age [i.e Chand Bibi]', a contemporary records, sent out emissaries to Bijapur and Golconda 'informing them of the strength of the enemy and the pitiable condition of the inmates of the citadel', seeking their aid.[95] And as the Adil Shah prepared 30,000 cavalry, and the Qutb Shah 30,000 of his own men to come to the aid of their neighbour, Chand Bibi readied herself to fight.[96]

The Mughals placed a number of mines under the fort – a strategy first introduced in India by Mahmud Gawan[97] – in order to explode their way in after the city failed to succumb to regular artillery attack. But in the hours leading up to the morning when these were scheduled to be blasted, the defenders began to countermine. When they were working on the third, and largest, store of gunpowder, the Mughals sprung the mines. The result was that at last there was a breach in the fortifications, and the invaders prepared to enter the city and fight on its streets, all the way up to the palace. That is when Chand Bibi, 'clad in armour . . . with a drawn sword in her hand, dashed forward to defend the breach'. Even as her men from above fired at the Mughals to slow them down, she from 'early morning until sundown . . . remained in the breach, encouraging her soldiers and endeavouring to repair the damage'. The invaders lost this round, and despite a furious, bloody attack to take the city, they were repulsed.[98] As the Mughals retired for the night, construction carried on in the breach till the fortifications were repaired, and the invaders found themselves the next morning back to square one, with harrowing prospects ahead. Though relieved, conditions on Chand Bibi's side were not promising either – perhaps for want of enough ammunition, at one point she is even said to have had opened her treasury and had cannonballs made of gold and silver![99]

As intelligence arrived that reinforcements from Golconda and Bijapur were on their way to Ahmadnagar, and that Chand Bibi's men in the hinterland had cut off their supply lines, the Mughals decided to seek a truce and come to terms. While hereafter, the invaders declared, they would refer to the queen not as Begum but as Chand Sultan, the title was mere flattery that came as a consolation alongside the main price of imperial withdrawal – they wanted Berar for Akbar.[100] At first inclined to reject the idea, Chand Bibi was persuaded that it might be wiser to take the offer, considering she was up against a behemoth on the one side, and on the other a court which, as soon as danger retreated, would lapse again into its petty rivalries. The Mughals were quite eager to exploit these dissensions: as one Mughal general remarked to his interlocutors in Ahmadnagar during the negotiations, 'You, like a eunuch, are keeping a woman in the fort in the hope that she will come to your aid . . . This man [the Mughal prince] is the son of His Majesty the Emperor . . . at whose court many kings do service. Do you imagine that the crows and kites of the Deccan, who squat like ants or locusts over a few spiders, can cope with the descendant of Timur . . .? You [Westerners] who are men of the same race as ourselves, should not throw yourself away for no purpose.'[101] Chand Bibi's nobles did not betray her, but Berar, till two decades ago the possession of the Imad Shahs, now became the 'first firm footing in the Deccan' that the Mughals obtained by treaty. In return Akbar recognized the Nizam Shah of Ahmadnagar, albeit now in tributary relations with his court.[102] An uneasy peace prevailed, but all involved were quite aware that as soon as an opportunity arose, there would once again rise the sceptre of war. As Ibrahim II warned from Bijapur, 'the enemy was still at their doors'.[103]

Unfortunately for the princes of the Deccan at large, the Ahmadnagar court was still in no mood to end its quarrels, even as the shadow of destruction was upon it. Disputes over rival candidates for the throne, backed by rival lords, resumed, and Chand Bibi was resented when, for the security of herself as well as the boy she had placed on the throne, she invited Ibrahim II's forces to the city.[104] Exploiting Ahmadnagar's weakness to assert its power and command obedience, the Mughals began to destroy the Nizam Shahi state by inflicting a thousand cuts – Nasik was taken one day, and then Lohgarh, and in this way over half a dozen forts were lost one after the other.[105] When in 1597 Chand Bibi combined with the Adil Shah of Bijapur and the Qutb Shah of Golconda and a joint attack was mounted against the Mughals during their latest attempt to steal territory, the allies lost. An effort at home was made to eject the queen from power, and civil war began to tear Ahmadnagar to pieces, even as the Mughals, emboldened by this news, prepared for their final assault on the capital. In 1599 Prince Daniyal arrived outside Ahmadnagar, and Chand Bibi had to take a tough decision: should she fight, while also fighting her own nobles with the other hand, or should she come to terms with the imperial army? After all, as someone had remarked, 'The enemy's force is double that of the Dakhan . . . It is absurd for a few drops of rain to claim an equality with the infinite ocean, or the insignificant motes to imagine themselves equal to sun-beams.'[106] She chose to make peace with the Mughals – and this was to be the cause of her death. As one narrator puts it:

Hamid Khan, one of the principal officers in the fort, and the head of [an] opposite faction, came to know of this, and at once ran into the streets exclaiming that the Queen wished to betray the people. The excitable and turbulent soldiers of Ahmednagar, forgetting all the noble devotion which Queen Chand had always shown, at once assembled in front of the palace. Headed by Hamid Khan they rushed inside, sword in hand, and not finding the Queen in the audience hall, they broke open the private apartment. There they were confronted by this courageous woman who was undismayed, though she saw that the end had come. Too excited to listen to her, the crowds rushed on, and Hamid Khan cut her down, and so died Chand Bibi, one of the noblest characters in the History of India.[107]

The assassination was pointless, though, for not only had Ahmadnagar lost a resourceful and capable leader, but the fort was going to fall anyway – learning from the mistakes of the past, the Mughals laid their mines determined to enter the city. And this time,

A Nizam Shahi nobleman's tomb, popularly called
Chand Bibi Mahal in her memory

they succeeded.[108] 'A scene of indiscriminate slaughter then took place, the treasury was pillaged, and the young King . . . was taken and sent to the Emperor Akbar.' (The only consolation, perhaps, was that the Mughals put to death Chand Bibi's assassin.[109]) In due course, the Nizam Shah was placed in Gwalior fort, far in the north, where he died a captive of the Mughals, in absolute obscurity. Formally, the kingdom of Ahmadnagar had come to an end. But as the conquerors would soon learn, the Deccan could not be easily subjugated, and resistance would carry on for decades. After all, the man they had locked away in Gwalior was only one of several claimants to the title of the Nizam Shah. And while one Sultan of Ahmadnagar had been toppled, the line could continue long after the capital had fallen, in the person of another. There were yet battles ahead, and Akbar's heir was destined to spend all his reign frustrated at the iron will of the defenders of the Deccan.

~

While the debris of Ahmadnagar fort had still not settled, in Bijapur Ibrahim II was shaken to his core by events in the Nizam Shahi kingdom. Remembering mournfully his aunt, in a tribute he reclaimed her for the Adil Shahs, now that her own house had stabbed her in the back:

> Though in battle's dreadful turmoil her courage never failed,
> In the softer arts of peace she was gentle and serene.
> To the feeble, tender-hearted; to the needy, ever kind,
> Was the noble Chand Sultana, Bijapur's beloved Queen.[110]

Combined with the defeat of 1597, Ibrahim II now saw wisdom in seeking an alliance with the Mughals, or, to put it more flatly, to buy peace. While he would not submit as a vassal of the emperor (Delhi refused to refer to any of the princes in the Deccan as 'Shahs' – they were always called merely Adil Khan, Nizam-ul-Mulk and Qutb-ul-

Mulk, after their original Bahmani court titles[111]), it was agreed that he would marry one of his daughters to Daniyal. An ambassador was dispatched in 1600 for this purpose from the imperial palace in Delhi, with additional charge to liaise and come to an arrangement with Golconda. The rulers of the Deccan, however, were clever. Instead of concluding the discussions promptly, during their negotiations they discovered a chink in the emperor's armour – the avarice of his own noblemen. For the next four years, thus, the Qutb Shah of Golconda and Ibrahim II together paid bribes running into hundreds of thousands in gold pieces so that matters could be prolonged as far as possible.[112] Akbar's envoy did not let them down, so enjoying his remunerative stint in the south that he couriered to the north excuse after excuse while granting the Adil Shah and his neighbour all the room they wanted to delay an actual settlement.

Eventually, by 1604, Akbar worked out what had been playing out behind his back, and commanded a new, more reliable man to ride to the Deccan and close discussions with its princes. When Asad Beg, this new envoy, appeared on the horizon, Ibrahim was ready with a bag of distractions for him – no sooner had he set foot in the Deccan than he was sent 'a fine, large elephant' (which had an appetite for Portuguese wine) and 'two Arab horses with gilded saddles, as well as silver accoutrements. Furthermore, nine trays of diverse cloths, and rare chintz from the Karnatak were given to him, together with a special golden tray with all sorts of jewels and rings on it.' An attempt was also made to seduce him with 200,000 hons in cash, but Asad Beg was made of tougher stuff, and continued his march to Bijapur.[113] For the Adil Shah, even as he recalibrated his approach, another factor in his efforts to delay the arrival of the ambassador was the reluctance of the princess promised to Daniyal; she had no desire to leave her father's palace and go into the hands of a man everyone knew was Bijapur's enemy. And if she was forced to go, she would not do it quietly.

But Asad Beg was determined – Akbar had given him express instructions to spend not more than one night in the Adil Shah's capital[114] – and so Ibrahim II cleverly decided to make a second attempt to keep the man at bay *before* he arrived in Bijapur for that one night. When he was a day's ride away, Asad Beg was asked not to carry on because the Adil Shah was suddenly grappling with some urgent business that would keep him occupied for the next two weeks. Reluctantly the Mughal cavalcade halted, only to be bombarded again with presents as well as with a train of conversationalists from Ibrahim II's court to keep the ambassador entertained. Ibrahim II also demonstrated his warmth in the form of food in his best china, till Asad Beg found, to his annoyance, that suddenly he was saddled with heaps of utensils, with no place to store them.[115] Finally, once the stipulated fortnight had passed, the man resumed his journey and entered Bijapur in state, reading out Akbar's farman to the Adil Shah in all solemnity. When the next morning he insisted, thereafter, on departing – and taking the princess with him – the Adil Shah said he could do so after a formal farewell party organized in his honour. Asad Beg consented, partly also so he could have a good look at the fort, and in the durbar the envoy saw Ibrahim II's beautiful golden throne, and a tempting display of the court's immense wealth, which included, incidentally, a collection of Chinese vases.[116]

In the end, the Adil Shah made yet another final, futile effort to delay matters. At the reception earlier, he had taken from Asad Beg a badge that Akbar had given him. This was a mark worn by followers of the emperor's new, eclectic religious group, the Din-i-Ilahi.[117] Ibrahim II was delighted to see it, and declaring himself a member, he now refused to return the badge to the envoy. The ambassador, in keeping with the emperor's command, left Bijapur, but halted at a distance and demanded the return of his property, which happened, understandably, to be of much sentimental value to him. 'It was only after elaborate negotiations that the Mughal envoy was able to have his precious symbolic object returned several days later.'[118] One other temporary delay was also caused in the ambassador's itinerary when the Bijapur princess he had with him abandoned the dowry and riches her father had sent in her convoy, and managed to escape the Mughal camp to make her way back to her father. 'In the morning, however, she was caught and was eventually safely handed over to her husband.'[119] Somewhere on the banks of the river Godavari, then, the Adil Shah's daughter became wife to Prince Daniyal of the house of Timur. And now there was a Deccan princess in the Mughal harem, whose fate it would be to watch over the dissolution of the kingdoms of the south, where she was born and raised, in happier days of the past.

When Asad Beg eventually returned to the Mughal capital, he had several presents for Akbar from his son's new father-in-law. Among these was a novelty that would soon catch on at the Mughal court: tobacco. As the ambassador records, 'His Majesty was enjoying himself after receiving my presents and asked how I had collected so many strange things in so short a time, when his eye fell upon the tray with the pipe . . . he expressed great surprise, and examined the tobacco, which was made up in pipefuls; he inquired what it was, and where I had got it.' When he was told, including that the substance was 'well known in Mecca and Medina' and could be consumed as 'a medicine', 'His Majesty looked at it, and ordered me to prepare and take him a pipeful. He began to smoke it, when his physician approached and forbade him from doing so. But His Majesty was graciously pleased to say that he must smoke a little to gratify me, and taking the mouth piece into his sacred mouth, drew two or three breaths.'[120] Akbar must have liked what the Deccan delivered up for him, for he is said to have commanded Asad Beg thus:

> You went before, in great discomfort to fetch . . . the daughter of Adil Khan and the presents because it was necessary. [Now] you must go in state to the four provinces of the Deccan and remain in each place so long as may be necessary, to collect whatever they may have of fine elephants and rare jewels throughout their dominions, to bring back with you. Their money you may keep. I want nothing but their choice and rare elephants and jewels. You must secure things of this kind for the Government, the rest I give to you. You must not relax your effort as long as there is one fine elephant or rare jewel out of your grasp in the Deccan.[121]

Soon afterwards, Akbar died, and his heir Jehangir ascended the Mughal throne, opening a new age of glory for his empire, with his Persian wife Nur Jehan by his side. Seeking Iranian aid to keep the Mughals at bay, the Adil Shah refused to send the new emperor his congratulations and pledge of fidelity. But it did not matter, for the imperial authorities were contemplating other designs themselves. And as it happened, these evolved far beyond the mere collection of the elephants and gems of the Deccan, and in three generations would conclude with the wholesale seizure of all the land that belonged to the southern princes. The only obstacle in the way, however, was one man – a warrior Akbar decried as 'arrogant' and 'evil-disposed' and whom Jehangir would violently, in his frustration, denounce as 'black-faced' and 'ill-starred'. His name was Malik Ambar.

VI

The Ethiopian Kingmaker
From African Slave to Rebel Warrior

The hero of the Deccan had skin the colour of coal. Emperors snarled at him from afar, while enemies at home quaked in fear when he marched into their neighbourhoods. Many were those who despised him, but many more still were the masses who discerned in him a champion. His story was certainly unusual, though he was neither the first of his people to serve in the Deccan, nor extraordinary in his antecedents. And yet he emerged as the strongest of them all, reigning indeed as king in all but name. 'He has a stern Roman face,' wrote one traveller, 'and is tall and strong of stature' though his 'white glassy eyes', it was added, 'do not become him'.[1] His charities were legendary, as was the valour of the men who pledged themselves to his service. When at last he died, not on the battlefield but secure in a formidable fortress, the Mughals admitted that this enemy was 'an able man. In warfare, in command, in sound judgment, and in administration he had no rival or equal . . . He kept down the turbulent spirits of [the Deccan], and maintained his exalted position to the end of his life, and closed his career in honour. History,' the obituary concludes, 'records no other instance of an Abyssinian slave arriving at such eminence.'[2] It was high praise, coming as it did from the imperial court, where two generations of emperors revealed nothing but spite for the man called Malik Ambar.

The Deccan, as we know, had long attracted foreigners to its shores, offering them wealth and a future in these eastern lands. Persians arrived, as did Arabs and Central Asians. Some graduated to princely ranks, while others soared to gratifying aristocratic heights. But among the legions of men absorbed by the Bahmanis and their heirs were also Africans who came primarily from the land we now call Ethiopia. And they too would thrive in the Deccan far above the stations where they began their lives. Some were associated with tales of treachery – Mahmud Gawan's confidant, who struck his seal on the forgery that delivered him his death warrant, was a habshi (an African) as was his executioner.[3] When Yusuf Adil Shah died, one of the regents who ruled in the name of his son was a black man from Ethiopia – the latter was stabbed to death for displacing Westerners and favouring the Sunni faith.[4] When years later Chand Bibi was imprisoned, her liberator who briefly stood at the forefront in Bijapur was a habshi,[5] as was the man Ibrahim Adil Shah II rejected after eight years of living under his guard.[6] In Ahmadnagar, during the wars of succession in the 1590s, one ruler, whose reign lasted less than a year, found himself without support from his nobles because his mother was 'a negress',[7] though when Chand Bibi was besieged by the Mughals, the man who led Bijapur's and Golconda's troops to her rescue was also a habshi called Suhail Khan.[8] And many years later, on the eve of the final Mughal conquest of the Deccan, in Bijapur once again would rise a habshi exercising as a short-lived vizier the full and tragic authority of power.[9]

The habshis had almost all of them begun their careers as slaves. And there certainly was a thriving market for men from Ethiopia in the courts and demesnes of the East. Writing as early as the fourteenth century, Ibn Batuta reports how habshis were 'guarantors of safety' for ships sailing in the Indian Ocean, with such fearsome reputations that 'let there be but one of them on a ship and it will be avoided by . . . pirates'.[10] Centuries later a Portuguese missionary noted how 'all the country of Arabia, Persia, Egypt, and Greece are full of slaves' who made for 'great warriors'.[11] In India too, this was true. The favour and affection shown by Raziya Sultan in the 1230s to Jamal al-Din Yakut, an Abyssinian warrior, provoked a rebellion and contributed to her brutal murder in Delhi at the close of that decade.[12] At the end of the fourteenth century, a habshi servant of the Delhi Sultans had established a near-sovereign state in Jaunpur, in present-day Uttar Pradesh, which sustained itself till 1479.[13] Firoz Shah Bahmani in the early fifteenth century had habshis in his harem, while in that same century a 1487 coup by Africans in the court of the ruler of Bengal led to the rise of a short-lived 'Habshi dynasty' hundreds of miles away, on the other side of the Indian subcontinent.[14] The exquisite Siddi Saiyyed Mosque in Ahmedabad was built by a habshi in 1572, and generations later the Mughal emperor Aurangzeb would appoint the African lord of the fortress of Janjira his naval commander, allocating to him an annual grant of 400,000 rupees to maintain the imperial fleet. In the old quarter of Delhi there is even an area by the name of Phatak Habash Khan, named, evidently, after a habshi courtier who bid farewell to the Deccan, embracing the cause of the Mughal emperor.[15]

While these are episodes that stand out, where Africans from humble origins arrived at positions of honour and power (and sometimes infamy), the beginning of their journeys on this path were never happy. The habshis were often taken as children and sold at a price to be transported abroad. Ethiopia, at the time, was called Abyssinia in the trading world, and the very word 'habshi' is a derivation denoting the origins of these slaves. Malik Ambar too emerged from this commercial exchange of human goods. Born around 1548 into the Oromo tribe, he was captured as a boy and sold to an Arab for twenty gold ducats.[16] In Baghdad he passed, temporarily, into the hands of another owner, who then sold him to the man who would bring him to India – and to his destiny. It was this master who educated him, though by now he had renounced his name, Chapu, and converted to Islam. 'Whether he assumed a Muslim identity at the time as an act of genuine faith or simply as a practical matter of assimilation is not known.'[17] But it certainly helped him in his life ahead, to share faith with the powerful kings and noblemen of the East, in whose service lay his ascent.

Around 1571, now in his early twenties, Ambar, as he was known, arrived in the Deccan where his long-time master sold him to the peshwa (chief minister) of Ahmadnagar. The sale itself was not unusual –

Malik Ambar

though his master had brought him up, the 'bottom-line was never in dispute: Ambar was property' and not 'an heir or son'.[18] However, the man who had just purchased the slave must have opened Ambar's eyes to a world of possibilities, for the peshwa was himself black and had arrived in the Deccan under similar circumstances. He would, in due course, be assassinated, but to Ambar it must have been clear that in India it was possible to rise beyond slavery and to come into great power and wealth – he himself was merely one of a thousand habshis the peshwa possessed.[19] None of them was intended for domestic service; they were all to become soldiers and function as men of war. It was a custom as old as time itself: when rulers found they could not trust implicitly their nobility, which wallowed in its feuds and vested interests, power was secured by obtaining slaves cut away from their own roots and loyal to masters who provided them protection and a purpose. In Egypt, Turkey, Persia and indeed in India, the formula had been applied many times over – the first kings of the Delhi Sultanate themselves were military slaves belonging to Muhammad Ghuri, the invader.[20] And as a beneficiary of the system once remarked, 'One obedient slave is better than three hundred sons; for the latter desire their father's wealth, the former his master's glory.'[21]

Ambar must have been devoted to his owner, for when the peshwa died less than five years after taking him on, his widow granted the young warrior his freedom and set him on course to shaping his own future. For the next twenty years, Ambar was a mercenary with a small force, primarily serving the interests of the Adil Shahs in Bijapur – who appear to have bestowed on him his title of Malik – after brief stints in Ahmadnagar and Golconda.[22] He also married (very likely purchasing his wife) and had two boys and two girls; one of his sons was named after the late peshwa, his former owner.[23] Like most other habshis in the Deccan's courts, the family was of the Dakhni faction. 'This was because the institution of slavery had permanently severed [the habshis] ties with Africa. Unlike the Westerners, who after several generations of living in the Deccan continued to cultivate the Persian language and to nourish close family or commercial ties with the

Middle East, the habshis had no option of returning to Ethiopia. The Deccan being their only home, they readily assimilated into Deccan society, embracing its regional culture and its vernacular languages.'[24]

It was really during the Mughal invasion of Ahmadnagar in the late 1590s that Malik Ambar truly came into his own. At the time of the first siege, he had less than 150 cavalrymen in his command, and he joined himself to a more established habshi lord.[25] But as war shred to pieces the nobility and challenged the loyalties of large numbers of men, within a year Ambar held in his control 3000 warriors; by 1600 this number rose to almost 7000, now including Marathas and other Dakhnis – a 'multiracial, multi-ethnic force that broadly shared a regional identity distinct from the northern Mughals'.[26] Indeed, there does appear to have emerged by now the signs of a pluralistic but shared identity among the peoples of the Deccan, so that years later, though Ambar fought under Ahmadnagar's flag, he obtained financial support from other rulers in the neighbourhood as well, in defending their common frontiers against a single, ferocious enemy from the north.[27] As he himself wrote to Ibrahim Adil Shah II, 'It is my design to fight the Mughal troops so long as life remains in this body.'[28] Ambar, in fact, would transform into such a legend that the Marathas invented a fable to couple his rise with a conscious design on their part, in harmony with divine forces. When the habshi was poor and still a nobody, they claimed, he was discovered by one of their noblemen, sleeping by the wayside. Finding 'marks of fortune' on his feet, this man promised the slave he would rise to great heights, and launched him on his career.[29] Within a decade of the fall of Ahmadnagar, thus, everybody seemed to want a piece of the most remarkable man still holding out and flying high the flag of the Nizam Shahs.

His actions were not motivated entirely by altruistic factors, of course, for Ambar's own future depended on his quest to restore a legitimate monarch. While the Mughals exiled Chand Bibi's Nizam Shah to Gwalior, Ambar decided to champion the cause of another member of the royal family. The candidate he selected was a nephew of Husain Nizam Shah, who had died in 1565, and a bona fide male-line descendant of the royal house. From his headquarters in Parenda, Ambar announced his resistance of the Mughals in the name of this new sovereign. He was successful in his early campaigns – Prince Daniyal was exhausted by the tireless wars the Deccan demanded, and agreed to peace with Ambar so he could concentrate on the brewing war of succession as Akbar declined (and return to his favourite habit of drinking in peace). While Ambar released Mughal soldiers he had captured, Daniyal, in return, recognized the Nizam Shah's right over the districts the habshi controlled.[30] In the meantime, Ambar also managed to shake off a potential rival for ascendancy over this new Nizam Shahi court. The Mughals held Ahmadnagar and parts around it, while Ambar was in possession of districts to the south and east, soon expanding to parts of the north and west of the capital.[31] Cleverly, using muscle when it was needed and trickery when that suited his ends, Ambar emerged as the principal force in what used to be the Ahmadnagar state. At the height of his power, it was said, 'the Nizam Shahi of the western Deccan was simply referred to as "Ambar's land"'.[32]

His feud with the Mughals lasted for decades. By 1610, as an Englishman noted, Ambar commanded 10,000 soldiers 'of his own caste' in addition to 40,000 Dakhnis.[33] Emperor Jehangir reserved a litany of calumnies for this defender of the Nizam Shahs, ranging from 'the black-faced' to 'the crafty Ambar' and, perhaps more revealingly, 'that disastrous man'.[34] His favourite technique was to unleash guerrillas on slow-moving Mughal armies, honing a military technique that the Marathas would improve to levels of perfection. In the same year Ambar suddenly descended on the Mughals with 50,000 horses and sacked Surat, the principal port of the Mughal empire, giving inspiration to the famous raid by Shivaji on that city five decades later. Of course, Ambar was not always successful. As one Mughal historian wrote, 'Malik Ambar was sometimes defeated, and sometimes victorious, but did not cease to oppose.'[35] Jehangir, in his hatred, even had a painting commissioned in which he featured shooting an arrow at the habshi's severed head. 'Rich in symbolism, the painting repeatedly associates the emperor with light and justice,

Emperor Jehangir

whereas the head of Malik Ambar, surrounded with owls both dead and alive, is associated with night, darkness, and usurpation.' The Mughals were, in fact, obsessed with the colour of their enemy's skin. But 'Most of all the portrait reveals the emperor's profound frustration with his failure ever to vanquish Ambar: he fantasized in art what he could not accomplish on the battlefield.'[36]

The habshi, in the meantime, had even won some domestic victories and battled court intrigue. When in 1600 he first sought to resist the Mughals in the name of a Nizam Shahi prince, the latter was uncertain about the chances of their cause. To persuade him, the African general gave him one of his daughters in marriage – the Nizam Shah, in other words, had a black queen.[37] Around 1610, however, there was trouble in the marriage. As a European traveller noted, 'At a certain time it happened that the king's [other] wife, who was a white Persian woman, scolded the daughter of . . . Melick Ambahaer with many bitter words, saying that she was only a kaffir woman and a concubine . . . and that her father had been a rebel against the king.' When Ambar – who was also growing irritated with the efforts by the Nizam Shah to assert himself, getting in the way of his authority – heard of what had transpired, he 'became so angry that he began to plot the murder of the king'. And that is what was done – both the Nizam Shah and his Westerner wife were poisoned, even as Ambar picked up their son, raised him to the throne and continued to exercise actual power as regent. 'The Mellick,' it was noted, 'goes to greet him solemnly twice each week as a token of his obedience.'[38] His detractors, meanwhile, grumbled that the habshi was 'addicted to sorcery' and given to human sacrifice to please the devil and keep the king in his thrall.[39]

After briefly expelling the Mughals from Ahmadnagar, and even occupying Daulatabad (old Devagiri), Ambar established a new capital for the Nizam Shahi kingdom at a place known as Khirki in 1610, filling it with palaces, fountains, avenues and every other mark that might invest in the place an air of nobility – the city eventually became home to as many as 200,000 people, settled across fifty-four quarters.[40] To demonstrate his gratitude to his loyal Maratha nobles, suburbs in the new city were named after a number of them – Paraspura, Vithapura, Khelpura and so on. One scholar notes that under Ambar the Nizam Shahi state 'effectively [became] a joint Habshi–Maratha enterprise'[41] and indeed the kingdom could be perceived 'as the nursery in which Maratha power could grow, creating the political preconditions for the eventual emergence of an independent Maratha state' under Shivaji (whose grandfather happened to be an associate of Ambar's).[42] For now, though, the state was wedded to Muslim ideals, and despite the little matter of Ambar's murder of a fidgety Nizam Shah, he was stern in matters of religious principle. It appears that a policy of prohibition was put in place, and if someone had the misfortune of being discovered drunk, the law had 'molten lead poured into his throat'. Nobody 'is allowed to sell liquor or even travel with it', a contemporary recorded.[43] Asad Beg, the Mughal ambassador to the Deccan, even noted that the thousands of Muslims in the habshi camp recited from the Quran every night, and that Ambar himself 'offered his prayers with the common people'.[44]

Still, in a ship steered so inflexibly by an iron hand, there were bound to be those with resentments. Malik Ambar, during the length of his career, survived a number of assassination attempts. We find the first of these recorded in 1613, and then again in 1614, orchestrated by Rajputs and Marathas under his command.[45] Hearing of their failure, Jehangir is said to have quipped, 'A very little more would have made an end of this cursed fellow.'[46] In 1621 and 1624 there were yet more attempts, first by trying to drown Ambar, and then by seeking to poison him. Their target, however, proved 'a consummate survivor'.[47] On the eve of his 1616 conflict with the Mughals – one he lost very badly and in which large areas and many forts had to be surrendered to the emperor – a number of his Maratha comrades deserted him and went over to the side of the Mughals.[48] Khirki was sacked by the Marathas and almost completely destroyed – a process that would be repeated a few years later by Prince Khurram, who eventually reigned as Emperor Shahjahan, and to whom the habshi lost fifty lakh rupees.[49] The town, it was noted at the time of the Maratha attack, 'which had taken twenty years to build will hardly recover its splendor for another twenty years'.[50] In due course Ambar did recapture the city and did what he could to repair it.

The losses Ambar suffered in 1616 were severe. The battle took place on the banks of the river Godavari near the city of Paithan. As a Bijapuri court chronicler records, 'Every day Ambar's nobles used to come and fight like *bargis* [i.e. guerrillas].' But when intelligence was received that Ambar himself intended to attack on a certain day with 40,000 cavalry, the Mughal army placed itself in 'a village encircled by the river . . . with a deep ditch in front, behind which they planted their artillery'. When the Nizam Shahi army arrived, the vanguard of horsemen landed straight in the ditch from where they 'could neither advance nor retreat, being huddled together as if they had been chained. In this position they were mown down by the Mughal artillery, like leaves of a tree under a destroying wind . . . The Mughals then advanced to the attack, slaying many of [Ambar's] slaves. A great defeat and flight' fell upon the whole of the habshi forces in this unfortunate episode.[51] It was in these circumstances that Ambar was compelled to sue for peace and give the Mughals what they desired. Despite such a catastrophic reversal, however, he was still strong enough to retain independence and half the kingdom he had conquered in the name of the Nizam Shah. There was yet hope, and as a biographer writes, 'Like the deciduous trees of the western Deccan, Ambar knew how to bend with the wind and shed his pride when necessary.'[52] And he knew also how to lie in wait.

There were more worrying betrayals he had to bear meanwhile. Ibrahim Adil Shah II of Bijapur – Saraswati's son and that patron of the arts – turned against Ambar. In 1613 he was brazen enough in his stand against the Mughals to refer to the emperor merely as the 'ruler of Agra and Delhi'[53]; in 1617, however, when Prince Khurram offered the Adil Shah an alliance where they would share territory conquered at the Nizam Shah's expense, Ibrahim II, for all his other virtues, was shortsighted enough to accept the offer.[54] The Flemish jeweller who railed against him for his 900 concubines even went to the extent of concluding that the Adil Shah of Bijapur was a coward,[55] though Ibrahim II's own defence was: 'Why would I want to make war on the Mogor [Mughal] . . .? I would rather offer him . . . money as a gift, and content him, and be his friend, and remain in my house with my peace and quiet.'[56] These offerings were all extraordinarily splendid – there were enormous diamonds, a sapphire and ruby of great value, and very expensive pearls, so that with other gems and treasures their total value surpassed two million rupees. Two famous elephants – Bakht Buland and Darjansal – were also transported to Agra, and when Emperor Jehangir beheld all that was laid out before him as the gift of the Deccan, he exclaimed, 'Such invaluable *peshkush* (tribute) was never presented to any ruler of this dynasty before!'[57] But in doing so, the Adil Shah had forgotten that invaluable lesson learnt from the fall of Vijayanagar: that the best bet for survival for the Sultans of the Deccan was to stand united against their common foe.

But while his neighbours ingratiated themselves with the Mughals, the habshi had his revenge in 1624. Five years before this, the clandestine arrangement the Adil Shah of Bijapur had reached with the Mughals was revealed when he attacked the Nizam Shah's territories. So far, not only had financial aid come from Bijapur, but also arms and armies. Now, however, Ambar had enemies to both his north and south. Where in 1616 Ibrahim II had sent an army against the Mughals to fight alongside the Nizam Shahi forces, in 1618/19 and again in 1624 he extended his considerable resources to the Mughal emperor as they conspired to bring down the man in Khirki. 'But Ambar was shrewd and knew that he had better strike before being struck himself.'[58] Unexpectedly he attacked the Adil Shah's capital, Bijapur, withdrawing soon afterwards and provoking Ibrahim II's armies into an engagement at a location of his choosing, waiting to inflict a 'crushing defeat' upon the allies.[59] Bhatvadi, which he selected for this battle, suited Ambar's guerrilla tactics very well. Water from a nearby lake was flooded out to create such a pile of slush in the path of the Mughal army that their movements were handicapped. Every night his men delivered the most frightful attacks on the enemy, so that 'Terror . . . seized the hearts of the enemies' troops' who 'spent their nights without sleep and their days without repose'.[60] By the end they were reduced to such humiliating straits that 'Ambar planted his own tent and the Nizam Shahi royal standard in front of the Mughal army with great pomp and demonstration'.[61]

The battle was won, and a 'great disgrace' fell upon the Mughals and their ally. 'Malik Ambar swollen to greatness by this victory, from an ant into a snake, [was] enriched with wealth exceeding the treasures of Corah, and troops numerous beyond imagination.'[62] He also sacked and destroyed the Adil Shah's pet city of Nauraspur where that ruler indulged his artistic inclinations and assembled his poets and painters.[63] In the next year, 1625, Ambar seized Solapur from Ibrahim II and continued his train of victories.[64] That is, however, till death took him away, for in 1626, approaching eighty, the legendary Ambar died of natural causes, in great comfort and in a state of supreme military confidence, inspiring even the Mughals to record his work in letters of gold. Jehangir, who never managed to vanquish Ambar and who everyone knew was the emperor's 'especial object of detestation', received some consolation, one imagines, in knowing that

Malik Ambar's tomb, c. 1865

Paul Fearn / Alamy Stock Photo

Emperor Shahjahan

at least his arch-enemy had died before him.[65] The habshi, meanwhile, was laid to rest in a mausoleum he himself designed, far away from the country where he was born, but in the land he made his own and served to the end.[66]

After Ambar, his son continued the struggle against the Mughals. But what the father had in tremendous quantities, the son seemed entirely to lack – Ambar's heir had neither energy nor strategic genius to turn weakness to strength against a superior enemy, and his crowning achievement was that he briefly named Khirki after himself.[67] By 1633, despite murdering the ruler whose parents his father had killed and planting another infant on the Nizam Shahi throne, Ambar's son failed to establish control. Part of his weakness might also have been due to circumstances beyond his control – starting in 1630, the region suffered such a terrible famine that 'Life was offered for a loaf, but none would buy; rank was to be sold for a cake, but none cared for it [and] . . . the flesh of a son was preferred to his love.'[68] Another factor was also that the latest Mughal onslaught was led by the emperor himself. In the terms that were finally struck, Ambar's successor was granted a generous pension, while the boy-king was sent to Gwalior, where three decades before a previous Nizam Shah had been imprisoned. Resistance continued weakly in some parts under the leadership of a Maratha nobleman, Shahji (who incidentally was the father of the Deccan's future hero, Shivaji). But by 1636 this effort too failed – Shahji was absorbed by the Adil Shah into Bijapur's service under terms agreed with the Mughals.[69] From that year, when the khutbah was read in all the provinces that belonged to the kingdom of Ahmadnagar, it honoured the name not of the Nizam Shah, but that of His Majesty Emperor Shahjahan.[70]

~

Ibrahim Adil Shah II did not live to experience the full consequences of his breach of faith with Malik Ambar, though he did receive a taste of what was to come. In 1617 an awestruck Emperor Jehangir, after surveying the presents from Bijapur, had written to Ibrahim II the following verse: 'Our merciful glance is always in your direction / Rest assured in the shadow of our felicity.'[71] At that time it had not been clear that such a 'glance' involved many more expensive demands for presents from the Deccan. Much treasure was lost – indeed as early as 1604, in Akbar's reign, the ambassador Asad Beg had asked for so much in Bijapur that by the end the Adil Shah had to plead that he had only personal jewels left to offer. And this after parting with his elephant Chanchal (who was so beloved as to appear in the 1590s illustrated romance produced at court called the *Pem Nem* or *The Toils of Love*), an Arabian horse called Chini, and even such household items as a 'bejeweled vase holder' that was a personal gift from his mother to Ibrahim II when he first succeeded to the throne.[72] The whole thing was, to borrow a scholar's phrase, 'institutionalized plunder' behind the veneer of ceremonious gift-giving, allowing the smaller ruler to buy peace while retaining some semblance of pride.[73]

In any case, in 1627, after a long reign that established Bijapur at the heights of prosperity (and brought the Mughals to its gates), the Adil Shah died in his capital. He had hoped for orderly succession, but with four sons anxious to inherit, bloodshed was inevitable.[74] The dispute soon came down to the eldest and the second in line, and the latter prevailed while the former lost his eyes. For thirty years thereafter, Bijapur was ruled by Muhammad Adil Shah, with Dakhni support. A teenager when he succeeded to power, two rival parties were formed at court during the early years of his reign – one urged strong cooperation with the Mughals so that the spoils of the Nizam Shahi state could be divided profitably, the other supporting those like Shivaji's father to prop up Ahmadnagar and pin the Mughals forever in a bloody quagmire of revolts and chaos. Oscillating between both sides, by 1635 Bijapur had formally expressed friendship towards the Mughals while also aiding rebels in Ahmadnagar (bringing to Bijapur that famous gun called the Lord of the Plain[75]) – the result was a Mughal invasion, culminating with the transfer, yet again, of a large sum of money to the imperial treasury.[76]

Clockwise from top left: The fall of Vijayanagar: After his heady rise to power and influence in the Deccan, Ramaraya of Vijayanagar was destroyed by the united forces of the Rebel Sultans in a devastating battle in 1565. The city was abandoned by its rulers, sacked by invaders and reduced to the ruins we now see in Hampi.

The scene of Ramaraya's execution after the 'Battle of Talikota' in 1565. Husain Nizam Shah, his most furious enemy, watches from his horse, while the elderly Ibrahim Qutb Shah, who was once Ramaraya's friend, makes an unsuccessful attempt to intervene.

Burhan Nizam Shah II, who lived in exile in Emperor Akbar's court, returned in 1591 to claim the throne of Ahmadnagar. With this the wheels were set in motion for the Mughal conquest of the Deccan, lasting nearly a century.

Facing page, top: The *Nujum al-Ulum*, a fascinating 16th-century work from Bijapur, covers topics ranging from magic and astrology to horses and halwa. Full of influences from across India and abroad, it abounds with images, such as this one of cow-headed angels.

Facing page, bottom: Ibrahim Adil Shah II was the greatest of Bijapur's rulers, and styled himself son of the Hindu gods Saraswati and Ganapati. He appears here in a moment of leisure, playing his tambura, in a happier time before his alliance with the Mughals rang the death knell of the Deccan's independence.

Left: A portrait of the goddess Saraswati commissioned by Ibrahim Adil Shah II, where she appears not as in conventional Hindu depictions, but like a Muslim princess, in costume, pose as well as setting, embodying the eclectic culture of the early modern Deccan.

Below: Chand Bibi, who advised kings and generals, fought valiantly against the Mughals and eventually fell before a treacherous assassin, is seen here as she goes out hawking. Like many royal women in the Deccan, she exercised great power and does not appear to have secluded herself in purdah.

Facing page: In the 16th and 17th centuries, the Deccan attracted not only European military talent and mercenaries, but also artists, travellers, doctors and others. Western influences – and European characters – begin to appear in the art of the Deccan, as seen in these two examples.

Left: Malik Ambar began life as a slave in Ethiopia but died in the Deccan as king in all but name. An unmatched warrior, he withstood the Mughal invasion of Ahmadnagar, married his daughter to a Sultan and became the greatest obstacle to the realization of Emperor Jahangir's ambitions in the early 17th century.

Below: Jahangir never succeeded in vanquishing Malik Ambar, giving vent to his rage by branding the African 'black-faced', 'crafty' and even 'that disastrous man'. So infuriating was Ambar to the emperor that he commissioned this painting depicting him shooting an arrow at Ambar's decapitated head – something he never achieved in real life.

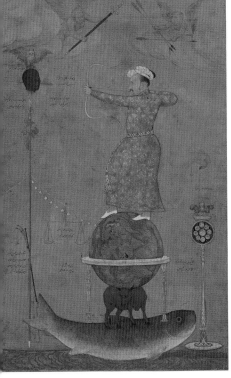

Facing page, top: Abdullah Qutb Shah (r. 1626–72) reigned for long in Golconda, though great authority was wielded by his mother, Hayat Baksh Begum, once sought as bride for the Shah of Iran. It was in his time that the Qutb Shah accepted Mughal suzerainty, submitting tribute and giving up his official religion of Shia Islam.

Facing page, bottom: Ikhlas Khan (*left*), another African nobleman in the Deccan, was the right-hand man of his childhood friend and sovereign Muhammad Adil Shah of Bijapur (*centre*). Unlike Golconda, Bijapur did not become a tributary to the Mughals, but Mir Muhammad Said was compelled to come to terms with Emperor Shahjahan to save his kingdom.

Left: In Golconda, Abdullah Qutb Shah handed over the reins of power in 1643 to Mir Muhammad Said (*pictured*), an ambitious administrator and business magnate who controlled diamond mines, had dealings with the English and had a vast commercial empire of his own. Mir Muhammad Said eventually fell out of favour and went over to the Mughals.

Below: Ali Adil Shah II of Bijapur, seen here with a courtesan, was rumoured to be illegitimate or adopted, providing the future emperor Aurangzeb his excuse to commence his campaign of conquest against Bijapur.

The House of Bijapur: On the extreme right here appears Sikandar Adil Shah, the last ruler of Bijapur, who surrendered his kingdom and throne to Aurangzeb in 1686. This painting depicts all the rulers of the Adil Shahi dynasty from the time of its founder, Yusuf (*enthroned*), down to Sikandar, who died a Mughal prisoner far from the kingdom his ancestors once ruled. The Shah of Iran appears in the background, handing over the key of temporal power to the first Adil Shah, while a ship in the distance symbolizes the vast overseas contacts of the Deccan.

Dinodia Photos / Alamy Stock Photo

Ibrahim Adil Shah II's tomb

In 1636 Muhammad Adil Shah became a vassal of the Mughal emperor, paying him twenty lakh rupees in lump sum, other presents, including an elephant called Gaj Raj, accepting his arbitration in any future disputes with Golconda and to generally keep peace with the empire.[77] In a letter to Shahjahan, the Adil Shah wrote: 'I gratefully acknowledge the illustrious farman and incomparable portrait of the King of Kings along with other gifts . . . I have no words to express to Your Majesty my gratitude for such a bountiful act. I performed *sijdah* [prostration] and *taslim* [salutation] in absentia to the Emperor before receiving such an honour. Day and night, I pray for the prosperity of Your Majesty, whose name I repeat like a *wazifah* [incantation].'[78] The document that was signed is known as the Ahd Namah (Deed of Agreement) – it could never be a 'treaty' for the two sides were not, it was now clear, equal. The terms, however, were interesting. The Adil Shah of Bijapur appears as the inferior but is not placed

Muhammad Adil Shah of Bijapur

under an obligation to transfer annual tribute, nor is he asked to terminate the custom of celebrating the Persian Shah in the khutbah during Friday prayers. This was in contrast to the Inqiyad Namah (Deed of Submission) signed with the Qutb Shah in Golconda at the same time, for this prince was made to pay annual tribute to the emperor of 200,000 hons, mint coins in the Mughal style and suspend veneration of the Iranian kings.[79] But despite being better off than the only other autonomous state left in the Deccan, the Adil Shah was at best a reluctant vassal – every time a letter came from Delhi, custom demanded he ride out of his capital to humbly receive it at a specified distance. And on each occasion, the Adil Shah invented a diplomatic 'illness' that served either to thwart such expectations altogether or allow negotiations to reduce the distance he would have to travel to receive the honour that was Shahjahan's farman.[80]

For all this, however, Muhammad's reign was a successful one, and the king was aided by his African favourite Ikhlas Khan (with whom he appears on the cover of this book, riding an elephant).[81] While he was prevented by the Mughals from acquiring territory towards the north, the south remained open to him, and fragmented lands in the Carnatic that once belonged to Vijayanagar were slowly picked up by the Adil Shahi state. In 1648 Shahjahan even permitted Bijapur's rulers to adopt the style of Shah – something they had always done, but which the Mughals, from Akbar's generation, diligently ignored.[82] But successes such as these were upset by other factors. By the 1650s the Adil Shah was unwell, and slowly his authority began to be flouted. External affairs also worsened matters – the Mughal governor in the Deccan at this time was none other than the future emperor Aurangzeb, and his policy towards the last two kingdoms of the Deccan, Bijapur and Golconda, was one of wanton aggression. Part of this was born from his disappointment with the Ahmadnagar territories under his charge – they were so destroyed by the famine of 1630 that even two decades later it 'could not pay even for the local administration'.[83] Naturally, as someone who felt that he would be disgracing the memory of his ancestor Timur 'if I did not seek to

extend the bounds of my present territories',[84] his attention quickly
turned towards Bijapur and Golconda, beginning with a series of
complaints that neither kingdom, acquiring territory after territory in
the Carnatic, had sought permission for such expansionist schemes
from the emperor, his father.[85]

With Bijapur, Aurangzeb obtained an excuse for intervention in
1656 following the death of Muhammad Adil Shah. His passing
provoked, with a little encouragement from the Mughals, rebellions
in the Carnatic territories, even as, in an interesting turn, Aurangzeb
insisted that Muhammad had had no sons and that his heir and
successor, Ali Adil Shah II, was illegitimate.[86] It is indeed believed
by some that the new prince was adopted – as Thevenot noted some
years later, 'The king [Ali II] . . . was an orphan, whom the late king
and queen adopted for their son.'[87] It also appears that in contemporary
Indian sources, Ali II is stated as raised by Muhammad's queen, but
the name of his actual mother does not appear. In any case, before
he had even made himself comfortable on his golden throne, the new

Dinodia Photos / Alamy Stock Photo

Gol Gumbaz, the tomb of Muhammad Adil Shah

ruler found Bijapur's lands under attack from the imperial armies, with Aurangzeb quite implacable.

Good luck, however, saved Ali II, for news arrived from the north that the emperor was not well, and soon his ambitious son would have to make haste to fight his own infamous war of succession for the Peacock Throne in Agra. But Aurangzeb had secured several very pleasing concessions from Ali II – all the Nizam Shahi territory that decades before had been taken by Bijapur (and confirmed as theirs by Shahjahan) now fell into Mughal hands. A crore and a half rupees was to be paid, in addition to more land, which included Bidar, the old capital of the Bahmanis and subsequently the seat of the Barid Shahs till they fell in 1619 to Ibrahim Adil Shah II.[88] It was a lot to ask, though, and soon, Bijapur was released from many of these terms by Aurangzeb himself in a bid to ensure that his rivals to the Mughal throne did not obtain any aid from the princes in the south.[89]

For quite some time hereafter, Aurangzeb was preoccupied with consolidating his power and waiting for his imprisoned father to die – the Persian Shah had sniggered when the former took the title of Seizer of the World (Alamgir) that it was somewhat exaggerated when the only thing Aurangzeb had actually seized was his own heartbroken father. Meanwhile, Ali Adil Shah II spent the early 1660s bringing order to his very many acquisitions in the Carnatic. By the middle of the decade, however, the emperor returned to the subject of the Deccan once again. He sent to the south a prominent Rajput general of his in order to put down Maratha rebellions, and to chastise the Adil Shah of Bijapur who was supposed to be aiding those very rebels. This does indeed appear to have been the case, for Ali II was 'playing a double or triple role, as dictated by his own survival' and its needs. 'Towards the Mughals he was overtly submissive, but secretly subversive, knowing that conflict with them was in the end inevitable.' In supporting Maratha rebels, he discovered, therefore, that he could at once keep the rebels from eating into his own territory while also using their resistance against the Mughals to his own advantage.[90] As Aurangzeb's general discovered and reported to his emperor, 'Adil

Khan in his folly played false with me. He outwardly sent an army into [Maratha] territory; but he considered the utter destruction of [the rebels] to be harmful to his interests and wished [them] to stand as a wall between the imperial troops and the Bijapuris.'[91]

In 1666, therefore, having succeeded in landing a substantial punch on the Marathas, the Mughal army made its way to Bijapur. In fact, in addition to his own 40,000 soldiers, the general also brought a Maratha army of 9000, supplied by the rebels themselves whom Ali II, till recently, had been subsidizing.[92] The Adil Shah prepared his capital for a long, terrible siege. 'The embankment of the tanks were demolished, poison and carrion were thrown into the wells, trees and lofty buildings near the fortress were destroyed . . . All round Bijapur the country was laid waste and not a trace of grass or fodder was left.'[93] This took the invaders by surprise – having paid large sums of money to bribe various Bijapuri nobles, the general had not actually expected to besiege the fort, and certainly not in conditions such as this with no water or food available for miles around. The plan had been to win over the court through money and promises of Mughal favour. Besides, while the Adil Shah's realms were vastly smaller than the Mughal empire, he was by no means a weak prince. Until recently Bijapur had an 'annual revenue of 78.4 million rupees, and in addition received 52.5 million rupees as tribute . . . it had an army of 80,000 cavalry, 250,000 infantry, and 530 elephants'.[94] This was in comparison with the Mughals, who enjoyed revenues in Shahjahan's reign of 220 million rupees.[95] Though now somewhat poorer due to his own campaigns and tribulations, the Adil Shah was certainly not prepared to allow any invader to make a potential annexation a convenient affair. For eight months, the Mughal general made aggressive sounds and tried to get his way, but in the end, having spent the four million rupees Aurangzeb had given him, as well as over twice that much of his own money, the Rajput saw light. The Mughals were compelled to retreat and return to their own headquarters, Khirki, which had now been renamed after the emperor as Aurangabad.[96]

Instead of strengthening his defences and bringing discipline to a

Bahlul Khan, one of the regents of Sikandar Adil Shah

court that had several factions willing to prosper as Mughal agents, Ali II now lapsed into a world of wine, and when he died in 1672, a four-year-old heir came to the throne. As always, a regency opened up avenues for plotting and counter-scheming: first there was a habshi regent, and then a Westerner, and then a habshi again, only the last of them surviving for more than two years. The Marathas took advantage of the quarrels in Bijapur, and one by one forts around the kingdom fell to them, at the cost of Bijapur's defence and integrity. Lords and governors refused to obey the commands of the court; the treasury was depleted. In addition to this, the third of the regents in charge of the young Adil Shah was rather favourable to the Mughals – in 1678 he agreed to an alliance by which the ruler's sister was to marry the emperor's son.[97] Such was the reaction to this news, not only at court but even in the city and other centres across the kingdom, that the regent was forced to go back on his word. And with Bijapur's troops on the brink of mutiny, he had to secure assistance from the Marathas for the defence of the state.[98] It was ironic, but for the time being it saved the capital. When the Mughal army arrived in late 1679, it was defeated. After bombarding the fort for some days, its commander 'marched through the country around it like a mad dog, plundering and burning the villages' before at last a humiliating attack by the Marathas in March 1680 caused him to be 'recalled in disgrace'.[99] Tragically, however, before this debacle had played out, in a bid to secure peace, the Adil Shahi princess had voluntarily gone over to the Mughal camp. She could not stop the invaders, and now, as they retreated, she could not avoid her marriage to the emperor's son either.[100]

For four years after this, Aurangzeb was preoccupied with his war against the Marathas and the rebellion of one of his sons – having himself displaced his father, the emperor was known to be anxious about the loyalties of his offspring. But by 1685 he had decided it was time to destroy Bijapur. He sent armies in April that year, but when the fort had not fallen even after thirteen months, Aurangzeb himself came to unseat the Adil Shah in July 1686. Famine raged in the countryside; stocks and reserves inside were almost over. The whole of the garrison protecting the Adil Shah numbered between 2000 and 3000 poorly fed and badly paid soldiers, disheartened by the sheer size of the Mughals gathered outside and by the presence of the emperor. For that could mean only one thing: that he was here to break the back of the kingdom, one way or another. On 22 September 1686, the Adil Shah finally opened the gates, and went in a sorry procession to the Mughal camp with the keys to the fort and his royal insignia. And there he surrendered the kingdom his ancestors had ruled for nearly two hundred years. 'I shall exalt you with many favours and gifts,' said Aurangzeb to him. 'Be composed in mind.'[101] In reality, the ruler was now reduced to the status of 'Adil Khan' and enlisted as a Mughal noble. With a pension of 100,000 rupees, he was sent away to Daulatabad, and then to Satara, where in 1700 he died in his early thirties. His name was Sikandar, and with him the Adil Shahi kingdom came to an end.[102]

In 1680, when Sikandar was about twelve years old, two artists at court by the names of Chand Muhammad and Kamal Muhammad had produced a painting called *The House of Bijapur*. The work is an interesting one, but also perhaps carried a foreboding of the destruction that lay just around the bend. In it, all the Adil Shahi rulers appear together, on the same carpet, creating a genealogical line, from Yusuf down to Sikandar himself. The founder is the only one among them seated on a throne. Behind him appears a Safavid figure, believed to be Shah Ismail, his contemporary in Iran, handing him a key – a key to both the temporal as well as spiritual worlds. There is even the sea in the background with a ship visible, signifying the important place Bijapur occupied in the wider, globalized world of the early modern age. Yusuf's successors all appear in the frame in their own distinct ways. Ali Adil Shah I, for instance, stands out as the only one wearing armour and not courtly attire – a marker of his legacy as the man who helped defeat Vijayanagar in 1565 at the 'Battle of Talikota'. Sikandar, as would be his place in history, is the slightest and smallest figure in the painting – even his turban is essentially an imitation of his father's style, for he was yet to carve out his own identity. Alas, he would have no opportunity. And the painting itself, as one scholar put it, goes down in history less as a genealogy of the Adil Shahs and more as a 'painted curtain call' on what had once been a great and glorious dynasty.[103]

The city of Bijapur too suffered. 'Aurangzeb entered [the city] seated on a portable throne, scattering gold and silver coins. He was, it turned out, performing the last rites of this once gracious and prosperous city. A devastating bubonic plague felled half the city's population soon after its fall, and it became a ghost city, its nobility impoverished, its artisans, scholars, and poets scattered and without sustenance.'[104] The fate that visited Ahmadnagar was now upon Bijapur too, reduced to serving merely as another provincial outpost of a vast empire, whose emperor had no interest in its prosperity but sought all its riches to carry out his wars and annex more lands from other kings. In the course of the eighteenth century, famine and neglect led to the Marathas and others plundering it for whatever was left, so that in 1808 when a British traveller came to this former capital of the Adil Shahs, he would describe it as a 'desert'. 'For fourteen miles' around it, the visitor noted, 'the only living creatures were some pretty parroquets, a partridge, a hare, and a herd of deer'.[105]

VII

House of Sheep
The Last Sultanate of the Deccan

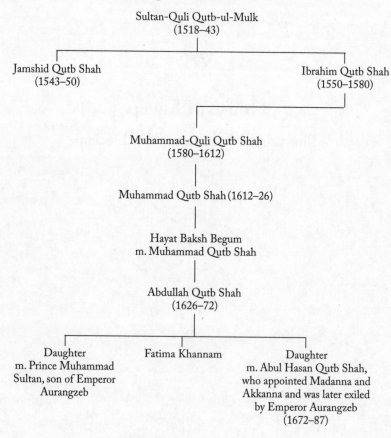

THE QUTB SHAHI DYNASTY

Sultan-Quli Qutb-ul-Mulk
(1518–43)

Jamshid Qutb Shah
(1543–50)

Ibrahim Qutb Shah
(1550–1580)

Muhammad-Quli Qutb Shah
(1580–1612)

Muhammad Qutb Shah (1612–26)

Hayat Baksh Begum
m. Muhammad Qutb Shah

Abdullah Qutb Shah
(1626–72)

Daughter
m. Prince Muhammad
Sultan, son of Emperor
Aurangzeb

Fatima Khannam

Daughter
m. Abul Hasan Qutb Shah,
who appointed Madanna and
Akkanna and was later exiled
by Emperor Aurangzeb
(1672–87)

If there was one dynasty in the Deccan that could claim a royal bloodline over and above its usurpation of Bahmani prerogatives, it was the house of the Qutb Shahs of Golconda. Their ancestors, in the fourteenth century, were vassals of the Sultanate in Baghdad, and belonged to the Turkic Qara Qoyunlu (Black Sheep) tribe, which controlled parts of northern Iraq near Mosul, in addition to Armenia and Azerbaijan. At one point, a member of the family rose to great prominence fighting Timur the Lame, and after the latter's death, essentially reversed the conqueror's work in that quarter of the world. Baghdad itself fell to him, though his successors were less than capable of defending his achievements, hastening the fall of their clan as brothers fought one another and sons toppled their fathers. By the 1460s the end was upon them, and a rival tribe, the Aq Qoyunlu (White Sheep), appropriated all that had been governed by their counterparts of the darker shade. In Hamadan in Iran, however, a fourth-generation scion of the hero earlier mentioned continued to retain some authority, with the result that the threat of assassination or war was ever looming – the White Sheep were determined to liquidate all males among their rival Black. And thus, taking the advice of the elders, so his line might not be extinguished, the man sent away his son to seek his fortune in the only land where the boy might have had a real chance and a clean slate: India.[1]

Of course, in the tradition of hagiographies, this flight from an unravelling tribal polity is presented in the *Tarikh-i Qutb Shahi* somewhat more glamorously as a 'decree of Providence' which guided the boy to 'kindle the light of Islam in the country of Unbelief'.[2] But the fact was that like Yusuf Adil Shah, the first king of Bijapur, and the immigrant Barid Shah in Bidar, the Qutb Shah of Golconda came to India seeking his fortune, albeit with more exalted genealogical credentials. He appears, in fact, to have taken an overland route to Delhi first, but finding it as dry as a desert there in terms of openings, he travelled south to the Bahmani court. Sultan-Quli, as the boy was called, was twenty at this time, somewhere in the 1470s.[3] His uncle who delivered him here returned to their homeland, while Sultan-Quli became 'Accountant General of the Imperial Harem'. In this position, he seems to have won the favour of the ladies at court, settling certain disputes on the battlefield on their behalf.[4] In 1487, when he saved the Bahmani Sultan from a ring of homicidal Dakhnis, he was granted a crisp new position, rising higher still in the sovereign's estimation. Seven years later, after he scotched a rebellion in Goa, he was created Qutb-ul-Mulk, the Sultan appointing him governor of the eastern provinces, adding Golconda to the estates that this nobleman already held.[5] By this time, though, it was obvious to everybody that the Sultanate was falling to pieces – and the man in Golconda did not hesitate to occupy his share. He did not, however, assert independence during the lifetime of the monarch who had first showered him with power and position: as late as 1518 he inscribed the name of the Bahmani sovereign on a mosque,[6] and paid a 'considerable amount of money' each year as tribute to the puppet in Bidar.[7] Loyalty, it appears, meant something to the first Qutb Shah of Golconda, even though the individual it was inspired by was a hopeless nonentity.

With the death of this Bahmani Sultan soon afterwards, however, Golconda ceased demonstrating any form of ceremonial obeisance to the former capital, and though he would never claim the title of king in his own day, for all real purposes Sultan-Quli was now an independent prince. Golconda fort was upgraded, its mud walls reinforced with solid rings of granite, making the citadel quite literally impregnable.[8] Unlike the other principalities, the state was also culturally homogeneous, its

Sultan-Quli Qutb Shah of Golconda

territories broadly encompassing the old domains of the Kakatiyas, with a Telugu-speaking population identifying itself as subjects of the kingdom of Telingana.[9] Hindu chiefdoms (many of which continued into the Mughal era and all the way till India's independence from the British in 1947), headed by lines tracing their origins to the days of the Kakatiyas, were absorbed as Qutb Shahi feudatories.[10] Sultan-Quli ruled, thus, with considerable success despite the troubles of his age – in addition to rivals in the Deccan, in the south he grappled with the towering presence of Vijayanagar under Krishnadeva, who did little to calm his neighbours' fears when he styled himself Paribhuta Suratrana (Vanquisher of Sultans).[11] In the north lay the realm of another enemy, the Gajapati of Orissa, and if Golconda was able to survive infancy, it was because its ruler was as decisive as he was unafraid of conflict. From Krishnadeva of Vijayanagar, Sultan-Quli snatched as many as nineteen forts,[12] not to speak of the port of Masulipatam, though from the second Adil Shah of Bijapur what he received, when he made a similar attempt, was a terrible slash of steel, leaving his face horribly mutilated for life.[13] Emboldened by the declaration of Shiism as the state religion in Bijapur, the Qutb Shah also proclaimed Golconda a Shia kingdom. Unlike the Adil Shahis, however, in Golconda there would never be a switch to Sunnism – that is, until the Mughals forced their Deed of Submission in 1636 and dragooned its rulers to refashion rituals as per imperial practice.[14]

In 1543, by which time he was a very old man said to have been in his nineties, Sultan-Quli was assassinated at the instigation of his son. Some versions show him stabbed to death during his prayers, while others suggest the disgraceful deed was done in the palace gardens, or inside a chamber where the Qutb Shah was examining his favourite jewels. But the general view is that the son, tired of watching his father age regally (and ever so slowly), decided to take matters into his hands and expedite his own succession.[15] In any case, blood was spilt. The new ruler then put aside one brother by blinding him, while the other fled into exile. Interestingly, the man who gave this refugee asylum was Ramaraya of Vijayanagar, who had himself once served the recently murdered Sultan-Quli as a nobleman at court.[16] But like his father, the new Qutb Shah of Golconda too deferred making any ostentatious displays of sovereign status.[17] He formed alliances with different princes in the neighbourhood for different purposes, and 'interfered far more than was the custom with his successors in conflicts between the [rulers] of the Deccan'.[18] 60,000 soldiers served his interests, and his right-hand man was a Telugu leader called Jagadeva Rao. His reign, however, was cut short, and by 1550 he was dead: the parricide was consumed by cancer if not by guilt.[19]

It was at this time, after a brief interlude when a son of the deceased was placed on the throne, that the exiled brother made his triumphant return from Vijayanagar. In this, he was aided by Jagadeva Rao and the Hindu soldiers who garrisoned Golconda fort.[20] The name of this new ruler was Ibrahim Qutb Shah. He was only in his teens when he fled his father's kingdom, and now, upon his return, his first act was to kneel at the old man's tomb.[21] And then, of course, he demanded absolute loyalty from his nobles – one inscription from his inaugural year confirms, somewhat inelegantly, that if anyone proved less than dependable, 'his moustache is as good as the hair on the private parts of public women'.[22] Despite such unusual language, Ibrahim's reign, which lasted for the next thirty years and saw him claim absolute sovereignty, was a period of great achievement. While Jagadeva Rao was expelled due to various intrigues, the Hindu nobility in general prospered during this era. Some of this might have been the result of the years Ibrahim spent as a youth in Vijayanagar, from where he is even believed to have brought back a wife.[23] The Qutb Shah was, besides, a lover of Telugu. 'His court was thronged by local poets of note, and he identified himself so much with indigenous culture that his name was affectionately Teluguised as Malkibharama and Abhirama.'[24] In the tradition of Hindu kings of the past, Ibrahim also patronized retellings of the ancient epics – a poet named Addanki Gangadhara was commissioned by him to expand a chapter from the Mahabharata that tells the tale of two lovers, Tapati and Samvarana.[25] One of Ibrahim's sons, meanwhile, became 'well versed in classical

Golconda fort, from *The Universal Geography with Illustrations
and Maps, Division XV,* by Elisee Reclus
(published by Virtue & Co. Limited, London), 1895

The Print Collector / Getty Images

lore and was a scholar of logic, philosophy, and medicine'.[26] Farmans
issued by the court from this time were bilingual,[27] and by the end
of the reign of the Qutb Shahs all proclamations were written in the
vernacular, 'with Persian summaries appearing only on their reverse
sides'.[28] Strong diplomatic relations, however, were cultivated with the
Shah of Iran, and the Qutb Shahs' fervour for their Persian friends
only grew with the eventual arrival of Mughals in the neighbourhood.

In military matters, Ibrahim was even-handed and rarely sought territory beyond the Telugu-speaking horizon. In 1565, however, it was he who joined the other Sultans of the Deccan in a league against Ramaraya, his one-time benefactor, and opened up a path for subsequent southward expansion. For a long time he had been on good terms with Vijayanagar, but Ramaraya's haughty annexation of Golconda property converted even this friend into a foe. Another provocation lay in that Vijayanagar harboured Jagadeva Rao, and at his instigation provoked a rebellion in Golconda – on one occasion, when the Qutb Shah returned from an extended outing, he discovered the gates of his own capital shut in his face. He became, possibly, the only ruler in India to have to suffer the embarrassment of besieging his personal headquarters simply so he could return to the business of heading it.[29] Moments like this brought out another side of Ibrahim Qutb Shah – he had all the soldiers who participated in this mutiny massacred. Similarly, when of the thirty children he fathered, some of the boys became a nuisance, Ibrahim had them punished: the eldest was poisoned, while another was drowned to death – perhaps the Qutb Shah didn't want to invite his father's fate upon himself.[30] These cruel decisions on dynastic questions, and his role in that sensational battle of 1565 against Vijayanagar mark the more aggressive events of Ibrahim's reign. For the most part, however, he was known for the prosperity he brought Golconda in a somewhat calmer frame of mind, which with most princes of his age was a rare characteristic.

Masulipatam, for instance, emerged during Ibrahim's long reign as an important centre of economic activity, integral to the welfare of Golconda's rulers. As a harbour it was a bad one, with 'one of the worst anchorages' on India's east coast. 'Ships were forced to anchor out at sea, and goods were transported to and from them in small boats.' But despite its weaknesses, Masulipatam's success derived from 'the fact that it was the major outlet for the products of the Golconda Sultanate' – and these were products in high demand in various centres of the trading world.[31] Textiles were a major export, and the Qutb Shah's realms offered 'painted' cloth – chintz – of a very high standard. This material, a traveller remarked, was 'famous throughout India' and

Ibrahim Qutb Shah of Golconda

was 'indeed the most exquisite' in its appearance and delicacy.[32] Ships from Golconda went east to Malaysia, the kingdom of Siam, and to Sumatra, while also sailing the other way for the annual Haj and to Iran. On board these vessels often were carpets, for outside Persia, 'the best Persian-style carpets were produced near Elluru' in Golconda.[33] As the Dutch and English East India Companies entered the Bay of Bengal, the Qutb Shah's textile industry was embraced in Europe as well, where Indian fabric became an everyday commodity – Golconda chintz, with its beautiful patterns and colours, saw especial demand in Holland and France besides England.[34] The 'welth [sic] and welfare of the kingdome of Gulcondah', observed the English, 'doth consist in itts inland manufactures'.[35] There were, of course, imports too, from not only Malabar and Bengal but also from lands as far as China and Japan, and items included 'clove, pepper, cinnamon, silver, copper, tin . . . and gold'.[36] The forests of the land, meanwhile, supported a 'thriving shipbuilding business', and its mines produced excellent steel swords for armies abroad.[37] Meanwhile, the mines of Golconda, twenty-three in number according to a 1677 English report, alongside the fifteen in Bijapur could, if they wished, 'furnish all the world plentifully with Diamonds' – mining operations were deliberately limited 'lest, as it is imagined, they should become too common' given the abundance with which these precious stones were available.[38] Such was the splendour associated with the very word Golconda that in as late as 1813 an American city in Illinois would change its name from Sarahsville to Golconda, to evoke a vision of the legendary wealth which was believed to have existed in the original city of that name.[39]

If Ibrahim Qutb Shah put his kingdom on to the path of prosperity, his successor settled his legacy upon a surer footing. As Golconda grew, Ibrahim had already initiated plans for the expansion of the capital and the construction of an unwalled city outside the fort. An effort in the west failed due to want of water, after which Ibrahim looked east, constructing a bridge over the river Musi. Ibrahim also built the Husain Sagar lake, as well as another town named after himself about sixteen miles away from Golconda. But the crowning jewel of the

Qutb Shahs was the city of Hyderabad, built by his heir, Muhammad-
Quli, who is described in one manuscript as nothing less than a
'Solomonic royal highness'.[40] Like his father, Muhammad-Quli Qutb
Shah had multiple talents. On the one hand, he composed poetry in
the *virahini* style, i.e. in the voice of a woman longing for her lover,
who is essentially god himself. Thus, we have the Qutb Shah cry, 'O
you of consummate charm / see how enslaved this poor girl is to you!'[41]
On the other hand, he was a great patron of the arts and the written
word as well, with a special department housed in one of his palaces
'where all manner of book-production activities took place, including
paper-making, manuscript illumination, gilding and painting', hosting
artisans from Persia, upper India and of course the Telugu countryside.[42]

   The special place he earned for himself, however, was on account
of his standing as a great builder. What Muhammad-Quli Qutb
Shah envisioned in Hyderabad was a city 'unequalled the world over',
a veritable 'replica of paradise'.[43] One story is that on a hunt across
the river, he met an exquisite woman called Bhagmati, and espousing
her, decided to honour her with a city: Bhagnagar, later rechristened
Hyderabad when she became Hyder Mahal. The story travelled – a
Mughal nobleman dismissed the whole project as the worthless doings
of a prince enamoured by 'an old prostitute'.[44] The city was named, he
spat, after 'a hardened whore'.[45] As it happens, it was named after Ali,
also called Hyder, who is venerated by Shias as their first imam and
certainly not after any of the Qutb Shah's mistresses. This is clear from
a composition of his own in which seventeen concubines are named,
including the special ones; none of them was called Bhagmati, and
in fact in this account the ruler refers to his new urban dream only as
Hyderabad. So too, coins of the time cite Golconda and Hyderabad
while a city called Bhagnagar never appears. More likely, once the
dynasty fell from power, Mughal gossip grew from a 'sneering sentence
. . . into a paragraph, the paragraph into a section, and the section into
chapters', repeating a falsehood till it was widely perceived as true.[46]

   The city, in any case, brought Golconda into the seventeenth
century with a huge splash of glamour, for it was utterly beautiful

Muhammad-Quli Qutb Shah of Golconda

and in a league of its own. The town was, wrote Tavernier during his travels here, 'little less than Orleans, well built and full of windows', while the bridge to cross into it across the river was 'no less beautiful than Pont-neuf at Paris'.[47] The Charminar, finished in 1592, stood at a major crossroads, right next to the main square, adorned with a fountain called the Cistern of Four Cardinal Points (Char-su-ka-hauz), octagonal in shape. Nearby appeared the new palaces of the royal family, and the Qutb Shah brought alive the whole place by having built a reported 14,000 shops, schools, baths, caravanserais and other public buildings.[48] Inside the Charminar itself, its design rich in Shia symbolism, on the higher floors was housed a mosque and a school, open to Hindus as well as Muslims. The place also doubled as a spot from where proclamations were read out for the benefit of the public.[49] The principal palace of the ruler is believed to have been even more splendid, with its seven or eight floors, each named after the Shia imams, after the Prophet and God himself. 'Of these, the storey named after Ali, the Haidar Mahal, was the most resplendent,

Charminar

and its roof and pillars are said to have been studded with precious stones and nails of pure gold.'[50] When the English merchant William Methwold came to Hyderabad, his review was rapturous. 'A citie that for sweetnesse of ayre, conveniencie of water, and fertility of soyle, is accounted the best situated in India, not to speake of the Kings Palace, which for bignesse and sumptuousnesse . . . exceedeth all belonging to the Mogull or any other Prince.'[51] Endearingly, Methwold lamented that while the 'Cotubsha' had four wives and 1000 concubines, 'his excellent Majesty our Gracious [English] Sovereigne' had 'three kingdoms . . . but [only] one wife'.[52] But royal boudoir contests aside, the man was pleased with the Qutb Shah's new capital.

The revenues of the kingdom around this time lay between twenty and twenty-five lakh rupees, and tax collection was farmed out to the highest bidder who agreed to deposit a certain sum every year in the capital.[53] As Jean de Thevenot, the French diarist, recorded, the king was 'proprietor of all the lands in his kingdom, which he rents out to those who offer most, except such as he gratifies his particular friends with, i.e. the nobles to whom he gives the use of them for a certain time'.[54] This applied to mines as well. Diamonds were found in Golconda, according to local legend, by a goatherd who accidentally came across 'a stone that shined somewhat bright'. The man sold it for some rice.[55] When the nature of the shiny pebble was understood, mining operations commenced in full force.[56] One of the mines, for instance, was rented to a man called 'Marcandoo, of the cast of the goldsmiths' for 300,000 gold pagodas a year, though if stones of more than a certain size were unearthed, they belonged automatically to the royal treasury in Golconda.[57] In one mine, Tavernier claimed there worked 60,000 people (one of whom was a thief who tried to conceal a diamond in the corner of his eye). Elsewhere, in the company of traders he encountered a 242-carat stone (the Great Table), which was 'the biggest [stone] that I ever saw in my life in a merchant's hands'.[58] The Hope Diamond is believed to have emerged from Golconda, from where it found its way to the French court, as is the Daria-i-Noor, now part of the Iranian crown collection in Tehran. As the centuries passed, massive gems like the Shah Diamond, the Regent Diamond and the Orlov Diamond (now in Russia) were thrown up by Qutb Shahi miners. Although the Koh-i-Noor may well have been found earlier in quite a different part of India, certain stories concerning even that most famous (and contentious) diamond connect it to Golconda, from where in the late seventeenth century it was supposedly smuggled by an opportunist minister after he had stabbed his sovereign in the back.[59]

Like Methwold, a Dutchman called Antony Schorer was also most impressed by all he beheld in Hyderabad. 'The state kept by the King of Golconda,' he wrote in 1609, 'is great. When he comes out, he is followed by a great crowd, some on horseback, and some carried in palanquins. He possesses many elephants and camels. He himself sits on an elephant when he comes out . . . It is said that the King has an annual income, in excess of all charges, of 19 tons of treasure . . . He bestows large sums in religious benevolence, especially on Persians, who come . . . in great numbers, men of noble ancestry but small means.'[60] The patronage to Westerners does not mean that the backing provided to Telugu Hindus in the previous reign had ceased – on the contrary, non-Muslims were employed in high places in Golconda, and the poet laureate of the court was a Hindu, Pattametta Somayaju Kavi, while the chief pandit of the Qutb Shah was a certain Ganesha Panditulu.[61] The celebrated Kshetrayya, ordinarily connected with the Vijayanagar splinter states of the Tanjore and Madurai Nayakas, similarly, notes in one of his poems that he composed in forty days 1500 *padams* to sing for the Qutb Shah.[62] English traders often recorded the presence of Brahmins in the administration and revenue department, their very caste becoming synonymous with clerical work – in 1678 there was even an instance of a mosque in Hyderabad seeking a 'writing Brahmin' for its use.[63] The reigning Qutb Shah, Muhammad, in his own composition, the *Kulliyat*, refers to customs of the Hindus, Muslims (favouring Shias over all other sects), and even the Parsis, whose ways of life and festivals he noted and appreciated[64] (this in addition to a discussion on games played in Golconda, including one peculiar to women, known by the memorable name *pokhari phu*).

Among foreigners living in the state both in its ports and occasionally in Hyderabad were 'Persians, Arabs, Turks, and Burmese', where by Burmese, Schorer seems to imply many of southeast Asian ethnicity.[65] In 1669 there was an Armenian in town working for the French who sought from the Qutb Shah certain trade privileges,[66] while sometime later the Italian Niccolao Manucci (on the run from the Mughals) would show up in Golconda and, in his avatar as a physician, treat an inmate of the royal harem – a Georgian lady of tremendous proportions.[67] A century earlier, the Portuguese, jealous of the trade emanating from Masulipatam, attempted to try and persuade the Qutb Shah, through a combination of armed conflict and diplomacy, to subscribe to their cartaz system (under which licences were granted by the Portuguese in return for security for ships at sea). It so happened that advising the Qutb Shah on how to handle the Portuguese was himself a renegade Portuguese subject by the name of Fernao Rodrigues Cadeira – Goa, miffed, gave orders for his assassination.[68]

That said, much of this prosperity so visible in the big cities and urban settlements of the kingdom was contained in those limited quarters by certain classes – where common country folk were concerned, poverty, in varying degrees, was the general state of existence. As Schorer remarked in 1609 on learning of the Qutb Shah's revenues, 'I have often wondered whence so much money could be collected, for [the people] usually live extremely poorly and meanly.'[69] This was not new – as early as the 1470s, in the days of the Bahmani Sultans, the Russian diarist Afanasy Nikitin had noted how the Deccan was 'overstocked with people', and that those 'in the country are very miserable, whilst the nobles are extremely opulent and delight in luxury', wont to being carried around in silver palanquins.[70] Corruption too existed in the state, and merchants – whose customs payments were precisely the source of much of the wealth accumulating in the cities – often found that within a distance of twenty leagues were lined up sixteen officers waiting to collect legal as well as illegal dues.[71] What struck visitors was also the ubiquitous presence of vice – some decades after Methwold, Thevenot and Schorer, an Englishman complained that tobacco was a rage in Golconda, and that even 'children of 3 or 4 years of age frequently take it, and it is made as frequent amongst them as meat and drink'.[72] From prosperity, then, the kingdom appeared to slowly slide towards general decadence and enervation by the eve of the Mughal onslaught.

It was not only Europeans who came to Hyderabad at the height of its fame, though. In 1603 a special Persian envoy was escorted into the city, and with him he brought a message from Shah Abbas, his emperor, along with several expensive presents, 'including a royal crown studded with rubies'. Their mission, which included a hundred senior Safavid officials, was to return to Iran with a princess from Golconda – Hayat Baksh Begum, the daughter of Muhammad-Quli Qutb Shah. For six years the Persian embassy remained in India, but was unable to achieve its objective. The princess was married to a cousin of hers and remained in the Deccan (where she had a role to play), despite the obvious prestige attendant upon a marriage into the royal house of Persia.[73] When Muhammad-Quli Qutb Shah died in 1612, in fact, it was this cousin, referred to in vernacular records as Sultanu Muhammadu Padusa Rajyana,[74] who succeeded him to the throne. He was, apparently, 'a very cultured man' but 'was not sufficiently enterprising to make history' – his reign proved to be 'the lull before the storm'.[75] When he died in 1626, his son Abdullah, barely in his teens, became the Qutb Shah, while actual power was exercised by Hayat Baksh Begum. Indeed, for the rest of his forty-six-year reign, this prince proved himself supremely lethargic, except perhaps in having his court poet prepare an Urdu version of the *Tuti Namah* (Tales of the Parrot).[76] As was subsequently stated, he lacked 'mental energy and . . . never appears in public to give audience and administer justice . . . nor does he venture outside the walls of the fortress of Golconda'. His noblemen naturally felt little respect for a timid monarch such as this, and exercised in their own small domains 'a disgusting tyranny' with nobody to control them.[77]

This depressive Qutb Shah had some strange habits. When Tavernier came to Golconda on his third visit in 1652, he

Abdullah Qutb Shah of Golconda

noted how a Dutchman had become surgeon to the ruler. One day the king 'summoned the Surgeon and told him that he wished him to bleed him on the following day in four places under the tongue as his physicians had directed, but that he should take care not to draw more than eight ounces'. The white doctor accepted the challenge and arrived at the appointed hour at the palace. There, to his alarm, he found that he was to have a bath first – he was 'conducted into a room by two or three eunuchs, and four old women . . . having undressed and washed him well, especially his hands, they anointed him with drugs and aromatics' and gave him Indian clothes to wear. After all, when going into the royal presence for such an intimate business as drawing blood, it was essential the surgeon appear and smell his best. When he treated Abdullah Qutb Shah and drew precisely the eight allowed ounces, the queen mother Hayat Baksh Begum and the king's wife decided they wanted to lose some blood as well. This, Tavernier believed, 'was more from curiosity' than any actual cause for treatment, 'for he [the doctor] was a young and well-made man, and probably in their lives they had not seen a stranger close'. Considering the dowager was in actual charge of power in the royal household, it is unlikely she was genuinely wrapped away from the world of men. But Tavernier's anecdote is a telling one about life in Golconda on the eve of its eclipse.[78] For while the court amused itself at the expense of a melancholy king, his lands were starting to sink.

~

In 1643, to manage affairs of the state, Abdullah appointed as mir jumla (chief minister) a man called Mir Muhammad Said. Morale in the kingdom was not high. Much had been surrendered, besides honour, by Golconda to the Mughals. By this time Bijapur and Golconda were the only states still standing in the Deccan. A tribute of 200,000 gold hons was due from Golconda to the emperor annually, and in 1636, with the Deed of Submission, the name of the Persian Shah was struck off the khutbah and replaced with that of Shahjahan.

Though the Qutb Shah made gains in the Carnatic in this period, harassment from the Mughals gave no peace to the ruler. The new mir jumla, whose career was proof of exactly how capable and energetic he could be, might have protected the fortunes of Golconda if he had not realized that his own fortunes could multiply many times over if he came to an understanding with the Qutb Shah's enemies. What provoked him to betray the king of Golconda was partly personal and partly a matter of survival – thirteen years into his rule, the mir jumla had grown so powerful and arrogant that when his son, drunk out of his senses, decided it was a clever idea to sleep on the Qutb Shah's throne and vomit all over it, he expected the king not to arrest the fool. Abdullah, though weak, had a little self-respect and refused to permit the affront to pass; in return, his minister sold himself to the Mughals, giving them an opening after two decades to interfere in Golconda and begin its slow but definite conquest.[79] Those more sympathetic to the mir jumla note that he was such a success at his job that jealous courtiers in Golconda poisoned the Qutb Shah's ears and brought about the downfall of his hitherto loyal minister.[80]

Mir Muhammad Said was born in Persia in the 1590s, and came to the Deccan in the entourage of a merchant. He was a man of phenomenal personality, and could have been expected to follow in the esteemed Mahmud Gawan's two-century-old footsteps. On the one hand he could maintain his own standing army, while on the other he purchased from the king rights to a diamond mine, reaping the most spectacular profits over and above the rent he paid for it. Thevenot records that the man had a personal collection of diamonds that weighed nearly 500 pounds.[81] At one time around 1634 he held the rank of *sardaftardar* (keeper of records) in Hyderabad, when he was still relatively low in the hierarchy, but deploying his mercantile profits, he purchased the position of havildar of Nizampattinam soon afterwards.[82] By the end of the decade, he had graduated to the rank of *sar-i-khail* (governor), and in 1643 paid his way to the post of mir jumla. All through this meteoric ascent, his financial star only grew brighter with a corresponding increase in the size of the bribes he paid.

The year he was appointed mir jumla he also began lending money to the English, repayment coming in diverse forms: in one instance, as 'a brass gun'.[83] Mir Muhammad Said was all at once a businessman, banker, merchant and the chief minister of Golconda in an age where nobody seemed to comprehend the dangers behind such incredible conflicts of interest. And yet it was clear to everybody that there were few who could claim more power than this Westerner in Golconda, which may explain why there was silence and slavish obedience.

'The whole kingdom of Gulcundah is governed by him,' the English recorded in 1651, 'of whome the people stand in feare and subjection unto as to the King himselfe.' Besides the two million pagodas he delivered in revenues to the Qutb Shah, 'Hee hath of his proper owne four thousand horse, three hundred elephants, foure or five hundred cammels, and tenn thousand oxen, which transporteth his goods up into severall countryes, as Gulcundah, Vizapore, and its dyvers partes of the Great Maguls country.' In terms of international trade, his 'ventures extended from the Red Sea to Basra to Makassar'[84] and he had 'ten vessels of his owne', to which more were added in time.[85] One of his ships alone had a burden of 500 tons, which apparently was perfectly normal at the time for a capitalist of his standing, who did commerce with the viceroy of Goa as much as with a high-profile Telugu warrior down the coast.[86] Either way, by the 1650s, the mir jumla was a man not only with tremendous influence over government, but also in possession of much private wealth through economic networks that ran across the Deccan, into Mughal territory and through several countries abroad. Alienating him, after having foolishly conceded so much power into his hands, proved to be the mistake Abdullah regretted for the rest of his mournful life.

It is likely that Abdullah Qutb Shah belatedly realized that he had permitted the servant to grow more stately than the master and made an effort to cut him down. Suspicions also simmered that with his economic connections in so many lands, the mir jumla was not altogether loyal to Golconda. But local gossip, besides the disgusting story about the minister's vomiting son, also offers another (very likely spurious) tale. In this, the king was informed that his mir jumla was having an affair with his mother, which is what provoked him to try and demolish the former's arrogance.[87] Either way, in 1655 we find the Qutb Shah dismissing Mir Muhammad Said, confiscating his property and making a fairly forceful effort to take charge of matters. The object of this princely wrath, though, appealed to higher powers. At first, the ex-mir jumla sought the intervention of the Shah of Iran,[88] which having failed, he reached out to the Mughal viceroy in the Deccan, with whom he appears to have maintained an open channel. This was none other than Aurangzeb who entertained only the shrewdest designs for the kingdoms of the Deccan, awaiting always an opportunity to meddle in places where he was not needed. An army with the viceroy's son set out for Hyderabad and parked itself near the city. Aurangzeb's views on what needed to be done were clear. The Qutb Shah of Golconda, he wrote to the ex-mir jumla, 'is devoid of any courage and sense of honour. He is irascible and impetuous. He is easily frightened. If you act strictly according to my instructions, you [will] succeed.'[89] Parts of the town, and reportedly even the king's palace, were looted, till finally the Qutb Shahi soldiers retaliated to defend their master's interests. Armed with the excuse of 'aggression' against Mughal troops, Aurangzeb himself arrived outside Golconda to take charge of the attack.

From inside the security of the fort, Abdullah sent a plea to the emperor directly in the north explaining the situation, and to Aurangzeb's regret his father commanded him to put an end to the whole exercise.[90] This was reportedly due to his sympathy for Golconda where once, as a rebel from his own father, Shahjahan had received help,[91] while some lobbying on the part of Aurangzeb's brother and rival, Dara Shukoh, may also have yielded results – Prince Dara had no desire to see Aurangzeb grow too strong in the Deccan, and had been in personal correspondence with the Qutb Shah for whom he expressed his 'unfailing solicitude'.[92] But Aurangzeb was clever – concealing the order till he had got what he wanted out of the Qutb Shah, he bullied the latter to offer the most unequal terms.[93] As he wrote to the ex-

Prince Dara Shukoh

mir jumla, 'Qutb-ul-Mulk is now craving pardon, but I wish to send him to the wilderness of destruction.'[94] This when Abdullah, despite his hatred for the Mughals, was more than tolerant of Aurangzeb's temper: a story goes that from the Qutb Shah's fort a gunner spotted Aurangzeb on his elephant and proposed to shoot him down during the siege. It was Abdullah who asked him to aim elsewhere instead, for 'the lives of princes must be respected'.[95] By the time the Mughals retreated in May 1656 to their base, Hayat Baksh Begum had met Aurangzeb, handed over her granddaughter for his son, confirmed that son as successor to Abdullah (who had no male heirs) and agreed to cede certain districts as the princess's dowry.[96] It was also now that the ex-mir jumla, who had participated in the proceedings on the Mughal side, went up to the imperial court in Agra and presented Shahjahan an uncut diamond of 360 carats, said to be none other than the Koh-i-Noor, in gratitude for coming to his rescue.[97]

The Qutb Shah was furious – it does not appear that the diamond belonged to Mir Muhammad Said to give away in the first place – and expressed all his concerns in a letter he wrote to the Persian emperor.[98] Referring to his ex-minister as a 'wretch', he describes how from Hyderabad, the Mughals looted 'thousands and crores of cash, and materials, valuable jewels, costly articles [like] . . . cups of gold and silver . . . and autographed books of learned men'. Once peace was agreed upon, and more money was paid, the ex-mir jumla was taken up grandly to the north with 'cash, materials of furniture, gold-embroidered weapons, diamonds, rubies' and other such valuables that the minister had 'acquired either by plunder or treachery'. Worse still, the emperor received him well at court and honoured him with titles and a Mughal rank. 'I hope,' concluded the Qutb Shah of Golconda, 'that the bond of religion would lead you to dislike the Mughal oppression. You will also not like that the religion of the Imams would be wiped away from this land . . . [where] the cry that Ali is the *wali* of God has resounded in the ears of the people for 170 years. In this crisis, what help you will render me will be dictated with an eye to religion. But I will pay the expenses of the soldiers after they reach the frontier.'⁹⁹ It was a plea approaching desperation, but for all the contacts the Deccan had cultivated with Persia, and for all the fortunes it had made for Persians in India, when it mattered no help came to save this last of the region's princes.

For the next many years, the Mughals left Golconda alone, preoccupied as they were with the Marathas and in Bijapur. In 1672 Abdullah died. Since the son-in-law who was meant to succeed him, Aurangzeb's son, had displeased his paranoid father – who was now the Mughal emperor, living in perpetual fear that his offspring were plotting against him – he was kept under arrest in Gwalior. Succession, then, had to be decided between the two other men married to the late Qutb Shah's daughters. For six years before his death, the older of these had exercised a dominating influence over the ruler. Hayat Baksh Begum had died, and this man stepped into the void. He was not altogether bad – evidently, he was a mathematician of sorts, who had got it into his head that Christians tended to be good at the subject. When a certain Father Ephraim was passing through Golconda, this prince made every effort to coax him into settling down there, offering him a house, a church and even a robe of honour (all in vain, sadly).¹⁰⁰ But despite such endearing eccentricities, this son-in-law was resented by the nobility of Golconda, and the majority at court preferred the dead king's juniormost daughter's husband. This was a man by the name of Abul Hasan, distantly related to the royal house. For years he had been living as an aspiring Sufi outside the fort, when overnight he found himself married to the king's daughter – her betrothed had arrived for the wedding, but an altercation at the last minute led to the marriage being called off. Instead of cancelling the ceremony, however, the bridegroom was simply replaced, the choice falling on Abul Hasan who was summoned to court and given an important wife.¹⁰¹

This last of the rulers of Golconda – for that is what he was fated to be – was not a very energetic monarch, weaker than even the Qutb Shah he had just replaced. He certainly had a number of artistic and musical talents, and popularity of a certain fashion, but in military affairs and in matters of the government, he left much to be desired.

Abul Hasan Qutb Shah of Golconda

Instead of making a proactive effort to revitalize his prospects, Abul Hasan ('a worthless voluptuary' in the acid words of one historian[102]) decided to hand over the actual business of ruling to a minister. This is precisely what many nobles had hoped for – a cipher they could control – but they were surprised. For the man chosen by the new Qutb Shah was not a Persian or even a Muslim – the last of the chief ministers of Golconda was a Brahmin. While Hindus had always served the state, never before had a position of such seniority been held by someone as clever and ambitious as Madanna, who began his career 'as a clerk and wormed his way to the highest office through talent, guile, and intrigue'.[103] Such was his power that a story told to Thevenot placed the origins of this non-Muslim influence on the fact that the late Qutb Shah Abdullah was actually born of a Brahmin mother, thereby opening avenues for Brahmins to rise to great heights.[104] It was rubbish, but it is telling that when Hindus made their way into the upper echelons of the government, those entrenched there for generations were upset.

Madanna was one of four sons born to a 'Banoojee Puntooloo' of Warangal. One of these brothers, Akkanna, was as influential as his sibling, and he too was appointed to court.[105] They certainly did see their rise to power as justice of a certain kind after many generations of playing second fiddle as a class. As Akkanna remarked to a Telugu-speaking Dutch merchant, 'You yourself can imagine which government serves the king best, ours or that of the Muslims; ours being fullheartedly devoted to the welfare of the country, [since] we are not people who have or seek other countries, [whereas] that of the Muslims is only to the end of becoming rich and then to leave for those places which they consider to be either their fatherland or holy.'[106] This was an extraordinary statement for its times, expressing perhaps a kind of proto-nationalism, though Muslims in this context seemed to mean the Persians rather than the Dakhni faction.[107] The Dakhnis too, it must be added, were not fully pleased with the advent of a powerful Hindu party, but worked with them to protect their own interests – they were closer to the Hindus than the Westerners.

Either way, while the claim was made that their government was a nobler one since it represented sons of the soil, the fact was that Madanna's regime was not a popular one. To begin with, the rapid elevation of large numbers of Hindus to senior posts at the cost of an established Muslim nobility invited too much hostility too soon upon the man.[108] Some also had prejudices of their own, including that Brahmins were not loyal – years before, a Brahmin officer was beaten to death after he was found to be in clandestine correspondence with the Mughals.[109] When Madanna tried to make the revenue system more transparent in the interests of the court, those who for decades had prospered under the old system further increased their hatred for the new man.[110] As mentioned earlier, the established method was that the highest bidder who paid the Qutb Shah the best annual figure for a district was given tax rights over that district. Madanna himself had once been such a tax farmer (and his brother owned merchant ships at sea, though not in the league of the former mir jumla), and his efforts to now place salaried bureaucrats and centralize the revenue system seemed duplicitous. The English East India Company in Madras certainly did not like him, writing in 1676: 'Madanna has sole control, and nothing is thought of but peeling and squeezing the people. The government of the country is now in so bad hands that nothing but fraud and oppression [prevail], and [the officials are] so void of shame that no credit can be given to either agreements, promises, *qauls* or farmans.'[111]

Madanna's complete opposition to wasting energy on war when enemies could be bought also divided the court. A number of the Muslim nobility championed aggressive action against the Marathas (who were making major inroads into Golconda territory) and the Mughals. Instead, to control the military better, Madanna appointed his brother *sarlaskar* (commander of the army), even getting him to pose for a painting with a sword (despite, as Daniel Havart, a Dutch agent, noted, the fact that 'he had never seen a battle except in a painting'[112]). To deal with the Marathas, Madanna persuaded the Qutb Shah to agree to a treaty with Shivaji whereby 100,000 hons were paid every year, starting in 1674, as a kind of protection money.[113] In 1677 it was agreed that the Qutb Shah would pay for a Maratha campaign in the Carnatic, where certain territories were to be handed over to Golconda.[114] Shivaji, the Maratha leader who had recently crowned himself and declared his territories a legitimate kingdom, was even received in Golconda by Abul Hasan. As Shivaji himself wrote, 'I have entered into a friendly understanding with the Kutb Shah . . . who recently called me for a personal interview, in an autograph-letter [sic] impressed with his own palm. I respected this invitation and met the Kutb Shah, who upon learning that I had already declared myself an independent king, excused me the usual Mohammadan ceremonials . . . namely, touching the ground before them with the head. The Kutb Shah and I met on equal terms, both coming halfway for the meeting . . . Holding me with his hand he seated me by his side and showed various marks of respect, thereby cementing a mutual relationship.'[115] There are, however, indications that Golconda had no option but to agree to ally with Shivaji, given his fearsome raids; as Havart rudely put it, Madanna had merely 'managed to plug the mouth of that barking dog with numerous gold lumps'.[116]

As with Shivaji, where money bought peace, with the Mughals too Madanna thought throwing gold would deliver the desired results. When in 1683 a Mughal army came close to Hyderabad, the Dutch recorded how 'no special preparations are made [for a siege] except that the castle, which has become very dilapidated since the reign of the present king, is being stocked up with some provisions'. The 'daft Brahmins', it was added, 'don't know of any military affairs, they let all bounce on the purse and know how to deflect all wars with money and blindfold the rulers, as can be seen from the substantial amounts of money that have been sent to Aurangzeb over a short period'. It was true, for in that year, over and above the formal tribute, between March and July alone Madanna paid nearly 900,000 rupees to the emperor, along with cartloads of mangoes.[117] By this time, even the Qutb Shah had no power over his minister. In 1683 Abul Hasan himself had to visit Madanna in his house on five occasions to ask for money. It may have been that the ruler was being extravagant and his minister was holding the purse strings tight, but the symbolism of the monarch going to his servant with a begging bowl was scandalous. And by 1685 it was said openly in Masulipatam that the Qutb Shah had practically retired, on an understanding that he would not interfere with Madanna's actions so long as 150,000 rupees were paid every month into his royal hands.[118]

Abul Hasan might have been content to take money and keep quiet, but Aurangzeb had no real need of bribes, and didn't intend to let Golconda rest for very long. Around the time Golconda's alliance with the Marathas was formed, the emperor had tried his best to provoke war with the Qutb Shah. An ambassador was dispatched to collect two enormous diamonds from Abul Hasan's custody – or at least that was the formal mission of the envoy to whom, in private, the emperor described the diamonds as 'useless bits of stone'. In actual intent, the Mughal representative was supposed to do his best and unearth some issue or another that could be construed as an affront to the emperor's dignity and allow him to declare war. The Qutb Shah of Golconda, however, for all his other flaws, was a man without a temper, and beat the ambassador at the game he had come to play. The man was terribly rough during his stay, trying constantly to obtain from the Qutb Shah one word that could be read as an insult. But Abul Hasan went out of his way to be obsequious. When the ambassador expressed outrage that he styled himself as a sovereign, the Qutb Shah laughed off the matter. 'If we were not to be called kings, how can Aurangzeb be styled king of kings?'[119] The mission failed. But if only Aurangzeb had let the matter rest there.

In 1685, when the war against Bijapur was ongoing, the Mughals finally found the opportunity they were seeking. A letter from the Qutb Shah to his ambassador fell into the wrong hands. In it the ruler was found to suggest sending aid to the Adil Shah of Bijapur.[120] An army was sent to Golconda immediately. At first its advance was halted, but then, after two months, the Golconda general in charge of the defence was successfully bribed – he moved his men to the side and welcomed

Madanna, a minister of Golconda

Akkanna, a minister of Golconda

the Mughal emperor's forces into the kingdom of the monarch he had just betrayed. The result of this invasion was that in October of the same year terms were agreed: Madanna must be removed from his position along with his brother; the tribute was to be raised; certain provinces were to be ceded to the emperor; and an indemnity of 1.2 crore rupees was to be transferred to the Mughals.[121] Some of these terms were agreed to, but the Qutb Shah was most reluctant to lose the services of his Brahmin, perhaps because he had no idea what to do without him. For Madanna and his brother, though, time was up. On 29 October, in a conspiracy hatched in the harem, they were captured and murdered, and a general massacre of Brahmins was carried out in Golconda.[122] It did not, however, mean Brahmin influence died – months later a third brother of the dead men, Vessanna, paid the Qutb Shah 250,000 hons and secured all the posts his brothers had enjoyed.[123] But it was all pointless, for only darkness lay ahead.

Abul Hasan had revealed himself during this invasion in 1685 as lacking the capacity to lead. When the invaders arrived, the Qutb Shah fled from his palace in Hyderabad for the fortress of Golconda, 'Without consulting with any of his nobles, or even caring anything for his property or the honour of his own women and family . . . he fled with a few servants by night with boxes full of such valuables as he could carry.'[124] Coming as it does from a Mughal account, this may be biased, but the picture it paints is devastating. As with Vijayanagar a century before when its rulers fled with treasure loaded on 550 elephants, on the Qutb Shah's flight from his own capital into the old city, 'A noise and tumult arose like that of doomsday.' An orgy of violence and plunder seized the city and the worst atrocities were propagated by some of its own people in the absence of the king's law and its enforcers. 'Carpets of great value, which were too heavy to carry, were cut to pieces with swords and daggers', and house after house was looted of its valuables. Another eyewitness noted that 'Even the doors were taken off their hinges' as noblemen and ordinary folk fled into the fort. What they left behind in Hyderabad was a tragic, ghost city that only yesterday was celebrated as one of the finest in the world.[125]

Although peace was agreed with the Mughals in this instance, when at the end of 1686 Bijapur was annexed, Aurangzeb had the full force of his armies to turn towards Golconda. In February 1687, therefore, he marched to destroy the Qutb Shah, using the magnificent graves and mausoleums of previous rulers as camps for his soldiers. Since no provocation could be invented at short notice, the reasons supplied were couched in moral terms. 'The evil deeds of this wicked man pass beyond the bounds of writing,' declared the emperor in melodramatic indignation, 'but by mentioning one out of a hundred, and a little out of much, some conception of them may be formed.' First, by handing over the government to 'vile, tyrannical infidels', i.e. Brahmins like Madanna, the Qutb Shah had sinned. With his 'debauchery and depravity', his 'drunkenness and wickedness' too he had invited the charge of sin. As a Shia, he failed to make a 'distinction between infidelity and Islam, tyranny and justice, depravity and devotion', and for this too he would be punished. And not least of all, 'it had lately become known that a lakh of pagodas had been sent to that wicked Sambha' – Shivaji's son and successor who was leading the Maratha resistance after his death.[126] All things combined, the emperor saw no reason why he should not take Golconda for himself. And if reasons did not exist, he was only happy to manufacture them.

The siege was to prove a nightmare for the Mughals, however. Though not as rich as Bijapur in recent years, Golconda was still a strong fort. On some occasions, providential help came to the defenders. One night, for instance, when the Mughals were trying to scale the walls, 'a dog was making his way . . . to eat the corpses of men killed yesterday', noted a chronicler. This dog 'true to his proverbial habit' decided to bark at the soldiers, with the result that the guards atop the walls were roused and thwarted the attack.[127] On another occasion, mines placed under the fort falls were successfully triggered, but the force was such that all the flying stone and debris fell on top of hundreds of Mughal soldiers, killing a large number then and there.[128] A curtain of flames descended down the walls so that 'the fort [itself] looked as if made of fire'.[129] The defenders, though less numerous, were not lacking in confidence. One night, guns from one of the bastions seem to have taken aim at Aurangzeb's pavilion – in response, the 'sun of royal wrath rose from the horizon of calamity' and 'cast its glare' upon the garrison within the fort.[130] But no amount of glaring by the emperor could win the war. And when the monsoons arrived, matters got worse. 'The wind tore into pieces every thing except the tent of the cloud, and what was spared by the wind, was drowned in water.'[131]

Aurangzeb also faced trouble in his own camp. The chief qazi insisted that the war was unjust, since there were two Muslim kings involved, with Muslim soldiers fighting one another. He advised that the 'crimes of Abul Hasan, who is sin incarnate . . . may be graciously forgiven' instead of continuing the violence.[132] There were, of course, a significant number of Shias too in the imperial camp who – despite the emperor's tendency to refer to people of their leaning as 'corpse eating demons'[133] – were half-hearted at the prospect of the last Shia king in India losing his crown and state.[134] But Aurangzeb suspected, correctly, that Golconda gold was softening the minds of people in his camp to persuade him to temper his stance. Abul Hasan himself wrote to him, trying a practical argument where all others had failed. He offered to rule hereafter as a Mughal vassal on even more generous terms, if the emperor ended hostilities. 'It will take seven or eight years to restore cultivation and population to this war wasted land and during that period [the Mughals] will get nothing out of it. If on the other hand Aurangzeb makes peace and retires beyond my frontiers, I shall pay him one crore of rupees as an indemnity, besides one crore in honour of every assault he has led in person.'[135] The emperor's dry, unforgiving response was that terms would only be discussed *after* the Qutb Shah came to him with a rope around his neck.[136] Aurangzeb's interests, after all, lay not so much in presiding over a thriving province as much as in utilizing Golconda's treasure for other military expeditions.

The siege continued, making things worse for the Mughals, who were also harassed in the rear by a Golconda army of 40,000 in the field. From the fort, meanwhile, in addition to guns, large rocks were being catapulted at the enemy. As a witness wrote during the time,

'When a stone struck the teeth of a man, he retorted, "Now I can realise very well the intelligence of the heavens. When I said I would get big stones in Hyderabad, diamonds and rubies were before my eyes. I never meant this stone."'[137] More brutally, the chronicle continues in its overblown language:

> In short, the guests of death and calamity sat at a table spread with the dishes of misery and adversity . . . In fact, it was a variety feast with rich food. Naptha-sheets were like hot bread and rockets like the Kabab. The arrow-points looked like vermicelli mixed with a deadly sherbet. From skulls the brains spilled out like *halwa*. The dying man enjoyed the pistachio of his lips and the lozenges of his tongue. The cannon balls were sweet water-melons, and hand-grenades were like too sweet melons. The naptha-bags dripped like sausages. As for bullets their taste was relished . . . Thus was the table spread on the battlefield. Heads and feet lay one upon another. Skulls crushed under horses' hooves seemed to be broken bowls.[138]

Finally, in October of 1687, what an emperor could not win with the might of all his armies and guns was delivered to him through treachery. An Afghan who had once served in Bijapur, and then the Mughals before coming to Golconda, was bribed to open one of the gates into the fort. At three o'clock one morning, columns of Mughal soldiers entered Golconda, and throwing open the main gates, allowed in the bulk of the invading forces to unseat the last of the Deccan's independent princes. This turn of events was so unexpected that most of the horrified garrison did not fight, though one captain personally stood up to as many of the invaders as he could, counting seventy wounds when he was finally captured – the emperor rewarded him for his fidelity to his patron.[139] Abul Hasan's own surrender was dignified. It was dawn by the time the armies arrived at the palace, and the Qutb Shah received them in all ceremoniousness in his throne room, dressed like a king, inviting them to join him for breakfast. Then he left the palace and went out to meet Aurangzeb in his camp.

Emperor Aurangzeb

After the catalogue of his sins was read to him, he was banished to Daulatabad fort with a pension of 50,000 rupees, and there he would die many years later. The Mughals, meanwhile, obtained millions of rupees in cash, and gold and silver in massive quantities from the keep in Golconda, not to mention the invaluable gems and stones collected by generations of princes who had ruled from the city.

The Muslim kings of the Deccan had fallen, and their story now reached its conclusion. Aurangzeb had all he ever wanted from the very start.

Epilogue
The Dawn of the Marathas

Shivaji

At the dawn of the seventeenth century, when Ibrahim Adil Shah II was composing his paeans to Saraswati and Ganapati, a very different kind of poetry was taking shape in the Nayaka raj of Madurai – a splinter state that claimed its sovereignty as the Vijayanagar empire collapsed. The Telugu *Rayavacakamu* (Tidings of the King) is ostensibly about the reign of Krishnadeva of Vijayanagar, who had died nearly eight decades before, but the work stands out primarily for its polemics against the Muslim kings of the Deccan. 'What are the Turks,' it declares, 'but drunkards and opium eaters!' while Brahmins, with 'their diet of rice with salt and *sambar*', are cast as the better sort who 'don't suffer from pride and malice'.[1] Elsewhere, Hindu agents of the Deccan's Sultans lament how 'Our lords are drunkards who have no faith in gods and Brahmins. They are,' these characters cry, 'barbarians and cow-killers.'[2] When spies from Vijayanagar travel to the Sultanates, all they witness are unspeakable horrors. 'People were being sliced into two at the waist or slowly cut apart with saws,' reports one informant, and even *officials* who fail to deliver gold to the greedy capitals of the north are 'tortured to death' in 'the middle of the street'.[3] The lands ruled by the Adil Shah of Bijapur, Nizam Shah of Ahmadnagar and Qutb Shah of Golconda, then, are likened to the realms of Yama, the god of death, and all three kings are painted as vulgar, unrefined upstarts who know neither honour nor dignity. Dharma as construed in classical texts is elevated while the adharma of the Muslims is violently castigated.

The *Rayavacakamu* is a fascinating text in retrospectively ascribing a hatred of Muslim princes to Krishnadeva's time. The reality, as the history of the Deccan shows, is that while rivalries existed, its world was not really perceived in terms of religious or communal acrimony. So where many popularly perceive the 'Battle of Talikota' that destroyed Vijayanagar as a plot by Muslim monarchs to annihilate a Hindu kingdom, the matter is complicated when it is remembered that Ramaraya of Vijayanagar was once a Qutb Shahi officer, and that the king of Golconda who fought him in 1565 spent seven years of his life living in Vijayanagar. Similarly, further complicating this 'Hindu–Muslim' narrative is the fact that there were a reported 6000-odd Marathas fighting on the side of the Sultans *against* Vijayanagar.[4] Generals and aristocrats too easily shifted between the Sultanates and the Hindu empire in the south. One, for instance, known as Ain al-Mulk Gilani began his career in Bidar towards the last years of Bahmani rule, before transferring his loyalties to the Adil Shah of Bijapur, and finally, in the 1550s becoming one of Ramaraya's most prominent courtiers in Vijayanagar, bringing with him 4000 cavalrymen.[5] Indeed, even a century before, in the reign of Devaraya II, there were prominent Muslims resident at court – Fath Khan, for instance, was a descendant of Firoz Shah Tughluq, and among the messages the Shah of Iran sent to Devaraya II was a request that he assist this northern prince in seizing the throne of Delhi.[6] The Turks, as Muslims were generically termed, were certainly different, but it was more politics and less religious difference that provoked the feuds and great battles of this time.

Such exchanges were not specific to Vijayanagar either. In Bijapur at one time there was a noble, Haibat Khan, who held half a dozen ranks at court, but whose actual name and religious identity might come as a surprise – he was a Brahmin called Daso Pandit.[7] Then, a little after the Bahmanis lost all political significance, there was a descendant of that Muslim house who became a significant figure in the Hindu Bhakti movement that enveloped much of the region. A senior contemporary of the well-known saints Tukaram and Ramdas,

Sant Muntoji, this scion of the old royal line, authored about ten works of devotion, all written in Marathi and concerning Advaita Vedanta. His guru even made an attempt to 'convert' him into a thread-wearing Hindu, giving him the name Mrityunjaya, but owing to resistance from other Brahmins, the man went to the grave with his Bahmani name intact.[8] Eknath, another prominent Bhakti figure in the sixteenth century, composed a satirical Hindu–Turk *samvaad* (dialogue), declaring of the two faiths: 'The goal is one, the ways of worship are different.' In it a Muslim and a Brahmin debate features of their faiths, and there is even mockery and the lampooning of their respective practices. And yet, in the end, they embrace, parting wiser than they were before, without rancour or hatred.[9]

The *Rayavacakamu*, however, signifies the beginnings of crystallization among Hindu elites of a sense of common identity in competition with the religion of the 'Turks' who ruled them – an indication of this is also evident later in the same century when Akkanna, the brother of the Brahmin chief minister Madanna of Golconda, refers to Muslims as building rich careers in the Deccan but removing their gains to fatherlands abroad. While the *Rayavacakamu*'s tone has been assessed by scholars to be a result of the fall of Vijayanagar – a 'culturally disruptive act' which left large numbers of poets and others without patronage – this mood did not yet, however, lead to what can be construed as a Hindu–Muslim *communal* divide. For instance, the very same work while degrading the Deccan's Sultans as low-born and mean, elevates the Mughals in Delhi to levels of Sanskritic divinity. Part of this might be on account of Mughal inroads into the Sultans' lands – they were enemies of an enemy and, therefore, friends. But what is striking is that the Mughals are painted as blessed by Hindu gods. India, in the conception of the *Rayavacakamu*, had three 'Lion-Thrones': Vijayanagar's was blessed by Vishnu in Tirupati, Orissa ruled by Gajapati had the blessings of Jagannatha; and the suzerains of Delhi shone in the glory of Visvanatha in Kashi. These three rulers, including the Mughals (who are described using the familiar term Ashvapati), are likened to the *devas* or gods of

Hindu mythology, while the Sultans of the Deccan are seen as *asuras*, or demons, inevitably destined for defeat.[10] In other words, while certain Muslim kings are disparaged as barbaric, others are seen as refined; and where the Adil Shah, Qutb Shah and Nizam Shah are demons, the Mughal emperor sits confidently among the gods.[11]

Power dynamics in the Deccan were certainly skewed in that a Muslim minority held political authority in the principal seats of the Sultanates, even though outside of urban nodes, power was shared with Hindu elites. These Hindu elites – 'co-sharers in the realm' – in the Deccan were Marathas, who first rose to prominence as a very consequence of the Sultanates. 'Marathas were', we are told, 'Marathi-speaking units in the armies of the Muslim kingdoms' of Bijapur and Ahmadnagar, and over time the term came to signify a community of sorts, extracted from the soil and local peasantry, and gaining an upward mobility through service in the Sultanates.[12] Many prominent Maratha families, in fact, recalled specific episodes in their tradition as moments when their elevation to prominence occurred. The Mores of Jawali, for example, were descended from a man called Chandrarao who won the Adil Shah of Bijapur's favour, the story goes, by fighting off a tiger. 'This achievement enabled him to ask for the lands of Jawali, as well as higher titles for twelve of his fellow Maratha chiefs', and over time the family came to enjoy near princely rank, before they were unseated by Shivaji.[13] The rise of the Marathas – who received favour from Malik Ambar too – was also due in some part to the strength of the Portuguese on the seas and the obstacles this raised. As it became difficult to import masses of men from Persia in the sixteenth century, the Deccan's Sultans, themselves absorbing Maratha blood through marriage and embracing the Marathi language, relied more and more on local talent.

That said, in 1642 when Shivaji was presented at court in Bijapur, there were few palpable indications that in only a matter of years the boy would transform into perhaps the greatest domestic challenge facing the Adil Shah, besides the nightmare that was the Mughal invasion. His father was one of the Deccan's best-known Maratha noblemen: in farmans, the Adil Shah addressed Shahji Bhonsle with the most overwrought superlatives. He was, for instance, 'the abode of intrepidity and grandeur', 'the support of faithful friends', 'the cream of tribes and companions', 'the pillar of the mighty state', and indeed even 'my son' to the ailing rulers of Bijapur.[14] What these grandiloquent titles concealed, though, was complicated history. Like many successful military men, Shahji had, at various points, been loyal to other states, sometimes even in rebellion. In the 1620s, for example, he served Malik Ambar, notwithstanding flirtations with the Mughals.[15] After the habshi's death, Shahji's fortunes led him back and forth between various camps – in 1629 he battled the Mughals under Adil Shahi banners, only to support Emperor Shahjahan a year later in his Deccan campaign. By 1634 he raised the standard of revolt by unearthing a new Nizam Shah in Ahmadnagar and making a scotched attempt to resurrect the latter's dynasty.[16] He was defeated and had to revert to Bijapur, prohibited, however, from military service in the Deccan – it was the Carnatic that attracted Shahji's energy hereon.

During his early childhood, Shivaji and his mother followed his father from fort to fort on his very many campaigns. But in 1636, when Shahji departed for his new posting in the Carnatic, he left his Deccan estates with his wife and son, and a trusted Brahmin administrator was placed in charge of everyday affairs.[17] While Shahji took a new wife in the south (there was a time when Shivaji did not see his father for as many as twelve years[18]), his son from Jijabai developed an appetite for adventure. Riding out into the lands around his home in Pune, by his teens he was more than familiar with the area and its strengths and weaknesses. The Brahmin manager involved Shivaji in administrative matters, so that when the former died in 1647, his seventeen-year-old ward was prepared for greater responsibilities. But mere oversight of his father's property did not interest Shivaji – he had superior ambitions, and the zeal to see them achieved. By the time he died thirty-three years later, not less than 50,000 square miles of territory (i.e. over 4 per cent of the subcontinent) was under his control, bringing him annual revenues that were between a fifth and sixth of the income of the Mughal emperor himself.[19] And most significantly, Shivaji also emerged as the greatest challenge to imperial authority, one who launched a movement that would break the very back of the empire. It was no wonder then that when intelligence of his death arrived in Agra, the mood in which it was received was condensed by a later Mughal chronicler with that infamous outburst of bitterness: 'The infidel went to hell.'[20]

Shivaji's motivations for seeking to establish his swaraj in the Deccan have animated many theories. The most popular romantic view conceives him as a champion of Hindu might resisting the evil designs of Muslim invaders, electrifying the minds of a downtrodden mass, and recovering for them their lost nobility and independence. While certainly charged with emotion and glamour, this narrative is not quite an accurate reflection of the Maratha leader's work. As shown earlier with other critics of Islamic rule in the Deccan, Shivaji had no hatred for a blanket category called 'the Muslims', nor did the Marathas heap love on 'the Hindus' en masse as witnessed in their campaigns against fellow believers in the Carnatic and elsewhere. The truth was more complex. Shivaji's father, for one, was named to honour a Muslim saint called Shah Sharif – while Shahji bore the first part of the pir's name, his brother took the second and was called Sharifji.[21] His grandfather, Maloji, was not only a loyal officer of the Nizam Shahs of Ahmadnagar, but his samadhi is, evidently, 'a completely Islamicate' structure that still stands in Ellora.[22] In the *Sivabharata*, when praise is heaped on Maloji, it is in words that confirm his loyalty to his Muslim sovereign: 'Whatever enemies did arise [to oppose] the Nizam Shah, mighty Maloji opposed them.'[23] Shivaji's mother's family too, similarly, had pledged affiliation to the Mughals years before and had no qualms serving a Muslim emperor.[24] And to top it all, Shivaji himself, when he was in his twenties, had Muslim Pathans in his armies, also employing qazis to administer Islamic justice within his dominions.[25]

Instead, his actions on the one hand were driven by a strong urge to be recognized as a powerful factor in Deccan politics, while on the other they were energized by genuine empathy with the common folk – since the famine of 1630, the year of Shivaji's birth, the Deccan had known only suffering, and endless wars due to the Mughal invasion, reducing the region to unprecedented desperation.[26] To this political effort was added, towards his last years especially, a new conception and idiom of power. Persian, for instance, was to be replaced by Sanskrit as the language of diplomacy: As the *Rajyavyavaharakosa* commissioned by Shivaji notes, 'Having completely uprooted the barbarians . . . a learned man was appointed to replace the overvalued Yavana words with educated speech.'[27] Shivaji even made an effort to write letters to Rajput princes in chaste Sanskrit instead of the standard Persian.[28] Similarly, when Maratha families he called to his side seemed uncertain on account of generations of loyalty to local Sultans, Shivaji appealed to greater loyalties than this – as he wrote to one chieftain, 'You and I are not being disloyal to the Shah.' They were merely being loyal, instead, to the local deity, whose blessings, Shivaji hoped, would 'fulfill the desire of creating a Hindavi kingdom'.[29] All this was certainly a rejection of an existing system of power built on Islamic ideals, but it does not appear to be a mark of hatred for that religion itself. It was also, simultaneously, the invention of a new court culture, derived from classical Hindu texts, something that came to be broadly encompassed in the term Maharashtra Dharma.[30]

In the early phase of his career, though, Shivaji primarily took advantage of a distracted Bijapuri court to improve his own standing in the vicinity of Pune, while, as noted earlier, the Adil Shahs also periodically utilized the Marathas as a bulwark against the Mughals. There was, to this, nothing new as such: powerful Maratha families were interlocutors of the royal court, negotiating with cultivators on the ground as well as with the ruler in the capital. In a fragmented landscape, if a Maratha chieftain or village head could expand his powers, repopulate lands, bring into force law and order and collect revenues in a systematic manner, Bijapur recognized him at a suitable level in the hierarchy, granting titles and rank.[31] Shivaji, essentially, was fortifying his own power to augment influence on the ground and negotiate with the faraway capital in Bijapur on terms favourable to him, when in the late 1640s he began to capture forts around his seat in Pune. In Torna, he bribed the commandant of the fortress to hand over its keys to him, with a similar formula applied in Chakan.[32] Sometimes Machiavellian methods were employed: when the commandant of Purandar fort died, his two sons quarrelled over who should be in charge. Shivaji offered to mediate, only to seize both candidates while they were in bed, taking the fort for himself.[33] By the middle of the next decade, thus, through force of arms or by exploiting the sheer stupidity of his enemies, Shivaji secured forts contiguous with Pune and demarcated his core territory. And aiding him in this were local men from the hills nearby, known as Mavale, who became 'the main stay of Shivaji's fighting machine'.[34]

By 1656 Shivaji was sturdy enough to clash with the aforementioned Maratha Mores of Jawali, who stood in the way of his southern and south-western expansion – an assassin masquerading as an ambassador successfully stabbed the chieftain to death in a brutal act of 'conscious treachery'.[35] Three years later, when the by now feared Shivaji raided the rich Konkan coast, he was in control of dozens of forts in the hills and large expanses of the plateau beyond, with 20,000 men in his service. At last, cognizant of the threat he posed not only to the Adil Shahi order but to the prestige of the court itself, Bijapur commanded a general, Afzal Khan, to march an army against the Maratha. The choice of antagonist could not have been worse. Though there were no orders from the court to do anything of the sort, Afzal Khan decided it was a good idea to take a long route, desecrating temples on the way – the shrine at Tuljapur where Shivaji's family went on pilgrimage, for instance, and Pandharpur which was of unparalleled importance to all Hindu groups in the Deccan. It is, we are told, 'doubtful that any act committed by a Bijapur officer could have alienated more people in a single stroke'.[36] Even those Marathas who paid homage to the Adil Shah now questioned their loyalties to a court that could permit unprovoked sectarian fury of this naked variety. Conversely, Shivaji's own cause received a moral boost, and the idea of Maharashtra Dharma took deeper root. As for Afzal Khan, Shivaji was not afraid: as one account has him declare in defiance, 'A goat with thirty-two teeth has come for slaughter!'[37]

As it happened, Afzal Khan died in his encounter with the Maratha warrior he came to destroy, his head neatly chopped off as a trophy.[38] And an emboldened Shivaji's ambitions were fanned into a whole new league, so that in 1664 he carried out the most audacious raid of his career, this time deep inside Mughal territory. In January 1664, news arrived at the rich port of Surat that Shivaji and his horsemen were on their way there. As the local English factors noted, 'This sudden surprise struck such terror to all, both men, women and children that the [Mughal] Governor and the rest of the King's Ministers and eminent merchants betook themselves to the castle; which the towns folk perceiving left their houses . . . and fled with their wives and children . . . [so] that in a few hours the whole town was dispeopled.'[39] Shivaji commenced his plunder, spending three days in Surat, seizing immense amounts of gold and other valuables. In the words of François Bernier, 'Burning what he could not take away, Sevajee returned without the least opposition, laden with gold and silver to the amount of several millions; with pearls, silken stuffs, fine linens and a variety of other costly merchandise.'[40]

The sudden influx of an estimated two and a half million rupees into Shivaji's treasury inaugurated a massive and sharp new project of expansion. The Marathas began to encroach on more and more Bijapuri territory, as well as lands of the erstwhile state of Ahmadnagar that were now officially the possession of the Mughals. Stories circulated that Shivaji had 'an airy body' with wings,[41] but where the masses were impressed, in Agra Aurangzeb was furious. Surat was, to quote Tavernier, 'the sole port for the whole empire of the Great Mogul'.[42] Twenty years before, it was calculated that the value of goods traded from Surat exceeded a crore of rupees every year, and revenues from the port were allocated to the emperor's beloved sister Begum Jahanara – Shivaji's raid, in short, was an affront to the imperial harem and only firm action could restore the emperor's prestige. Furthermore, the Mughal court had not recovered from the humiliating defeat of Aurangzeb's uncle who had been sent in 1661 to deal with Shivaji, when it was assumed that he was still relatively small fish. As it happened, instead of putting the Marathas in their place, after two years of playing hide-and-seek, the Mughal general received a surprise night visit from Shivaji's men who burrowed into his house, took, besides the royal uncle's dignity, his fingers, and killed one son and several retainers of his household, in an attack only marginally less provocative than the sack of Surat.[43]

Given how, as Manucci recorded, Aurangzeb 'could no longer endure the insults of Shivaji',[44] in 1665 he sent to the Deccan a famous Rajput general to bring the Marathas to their knees. This man was not only capable but was also known to be loyal to the empire – Aurangzeb addressed him in a farman as 'Faithful and obedient to Islam, an object of glory, exalted Mirza Rajah Jai Singh'.[45] By June, Jai Singh had outwitted the Marathas and cornered Shivaji in his own lands. As many as twenty-three forts were seized, the Marathas being left with only twelve in their control. Terms were agreed, under which Shivaji's son, Sambhaji, was granted a Mughal title, Shivaji himself receiving a robe of honour.[46] (And it was at this time that Manucci personally encountered Shivaji, who called him a 'Firangi Rajah' and discussed with him both European politics and the Christian faith.[47]) Delighted with the turn of events, Aurangzeb sent his Rajput general another farman, sixteen feet long, expressing approval of the latter's actions and giving instructions for future moves.[48] 'We appoint the said person [Shivaji],' states the document, 'to the glorious and proud wing of the army, so that he takes strong efforts continually in the service and remains obedient.'[49] If only.

In 1666 Shivaji was summoned to Agra to attend court as a member of the Mughal order. 'A large elephant goes before him carrying his flag,' an eyewitness recorded. 'An advance guard of troopers also precedes him; the horses have gold and silver trappings. The Deccani infantry [of 4000] too marches before him. In this manner he has come to Agra, with the whole of his contingent moving with great

care and pomp ... His [own palanquin] is completely covered in silver
plates. With this splendor has he come.'[50] In the imperial assembly,
however, things began to unravel. There was, on both sides, an ocean
of miscommunication: where Jai Singh had confirmed that Shivaji
was only a zamindar, the Maratha himself was under the impression
he would be received as a vassal prince. Unlike Rajputs who for
generations had been part of the Mughal system and understood its
protocols and etiquette, Shivaji was a little out of his depth in the
ceremonious atmosphere of a Persianized court. When he was made
to stand among nobles of a much lower rank than he expected, he
objected and left the gathering, which was part fury, but also 'a reflex
action designed to cover his embarrassment at his lack of ability to
fit in with Mughal courtly etiquette'.[51] Either way, the one principal
opportunity the Mughals had to co-opt the Marathas into their world,
as was done with the Rajputs in Akbar's day, was squandered. And
with that turned the course of history, not merely of the Deccan but
of India itself.[52]

Shivaji was placed under house arrest, while rumours floated about
possible attempts to poison him to death. Aurangzeb himself was not
certain what to do. On the one hand there were those who resented
even the low rank he had bestowed upon Shivaji – powerful persons
such as Jahanara, whose port he had ransacked, and the fingerless
uncle's sister.[53] On the other hand there were men like Jai Singh,
actively lobbying against those who wanted the Maratha warrior
murdered. At one point, Shivaji even offered to retire as a fakir to
Benares if he were restored to liberty,[54] but two months into his stay,
at last he managed to escape. While a compelling story tells that he
hid inside a box of sweets on their way out, what seems also likely
is that Jai Singh secretly lent him money with which to bribe the
guards watching him.[55] Either way, the emperor was outraged – and
many years later, on the eve of his death, by which time he had spent
a lifetime attempting to subjugate the Deccan, breaking the back of
the Mughal empire, he would ruminate sadly: 'Negligence for a single
moment becomes the cause of disgrace for long years. The escape of

the wretch Shiva took place through carelessness, and I have had to labour hard to the end of my life [as a consequence].'[56]

Back in the Deccan, Shivaji prudently opened channels of diplomacy with the irate Mughals, while focusing on gathering pieces of the disintegrating Bijapuri state – by 1675, for instance, the entirety of the coastline of Bijapur would come into his possession.[57] Three years after his escape, however, the Marathas were ready for conflict once again. In 1669 Shivaji retrieved five forts from the Mughals, and in 1670 raided Surat a second time, taking even more plunder with him on this occasion valued at nearly seven million rupees. In Berar, which the Mughals had obtained decades before from the Nizam Shah of Ahmadnagar, Shivaji's raids yielded him over two and a half million rupees in booty. With Jai Singh having died in 1667, a succession of new governors were sent to the Deccan by Delhi to demolish the Marathas, but they all failed while Shivaji grew not only stronger but also bolder. As Bernier noted, Shivaji was 'exercising all the powers of an independent sovereign'. He 'laughs at the threats both of the Mogul and the King of Visapour [Bijapur] . . . How to put down Seva-Gi is become the object of chief importance.'[58] Unfortunately for both the Adil Shah as well as the Mughal emperor, what Shahji's son had begun could not be easily ended.

Six years after his coronation ceremony, Shivaji died in 1680, confident and strong.[59] Aurangzeb, consumed by his fury, himself descended on the Deccan to destroy all resistance once and for all. As it happened, the man ended up shattering his own empire in the twenty-six years he spent in the south. In theory, events went his way. The conquests of Bijapur and Golconda added as much as fifty-three million rupees to the imperial treasury in revenues, i.e. a full 23 per cent more than its previous income. But instead of nurturing this new land, Aurangzeb exploited it to finance campaigns further south, and to battle the Marathas. Then there was a crisis among the nobility of the empire – there were more aristocrats clamouring for estates than there were estates to distribute. The shortage was an artificial one: 'In his anxiety to pull resources out of the two conquered kingdoms, Aurangzeb skimped on the administrative and military manpower necessary to maintain political stability and order.'[60] He made, meanwhile, implacable enemies of the Marathas – by the time Shivaji died, thirty-one of the top fifty nobles, and as many as fifty-seven of the leading hundred nobles of the Mughal court had been directly engaged with attempting to put them down.[61] The emperor's sectarianism and high-handedness did not help find a diplomatic solution either: when Shivaji's heir, Sambhaji, was captured, he was tortured and killed in a most savage fashion, burning any real bridges that might have remained.

For decades the Maratha state only survived because various factions kept the flag flying from their hill forts.[62] Their preferred technique of guerrilla warfare also gave the Marathas a disproportionate advantage over the Mughals. The latter deployed hundreds of thousands of men in the Deccan, but with them came cooks, dancing girls, eunuchs, traders and a whole host of others, slowing down progress and tying them up in large camps. When the Mughal army was on the road, Manucci reports, they never marched in formation 'but always in long files. Almost every soldier has with him in camp his wife and children. Thus a soldier may be seen carrying under his arm an unweaned infant, and on his head a basket of cooking pots and pans. Behind him marches his wife with spears, or else his matchlock, upon her back. In place of a bayonet they stick into the muzzle of the gun a spoon, which, being long, is more conveniently carried there than in the basket borne by the husband upon his head.'[63] It might have been a comical scene were it not for the tragedy that unfolded when swift Maratha cavalry corps descended on these cumbersome Mughal parties, so that before the soldier could swing the pan in his hand, he probably lost his head to a rider zooming past.[64] All of this, we are told, 'baffled Aurangzeb. He could not comprehend what he was up against. He thought that all that remained for him was to take a few hill forts. But taking a fort or a town or even crushing a particular army meant nothing in the fight against the Marathas. They had no centre, no particular base. Not even any regular army . . . As the Mughals kept spinning around, chasing the elusive Marathas everywhere, they lost all bearing and all control.'[65]

By the time Aurangzeb was on his deathbed in 1707, the Mughal empire was starting to unravel, and nearly three decades of persistent, furious effort had failed to crush the Maratha resistance. Such, as one authority wrote, was the emperor's angst to seize the Deccan and so strong was his 'longing and passion for taking all the [Maratha] forts, that he personally runs about panting for a heap of stones'.[66] In the meantime, as this descendant of Akbar and Jehangir spent the final years of his life in the tents and battlefields of the south, governance in the north fell by the wayside, the imperial treasury slowly crumbling into an empty darkness.[67] Emboldened by the success of the Marathas, rebellions broke out across the empire, even as there loomed on the horizon a terrible war of succession between Aurangzeb's sons. In less than a century and a half – when the last of the Mughals was exiled to Burma on a bullock cart – the imperial line was destroyed, even as the Marathas prospered and thrived; less than fifty years after Aurangzeb, they would become such a force that the Mughal emperor who ruled in 1752 named them 'protectors' of the Peacock Throne, a dignity unthinkable two generations before when Shivaji was contemptuously dismissed as a mountain rat.[68] A line of Brahmins would emerge to rule from Pune, where Shivaji was raised, while warlords established Maratha houses in such faraway lands as Gwalior, Indore, Baroda and Nagpur.[69] The Mughal emperor, in the meantime, was reduced to a 'tinsel sovereign', whose power survived only in the make-believe world of court ritual and ceremonious protocol.[70] A new age had dawned in India.

For most of its late medieval history, rulers of the Deccan had come from the north or from lands beyond the Indian subcontinent and reigned here as kings. Now, however, it was children of the Deccan who went out and dominated the heart of India, striking terror in distant provinces where they were feared and sometimes even abhorred.[71] The power of the Marathas did not endure, though, and in due course the

British would unseat them, launching India into the colonial age. And yet this phenomenal force unleashed by Shivaji – heir, ultimately to the Bahmanis and all the Rebel Sultans who came thereafter – did not easily give up, fighting hard till the very end. The British may ultimately have triumphed in 1818, but by then the Marathas had reshaped India itself.

That, however, is another story.

Notes

Introduction

1. Allen, *Coromandel*, 7.
2. Beal, *Travels of Fah-Hian and Sung-Yun*, 141.
3. Davis, *Lives of Indian Images*, 71–75. In 690 CE we also have the Deccan's Chalukya king Vinayaditya claiming great victories in the north, a little before the Rashtrakutas. Richard H. Davis in his study notes at some length how, prior to the emergence of strong powers in the south, 'imperial formations' in India were heavily focused on the Ganga–Yamuna belt. Subsequent attempts by the Deccan rulers to claim ritual sovereignty and plunder in the north was also an effort to 'remake the imperial topography of the subcontinent'.
4. Phillips, *Tavernier's Travels in India*, 355. This is the diamond that would come to be known as the Great Table, of which Tavernier included a sketch. It was, he commented, 'the biggest [stone] I ever saw in my life in a merchant's hands'. Its fate remained unknown for many years afterwards, till in the 1960s it was fairly conclusively stated that the Daria-i-Noor of the Iranian crown jewels was cut from the Great Table.
5. Lovell, *Travels of Monsieur Thevenot*, 102.

Prologue

1. Eaton, "Kiss My Foot," 289–313.
2. Raichur's importance was to continue into modern times. The British, as part of their subsidiary alliance with the Nizams of Hyderabad in the mid-

nineteenth century, ensured that Raichur was part of the territory ceded
by the Nizam into their own control.

3.   Eaton, "Kiss My Foot," 293.

4.   Ibid., 299. Some writers like P.M. Joshi in *History of the Medieval Deccan*
have stated that Vijayanagar seized Raichur in 1512 and what we witness
in 1520 is an attempt by the Adil Shah to retrieve the region. However,
according to Eaton, this is belied by inscriptional evidence which shows
Ismail Adil Shah's rule in the district well after 1512 and before 1520.

5.   The Vijayanagar throne is also sometimes referred to as the Lion Throne,
particularly in the Telugu *Rayavacakamu*, where it is one of three divinely
blessed Lion Thrones – the other two belong to the Sultans of Delhi and
the Gajapati of Orissa.

6.   Rau, *Neglected Emperor Poet*, 11. See also Ekambaram, *Krishna Deva Raya*,
52.

7.   Rao, *Sri Krishnadevaraya*, 15–16. Others like Suryanath U. Kamath in his
Krishnadevaraya of Vijayanagar, 26, say that this story about the goat's eyes
is untrue.

8.   See Rau's *Neglected Emperor Poet* for a list of Krishnadeva Raya's Sanskrit
works, most of which are now lost. His *Amuktamalyada* offers his heirs
words of practical wisdom: 'If you are partial to learning / And give lands
and money away to the learned / Mendicants, monks and men with
matted hair / Will become swollen headed . . . / Just show devotion to the
learned / And if they resent their poverty, don't be concerned.' Similarly,
when discussing tribal leaders in the forests of the kingdom: 'Trying to
clean up the forest folk is like trying to wash a mud wall. There is no end
to it. No point in getting angry.'

9.   Rao, *Sri Krishnadevaraya*, 20–21. Interestingly, Krishnadeva brought back
from the Gajapati's territories, from a temple in Udayagiri, the image of
Balakrishna, which was then consecrated in his own capital. So too, after
defeating Ismail Adil Shah, he would take possession of the idol of Vitthala
in the Pandharpur temple, though this was evidently later returned to
Bhanudas (an ancestor of the saint Eknath) who carried the deity back to
his original shrine in Maharashtra. See Davis, *Lives of Indian Images*, 67.

10. Ibid. Also see Fernao Nuniz's account in Sewell, *Forgotten Empire*, 318,
which refers to a wife and son of the Orissa king having fallen into
Krishnadeva Raya's hands in an earlier battle in 1515. Some scholars are
undecided about this Orissan wife of the Raya, since, unlike Krishnadeva's

other two consorts, she doesn't feature in many sources. However, basing himself on the *Prabodha Chandrodaya Vyakhya*, authored by a close relation of the Raya's minister, Krishnaswami Ayyangar, in his *Sources of Vijayanagar History,* 11, concludes that a marriage did indeed occur and that 'she was neglected'.

11. Wagoner, *Tidings of the King*, 58. The *Rayavacakamu*, written decades after Krishnadeva's time, sometime in the early seventeenth century, tells that when this king was born, astrologers in the Muslim courts of the Deccan warned: 'A king has been born in Karnataka who is an emanation of Vishnu. This kingdom of yours—as well as the Ashavapati and Gajapati kingdoms [i.e. in this context Delhi and Orissa]—all are to be conquered by that king!'

12. Sewell, *Forgotten Empire*, 145. Faria y Sousa was originally Portuguese but moved to Spain and preferred writing in Castilian. It should be noted here that he makes this mention while writing his *Asia Portuguesa* much later and was not a contemporary of Krishnadeva's.

13. Quoted in Stoker, *Polemics and Patronage*, 33.

14. Rao, *Sri Krishnadevaraya*, 15.

15. Quoted in Filliozat, *Vijayanagar Empire*, 29.

16. Ibid., 29–33.

17. The presence of eunuchs in Hindu courts was adopted from India's Islamic courts, which in turn first began to employ eunuchs in imitation of customs in Central Asia, Persia and beyond.

18. Eaton, "Kiss My Foot," 293. Reference is to a Sanskrit inscription at Bidar. The battle that led to tribute in the reign of Devaraya II, in 1444, appears in Chapter 3.

19. Sherwani, *Bahmanis of the Deccan*, 387, 414.

20. Ibid., 419.

21. Eaton, "Kiss My Foot," 293.

22. Ibid.

23. Ibid., 301–02. T.V. Mahalingam in his *Administration and Social Life in Vijayanagar*, 138, provides a tabular breakdown of the chief nobles and the forces they individually led, based on Nuniz's account. For instance, 40,000 infantry, we know were led by three eunuch nobles.

24. Ibid.

25. Waring, *History of the Mahrattas*, 12.

26. Sharma, *History of the Vijayanagar Empire,* 28.

27. The hon weighed, according to P.M. Joshi, some fifty-three grains. In

1567 it was valued in English money as worth a little over six shillings and equivalent to three Indian rupees. By the middle of the seventeenth century this appears to be revised to four Indian rupees.

28. Subrahmanyam, 'Vijayanagar,' 94.

29. Sewell, *Forgotten Empire*, 62. There is even a book that draws inspiration from this tale of the goldsmith's daughter for its title. See Watson, *War of the Goldsmith's Daughter*.

30. Rotzer, 'Deccani Guns,' and Pushkar Sohoni, 'From Defended Battlements,' 118. The Muslim rulers of the Deccan had adequate manpower and skill to work guns, thanks to Islamic networks that spread far and wide, unlike Vijayanagar, which was at something of a disadvantage where artillery was concerned, even its fortifications relatively inferior when compared to those designed by its rivals in the north.

31. Eaton, "Kiss My Foot," 302. It appears that the men were paid in proportion to the stones they were successfully able to dislodge! See Eaton and Wagoner, 'Warfare on the Deccan Plateau,' 19.

32. Ibid., 304. Rotzer in 'Deccani Guns' explains in some detail how Deccani guns were extremely heavy and used primarily for defensive purposes atop forts – their use in the battlefield was rare, the Adil Shah's effort in 1520 being one example. So the guns at Raichur were probably mounted on the walls of the fort on a permanent basis, unable therefore to manoeuvre downwards towards the enemy at the foot of the walls.

33. Quoted in Filliozat, *Vijayanagar Empire*, 140.

34. Eaton, "Kiss My Foot," 302.

35. Sewell, *Forgotten Empire*, 340.

36. Ibid., 300–01.

37. Joshi, 'Adil Shahis,' 309.

38. These were under the command of one Cristovao de Figueiredo, a horse trader.

39. Eaton, "Kiss My Foot," 305.

40. Ibid., 306. See also Mitchell and Zebrowski, *Architecture and Art*, 36.

41. Ibid., 289.

42. Fernao Nuniz quoted in Sewell, *Forgotten Empire*, 348.

43. Ibid., 352.

44. Ibid.

45. Rau, *Neglected Emperor Poet*, 12.

46. Fernao Nuniz quoted in Sewell, *Forgotten Empire*, 353, and Eaton, "Kiss My Foot," 306.

47. Fernao Nuniz quoted in Sewell, *Forgotten Empire*, 353–54.

48. Eaton, *Social History of the Deccan*, 90. Some authors like M. Rama Rao and K.G. Gopala Krishna Rao give the year as 1512 or 1514, but general consensus is that it was in 1523 that Krishnadeva Raya took this title. In some sources, the title also appears as *Yavana Rajya Pratishta Sthapana Acharya*. The word 'Yavana', evidently a Sanskrit version of Ionian, was initially used to refer to Greeks but soon came to stand for foreigners in general and applied to Muslims and Turks, the exact meaning varying from context to context. The Portuguese, in due course, during what is called the Nayaka period in southern India, would come to be called 'Parasikas', distinguishing them from the Muslim Yavanas, though this term was also used for Persians. And in a much later period, the French in Pondicherry would be described as Yavanas too. Muslims also continued often to appear as Turks or 'Turuskas/Turukas', including as late as 1846 when, for instance, Seshachala Kavi wrote his *Nilagiri Yatra*.

I. Sons of Fury

1. Eaton, 'Sufis of Bijapur,' 30. The oldest mosque in India is popularly believed to have been constructed in 629 CE in Kodungallur, Kerala, three years before the death of Prophet Muhammad. In the Deccan, Al Masudi saw in 916 CE 'a settlement in Chaul of ten thousand Muslims whose ancestors had come from Arabia and Iraq to engage in the pepper and spice trade', and who had gone on to intermarry with locals.

2. Khalidi, *Muslims in the Deccan*, 13–16. Jalal al-Din al-Suyuti recorded that Muslims arrived on the Konkan coast within seven decades of the Prophet's death, fleeing Basra where they were unable to live under the tyranny of the Umayyad governor.

3. Ibid., 16. There is also an inscription from the time of the Kadamba king Jayakesin I, dated 1053 CE, in which reference is made to a *mijigiti* or mosque, while another from 1059 refers to one Chadama, son of Madhumada (i.e Muhammad), son of Aliyama (or Ali) who was a Tayika (Tajik). A century before, in 926, we have the Chinchani copper plates of the Rashtrakutas where Madhumati (Muhammad), son of Sahiyarahara

(Shahriyar) appears as a governor of a coastal town. The exchange worked in the reverse as well, and as early as 771/773 CE there was an Indian scholar who was present in Baghdad bearing astronomical and other Hindu texts from Sindh, while in the ports of southern Iraq, Indian merchants had the religious freedom to found temples to Hindu gods. See Flood, *Objects of Translation*, 21, 23.

4. Al Biruni quoted in Smith, *Hinduism and Modernity*, 51. The rhetoric here, however, should not be overstated – even the Ghaznavids (of whom Mahmud of Ghazni is notorious for his destruction of the Somnath temple), had Hindus in his armies (the salar-i Hinduyan) and some of their generals are known by name, such as one Tilak. He was from Kashmir, began his career as a translator, and earned such royal favour as to be granted the right to use a parasol, banners, and drums, leading soldiers against both Hindu kings and rebellious Muslims in the name of the Ghaznavid Sultan. Decades before Tilak, similarly, in 1009 the Rajput ruler of Narayanpur (Alwar) sent Mahmud of Ghazni as many as 2000 Hindu soldiers to serve in that Muslim king's armies. See Flood, *Objects of Translation*, 78–79.

5. Joshi and Husain, 'Khaljis and Tughluqs,' 31.

6. Quoted in Chattopadhyaya, 'Other, or the Others?' 315–16.

7. Quoted in ibid., 319.

8. Joshi and Husain, 'Khaljis and Tughluqs,' 32–33. They were the daughter and wife respectively of the uncle Alauddin murdered and replaced.

9. Khan, *Deccan Policy*, 35. Sikandar al-Thani, the Arabic version of this title, also appears in a 1299 inscription in a mosque near Allahabad.

10. Joshi and Husain, 'Khaljis and Tughluqs,' 36.

11. Eaton, *Social History*, 2. The Biblical claim was in keeping with the view that Africans and Asians were all descendants of Ham. This was not unusual and until late in the eighteenth century even European visitors to India tried to fit Hindus into the Biblical narrative as a lost and misguided people. See also Waring, *History of the Mahrattas*, 4–5.

12. Joshi and Husain, 'Khaljis and Tughluqs,' 35. The Great Boar, of course, is one of the avatars of Vishnu from Hindu mythology. This, like Balban's earlier inscription, is an example of what the scholar Sheldon Pollock calls 'the creation of the fame and virtue of the king through a celebration of his fame and virtue', a regular feature of Sanskritic kingship. It should also be noted that in 1291 the poet Narendra in a composition also refers to Turkish cavalry, suggesting that awareness of Turks and their strong cavalry

units had travelled to southern India even if the Turks themselves had not.

13. Phillips, *Tavernier's Travels in India*, 116.

14. Joshi and Husain, 'Khaljis and Tughluqs,' 37.

15. Ibid., 38.

16. Quoted in ibid.

17. Ibid., 39.

18. Barani quoted in Kidwai, 'Khaljis in Love,' 132.

19. Barani quoted in Elliot and Dowson, *History of India*, 199.

20. Some authors give 1306 and 1307 as the dates for this event, but it is now believed that Barani's account that offers 1308 is the correct one.

21. Joshi and Husain, 'Khaljis and Tughluqs,' 45. See also Eaton, *Social History*, 13. There was by now the emergence of defined identities in these regions. So as early as 1053, 'the term andhra bhasa, "the language of Andhra", was being used synonymously with Telugu, indicating that people were mapping language onto territory', and by the late thirteenth century, we have a Marathi text instructing locals 'not to go to Telugu or Kannada countries'. So too in 1163 after the Kakatiyas freed themselves from their Chalukya overlords, they 'switched from Kannada to Telugu, indicating official recognition of Telangana's vernacular language'. These identities were also regional rather than religious, as is often believed.

22. The *Prataparudracaritramu* has an interesting origin myth for this dynasty. It claims that the house was founded by one Madhava Varman. As a little boy, he once left his books in a temple to Padmakshi to run off and play with other boys. Late in the evening he returned to the temple only to find the goddess seated on her throne, 'attended by a horde of terrifying demons'. But unafraid, he walks straight into this strange assembly of ghosts and goblins and picks up his things. Then the goddess tests him by taking a particularly frightening form, but he is not scared and instead sings her praises. Impressed, she grants him a boon, and he says, 'Please grant me the ability to vanquish the lord of Cuttack and to get our royal herds back.' She agrees, bestows on him a divine sword and shield, and promises him an army that will emerge from a cave, guaranteeing 1000 years of sovereignty to his family.

23. Isami quoted in Eaton, *Social History*, 17.

24. In an earlier time, Sultan Mahmud Ghaznavi incorporated the Rajah of Kalinjar in northern India into his court order in 1023 by similarly bestowing upon the latter a robe of honour. The rajah did not, evidently,

warm to this immediately: according to one source, he said to Mahmud's ambassador, 'I beg you to excuse me from wearing it [but to] tell your lord that I have put it on.' The ambassador, though impressed by this 'splendid youth of great beauty, glorious in blackness', said he could not deceive Mahmud, and in the end the rajah had to wear the khilat after all. The robe, theoretically from the overlord's own wardrobe, symbolized both his presence as well as essence, so that the wearer of the khilat was, in a way, wearing the authority (and recognizing the suzerainty) of the overlord, and governing with his blessings. See Flood, *Objects of Translation*, 82.

25. Eaton, *Social History*, 11.
26. Ibid., 16.
27. Ibid., 18.
28. Ibid., 20–21. Such ritual suicide was not unknown. The Chalukya king Somesvara, after his defeat at the hands of all three sons of Rajendra Chola I, challenged one of them to man-to-man combat. On the day, however, suffering from a fever, he could not fight, and instead he threw himself into the Tungabhadra in what was a similar case of ritual suicide. See Davis, *Lives of Indian Images*, 81.
29. Ibn Batuta quoted in Sewell, *Forgotten Empire*, 18. See also Sharma, *History of the Vijayanagar Empire: Beginnings and Expansion*, 14.
30. Rao, *Sri Krishnadevaraya*, 3.
31. Watson, *War of the Goldsmith's Daughter*, 52.
32. Husaini, 'Sultanate of Ma'bar,' 59. Ibn Batuta's wife was this commander Jalaluddin Ahsan's daughter, Hur Nasab.
33. Flood, *Objects of Translation*, 246. Here the Sultan reminds one of the Cholas who too transported sacred waters from the Ganga across distant lands, pouring it into a man-made lake called Chola-Ganga at first and now identified as the Ponneri tank.
34. Barani quoted in Elliot and Dowson, *History of India*, 239.
35. Sewell, *Forgotten Empire*, 14.
36. Sherwani, *Bahmanis of the Deccan*, 19–20.
37. Ibid., 25.
38. Joshi and Husain, 'Khaljis and Tughluqs,' 55.
39. Sherwani, *Bahmanis of the Deccan*, 26.
40. Rao, *Mysore Gazetteer*, 1469.
41. Eaton, *Social History*, 41.
42. Ferishta quoted in Wheeler, *History of India*, 83.

43. He appears often with his title 'Zafar Khan' in contemporary records.

44. Sherwani, *Bahmanis of the Deccan*, 37.

45. Ibid., 64. The inevitable talk of conspiracy by the ex-ruler against Hasan existed but this could very likely also have been simply a pretext to get rid of him.

46. Wheeler, *History of India*, 84.

47. Sherwani, *Bahmanis of the Deccan*, 49–50. 'Gangu' being a corruption of 'Kanku', which in turn was a variant of 'Kakuyah', the name of an aristocratic clan that once controlled Isfahan and Hamadan in Iran.

48. Ibid.

49. Ibid., 64.

50. Eaton, *Social History*, 40–42. As part of the project of building a new kingdom, a new narrative, and to construct legitimacy, Hasan also invited poets from Delhi to his new court. Abdul Malik Isami, whom we encountered earlier in the context of Devagiri's annexation, was poor and without patronage in Delhi when he received an invitation to come to the newly founded Bahmani court. Here, in the 1350s he composed his *Futuh al-Salatin* in which he sings praises of Mahmud of Ghazni and essentially encouraged Hasan and other Muslim kings to follow in that invader's footsteps. Hasan, thankfully, did nothing of the sort and while he founded an Islamic kingdom, the first Bahmani Sultan did not embrace suggestions to also destroy temples and idols. See Davis, *Lives of Indian Images*, 190–91.

51. Sherwani, *Bahmanis of the Deccan*, 66.

52. Ibid.

53. Eaton, 'Sufis of Bijapur,' 33.

54. Michell and Zebrowski, *Architecture and Art*, 63. See also Eaton, 'Tughluq and Temples,' 178.

55. Eaton, *Social History*, 45–46.

56. Sherwani, *Bahmanis of the Deccan*, 86–87. Three elements – the khilat, the khutbah, and sikka or right to mind coins – were essential in Islamic statecraft to demonstrate authority.

57. Sardar, 'The Bahmanis,' 34. See also Wagoner, 'Money Use,' 457. The popularity of Vijayanagar currency, as Wagoner shows, was because it offered coins in smaller values that were more convenient for transactions, and also because, unlike the Bahmani system imported from the north, this had evolved over 400 years locally. It is also believed by some that Muhammad bin Tughluq's attempt at circulating copper coins in the country led to a

general loss of confidence in currency minted by Muslim kings, given the disastrous results of that infamous experiment.

58. Sherwani, *Bahmanis of the Deccan*, 77.

59. Sewell, *Forgotten Empire*, 30.

60. The Turquoise Throne was presented by the Kapaya Nayaka of Telingana after his defeat at the hands of the Sultan, with the second Bahmani Sultan taking his seat on it 'when the sun was supposed to pass from the constellation of Taurus to the constellation of Aries' on 21 March 1363.

II. The Turquoise Throne

1. On this, more information is available in the section titled 'Muhammad Qasim Firishta on the Introduction of Firearms in the Bahmani Kingdom,' in Iqtidar Alam Khan, *Gunpowder and Firearms*, 205–09. Ferishta also suggests that Vijayanagar had firearms as early as 1366, though there is some debate on the veracity of this claim (ibid., 210).

2. Sherwani, *Bahmanis of the Deccan*, 90.

3. Ibid., 92.

4. Ferishta quoted in Sewell, *Forgotten Empire*, 41.

5. It is important to remember that these are not merely silly pretexts. Waging war was part of a king's legitimate demonstration of kingliness, both in Hindu and Indo-Islamic thought, and a king who could not prove his military prowess also opened himself up to the charge of weakness, and to the prospect of refractory subordinates.

6. Sewell, *Forgotten Empire*, 46.

7. Or collarbone, according to another retelling of the episode.

8. Sherwani, *Bahmanis of the Deccan*, 120.

9. Ibid., 124–25. One prominent exception was the Mughal emperor Shah Alam II (r. 1759–1806) who was blinded by a rebel in 1788 but later restored to the throne (incidentally, by a Hindu, the Maratha warlord Mahadji Scindia). The Mughal throne itself, however, had little political heft by then, and as a popularly saying went, the aged, declining Shah Alam's 'kingdom' extended merely from Delhi to Palam!

10. Siddiqi, 'Mohammad Shah II Bahmani,' 584. The *Bahman Namah* was composed in Sultan Ahmad Shah's reign by Sheikh Azari.

11. Rao, *Mysore Gazetteer*, 1529.

12. Eaton, *Social History*, 61.

13. Khan, 'Condition of Education,' 588. This author, however, states that Hafiz was invited by our ruler's predecessor, which is unlikely given that he sat on the throne for less than two months.

14. Eaton, 'History of the Deccan,' 3.

15. Sherwani, *Bahmanis of the Deccan*, 130.

16. Ibid.

17. Ibid., 131–32.

18. Ibid., 145.

19. Khan, 'Condition of Education,' 589.

20. Sherwani, *Bahmanis of the Deccan*, 149.

21. Shirazi, in his version, however, declares that Firoz Shah had only one wife! Even if the number of his concubines is an exaggeration, the suggestion of chaste monogamy swings to the other extreme, so that this might have been an attempt to win the Sultan retrospective redemption in the eyes of the orthodox.

22. Sherwani, *Bahmanis of the Deccan*, 146. See also Siddiqi, *Bahmani Sufis*, 138. Switching between Sunnism and the Shia sect was not altogether unusual – the Mughal emperor Shah Alam II mentioned above, according to Sanjay Subrahmanyam and Muzaffar Alam's reading of his *Ajaib al-Qasas*, might have secretly been a Shia, for example.

23. Chandra, *Medieval India*, 184.

24. Eaton, *Social History*, 74, and Sherwani, *Bahmanis of the Deccan*, 233–34. The invading father-in-law, the ruler of Khandesh, which was another Muslim principality, lost the battle as well as a lot of gold to his son-in-law. Khandesh was founded in the reign of Firoz Shah Tughluq of Delhi, before it split from the Delhi Sultanate and asserted its own power. It was closely involved in feuds with the rulers of Malwa and Gujarat, as well as with the Bahmanis and their successor states, even though, to avoid making our narrative unwieldy, these states have been left out of this book.

25. Sherwani, *Bahmanis of the Deccan*, 233–34.

26. Chandra, *Medieval India*, 184. Ferishta also gives a fascinating, although certainly exaggerated, account of the life of these women in Firozabad: 'Separate villas as lovely as moons were also built, and each one was conferred upon one of the women of the sultan's harem. Having reflected upon the problem of throngs of women jostling in his palace, the sultan established rules that were never violated in his lifetime. The essence of these rules was that there would be no more than three maidservants for

each apartment in which each one of his favourite women resided, and these servants would speak the same language as their mistress. Accordingly, when he wanted to speak in Arabic, he would go to the "Arabic Mahal", located next to the "Deccani Mahal" where Sultan Mahmud Shah Bahmani's daughter was kept. In the "Arabic Mahal" he would find nine Arab women, who, having been raised in the Hijaz, in Mecca, or in other regions in Arabia, possessed perfect linguistic eloquence. The maidservants of these mistresses were either Abyssinians or born of Abyssinians, and were fluent in Arabic. Women who did not speak Arabic were not permitted to frequent that apartment, lest its inhabitants lose their Arabic proficiency or allow their tongue to become mixed with other languages. Moreover, the sultan constantly ordered deputies to be sent to Arabia to procure women in order to fill vacancies created by the deaths of the mistresses or their maidservants. Similarly, he also kept nine women from non-Arab lands, and their maidservants were Persian-speaking Caucasians, Turks, Russians or Georgians. In the same manner, the sultan kept Turkish, European, Afghan, Rajput, Bengali, Gujarati, Telugu, Kanarese, and Marathi women in his harem, and knew the native language of each of them. Each day he would visit one of these apartments and comport himself in such a way that each woman considered herself the sultan's most beloved.' See Michell and Eaton, *Firuzabad*, 10.

27. As Gibbon said of Emperor Gordian II of Rome, whose penchant for books and women parallels Firoz Shah's own, these were both 'designed for use rather than ostentation'!

28. Her name is supposed to have been Parthal.

29. This was the fort of Bankapur.

30. Sherwani, *Bahmanis of the Deccan*, 162. In the 1430s, in a similar offering, the Raya is supposed to have delivered to Vijayanagar 200 accomplished artists and musicians. See C. Rao, *Mysore Gazetteer*, 1573.

31. Ibid. See also Sewell, *Forgotten Empire*, 60–61.

32. Ibid., 60.

33. Ferishta quoted in ibid., 60–61.

34. Ibid.

35. Ibid., 172.

36. Sherwani, *Bahmanis of the Deccan*, 143–44, and Khalidi, *Muslims in the Deccan*, 41–44. The Sayyids would later be welcomed at the Mughal court as well – in 1560, Haji Begum, on her way back from Mecca, brought 300

Hadramis with her to recite the Quran around the tomb of her husband, Emperor Humayun.

37. Eaton, *Social History*, 51. Eaton here refers to Goa instead of Dabhol, but Goa in Firoz Shah's time was a Vijayanagar possession.

38. See also Subrahmanyam, 'Iranians Abroad,' 340–63.

39. Khan, *Deccan Policy*, 5.

40. Harris, *First Firangis*, 32.

41. Barendse, *Arabian Seas*, 107.

42. Eaton, *Social History*, 51. The Jami Masjid, believed to have been completed around 1406, runs 343 feet by 202 feet covering nearly 70,000 square feet, and is perhaps the only majestic reminder of the city Firozabad once was – it is now in ruins, having been abandoned soon after Firoz Shah's death and neglected for centuries.

43. Sherwani, *Bahmanis of the Deccan*, 149.

44. Eaton, *Social History*, 51. The qaba is another word for the khilat or robe of honour, also known sometimes as *saropa*. The khilat could, however, include more than a robe and as a word could be applied to a whole ensemble featuring robes, turban, etc.

45. It should be noted, though, that the Mughals too grew preoccupied with Persian once they were established in their power – a descendant, Mirza Ali Bakht Azfari in his *Marghub al-Fuad* of 1793–94 laments that his royal ancestors lost much of their virility when they forgot their martial Turkish roots and allowed themselves to be seduced by all that was Persian in art, aesthetics, culture, and deportment.

46. Eaton, *Social History*, 51.

47. Ibid.

48. Sherwani, *Bahmanis of the Deccan*, 163.

49. Rao, *Mysore Gazetteer*, 1547. See also Sharma, *History of the Vijayanagar Empire: Beginnings and Expansion*, 51.

50. Eaton, *Social History*, 54.

51. The story goes that the Sufi took his turban and divided it into two parts, giving one to Ahmad and the other to his son, indicating that they would both be Sultans. The power of spiritual leaders could, thus, play a great role even in non-spiritual domains.

52. Sherwani, *Bahmanis of the Deccan*, 168.

53. Rao, *Mysore Gazetteer*, 1547. This son, Hasan, was created a nobleman of 500-horse, and Firozabad was first given to him as his fief, and he was

'permitted to promenade or hunt within an eight-mile radius of the palace'. But since his very existence was a threat to Ahmad's power, he was blinded. See Michell and Eaton, *Firuzabad*, 17.

54. Haig, 'The Religion,' 75. Other versions have him strangled or stabbed, though there is also a version in which he dies a natural death after his reconciliation with Ahmad.

55. Eaton, *Social History*, 54.

56. Ibid., 55–56. Ahmad also funded the construction of Shah Nimatullah Walli's mausoleum in Mahan, Iran.

57. Sherwani, *Bahmanis of the Deccan*, 192.

58. Ibid., 199.

59. Thangasamy, *Vijayanagar Empire*, 38.

60. Sewell, *Forgotten Empire*, 67, and Sherwani, *Bahmanis of the Deccan*, 198–99.

61. Rao, *Mysore Gazetteer*, 1562. Stories such as this are as difficult to fully negate, despite the comedy, as they are to verify. But they exist and perhaps reflect that while the stakes were high, there were also petty, and indeed hilarious, exchanges between both kingdoms and their respective kings.

62. Sherwani, *Bahmanis of the Deccan*, 201.

63. As Arjun Appadurai explains in *Worship and Conflict Under Colonial Rule*, 63, 70–71, under the Vijayanagar kings, and in general in southern India, kingly duty included protecting the subjects of the kingdom, but also endowing and protecting temples (where protection included settling disputes that could not be resolved locally by the local elites in actual control of these temples). And as the kingdom expanded, assuming protective powers over important temples in new areas was a means also to entrench the power of the state in these conquered territories.

64. Sharma, *History of the Vijayanagar Empire: Beginnings and Expansion*, 56.

65. Sohoni, 'Vernacular as a Space,' 260.

66. Sherwani, 'The Bahmanis,' 195. See also Ali, 'Contributions,' 594.

67. Sherwani, 'The Bahmanis,' 209.

68. Michell and Zebrowski, *Architecture and Art*, 3.

69. Eaton, *Social History*, 63.

70. Sherwani, *Bahmanis of the Deccan*, 180–81.

71. Ibid., 184.

72. Nikitin quoted in Fisher, *Visions of Mughal India*, 20.

73. Ibid., 19.

74. Ibid., 20.

75. Eaton, *Social History*, 75.

76. Sherwani, *Bahmanis of the Deccan*, 191. This was not unprecedented. Ali in 'Between Market and Court' narrates how even in the Hoysala empire there were two merchant houses that accumulated political clout at court. Interestingly, this importance given to merchants is quite a contrast to classical Indian texts such as the *Arthashastra* where the merchant is placed among 'thieves known under other names' and a 'thorn' in the side of the state! Quoted in Heesterman, 'Was There an Indian Reaction?' 39.

77. Subrahmanyam, 'Iranians Abroad,' 348–49.

78. This included also, however, Muslims of Arab descent from the coastal enclaves and Hindu converts.

79. Sherwani, *Bahmanis of the Deccan*, 192.

80. Nikitin quoted in Michael Fisher, *Visions of Mughal India*, 20.

81. Ibid., 19.

82. Subrahmanyam, *Courtly Encounters*, 45.

83. Eaton, *Social History*, 76.

84. Sherwani, *Bahmanis of the Deccan*, 190.

85. Haig, 'The Religion of Ahmad,' 75. There is a legend associated with Ahmad Shah's transformation from Sunni to Shia Muslim. After Gisu Daraz gave him his blessings, Ahmad Shah is supposed to have had a dream in which, while he rested under a tree, a stranger appeared and handed him a green crown with twelve points, telling him it was sent by 'one of the shaikhs who sits in seclusion'. When many years later Shah Nimatullah Walli's grandson was to come to the Deccan, one of the men who travelled in advance carried with him such a crown – Ahmad Shah recognized in him the man from his dream, and the 'shaikh who sits in seclusion' was, of course, Shah Nimatullah Walli.

86. Sherwani, *Bahmanis of the Deccan*, 192.

87. Eaton, 'Sufis of Bijapur,' 50. The first available Dakhni work of literature is *Kadamrav Padamrav* by Fakhruddin Nizami in the 1420s. In the 1650s, Jayarama Pindye, who claimed he could compose in twelve languages, described Persian as Yavani while Dakhni is given the name Daksinatya-Yavani.

88. Sherwani, *Bahmanis of the Deccan*, 224. In Vijayanagar also we see this division in the form of left-hand Idangai castes and right-hand Valangai castes, 98 on each side, evidently, that often clashed but could also ally to realize common goals. See also Rao, *Mysore Gazetteer*, 1660–61.

89. Bayly, *Indian Society*, 19. This problem would, centuries later, come to spook the Mughal empire as well, especially in the eighteenth century when the empire was in decline. Factional rivalries between 'foreign' nobles and Indian-born aristocrats resulted in several grandees departing from court and slowly building up their own power bases (for instance, the first Nizam of Hyderabad and the Nawab of Awadh), which in turn hastened the disintegration of the empire.

90. Sherwani, *Bahmanis of the Deccan*, 258.

91. Ibid., 263.

92. Ibid., 264.

93. Eaton, *Social History*, 59.

94. On Gawan's letters and the culture of epistolary friendships, see Flatt, 'Practicing Friendship' in *Studies in History*, 61–81.

95. Sherwani, *Bahmanis of the Deccan*, 258.

96. Ibid., 317.

97. Eaton, *Social History*, 66.

98. Sherwani, *Bahmanis of the Deccan*, 296.

99. Eaton, *Social History*, 66–67.

100. Sherwani, *Bahmanis of the Deccan*, 296.

101. Fisher, *Visions of Mughal India*, 23.

102. Ferishta quoted in Eaton, *Social History*, 72.

103. Sherwani, *Bahmanis of the Deccan*, 314.

104. Eaton, *Social History*, 70.

105. Sherwani, *Bahmanis of the Deccan*, 334.

106. Gawan quoted in Eaton, *Social History*, 73.

107. Sherwani, *Bahmanis of the Deccan*, 358.

108. Eaton, *Social History*, 73.

III. Hindu Sultans

1. Ferishta quoted in Sherwani, *Bahmanis of the Deccan*, 236–37.

2. Eaton, *Social History*, 104.

3. Mahalingam, *Administration and Social Life*, 319.

4. Sherwani, *Bahmanis of the Deccan*, 236–37. This first group of 2000 is believed to have consisted of mounted archers.

5. Stein, *Vijayanagara*, 20. Subsequently, in the post-imperial era of Vijayanagar's Nayaka successor states, there remained this appetite for

foreigners in service. In the 1630s, Antonio Bocarro, the Portuguese diarist, noted that Tanjore's king hosted many Portuguese mercenaries who were 'allowed to sit down and to wear hats in his presence, and to address him merely as Senhoria'. In the next decade, the Madurai Nayaka was noted by Baltasar da Costa as having 'three or four hundred' Turks in his bodyguard. See Rao, Shulman and Subrahmanyam, *Symbols of Substance*, 232–33.

6. Stein, *Vijayanagara*, 70.

7. Rao, *Mysore Gazetteer*, 1606.

8. Sewell, *Forgotten Empire*, 126–27.

9. Shivarudraswamy, 'Hindu–Muslim Relations,' 394–98.

10. Sarma, 'Rama Raya's Policy,' 144. Rama Raya, the regent and kingmaker during whose time Vijayanagar was destroyed, was originally in service of the Qutb Shah of Golconda.

11. Eaton, *Social History*, 78.

12. Saletore, *Social and Political Life*, 1.

13. Ibid., 14.

14. Sewell, *Forgotten Empire*, 5. See Reddy, *Vijayanagar and its Lessons*, 5, where he lists the 'Hindu' motives behind the founding of the kingdom.

15. Sherwani, *Bahmanis of the Deccan*, 105. This was not peculiar to Ferishta alone. Mary Beard's *SPQR* which studies the early history of Rome also records fantastic numbers that show up in sources, with Beard recommending we read them not as exact figures but as exaggerations of what were certainly large, but not *so* large, numbers.

16. Thangasamy, *Vijayanagar Empire*, 22.

17. Rao, *Mysore Gazetteer*, 1469, and Sewell, *Forgotten Empire*, 32. The ruler was Bukka I who, along with his brothers, is credited as the founder of Vijayanagar. This is not all that surprising – centuries before, the (Hindu) Rashtrakutas had made common cause with the (Muslim) Arab rulers of Sindh against the (Hindu) Gurjara-Pratiharas. Ironically, even the Gurjara-Pratiharas, who appear as staunchly opposed to Arabs in Arab texts, evidently had a jami mosque near their capital in tenth-century Kannauj. See Flood, *Objects of Translation*, 20, 23.

18. Rao, *Mysore Gazetteer*, 1466.

19. Of course, it is important to note that both sides, coming from different cultural contexts, had different conceptions of kingship and what a 'good' king was to do. Thus, for instance, one inscription in Tamil territories, after the fall of the short-lived Madurai Sultanate, lauds the Telugu rulers

of Vijayanagar with the words: 'the times were Tulukkan [i.e. Muslim or Tughluqan even] times and Kampana-Odeyar [the Vijayanagar prince] came on his southerly campaign, destroyed the Muhammedans, established orderly government throughout the country and appointed many nayakkanmar [officials] for inspection and supervision in order that the worship of all temples might be revived and conducted regularly as of old'. See Appadurai, *Worship and Conflict*, 83–84. Here, the Rayas are celebrated ostensibly for restoring the world as it existed before the encounter with Muslim armies and, on the face of it, for protecting classical Hinduism in a time of crisis. But by doing so, these Telugu emperors building a new empire also gained a degree of legitimacy in freshly conquered Tamil territories. In other words, while Bukka could seek an alliance with the Muslim Sultan in Delhi against the Muslim Bahmanis, his son could be cast, without irony, as the protector of high Hinduism in the south against Muslims who had emerged originally from the same Delhi Sultan's court, given that the audiences and intentions were different in both cases. In the former instance, Bukka had strategic interests against the Bahmanis; in the latter, Vijayanagar had a strategic interest in gaining legitimacy and consolidating their power in their new Tamil provinces. This becomes clearer also when further inscriptional evidence shows that the Vijayanagar rulers used the resources of these temples to distribute largesse to local groups, thereby causing these local groups to be beholden to the emperor and to the new Telugu order that was being constructed in Tamil country. Old families and agents lost influence while those placed by Vijayanagar in order to further the imperial centre's interests gained power and economic control. See Appadurai for a more detailed analysis of this period and process.

20. Rao, *Mysore Gazetteer*, 1467.

21. Talbot, 'Inscribing the Self,' 705.

22. Michell, 'Migrations and Cultural Transmissions,' 80–82.

23. Stein, *Vijayanagara*, 28.

24. Rao, *Mysore Gazetteer*, 1601. Even at smaller levels, we see evidence of the same process. The Gadwal Reddy family was originally part of the Kakatiya order. With the fall of Warangal, they eventually transferred their allegiance to the Bahmanis, followed by the Muslim rulers of Bijapur, and then at last the Nizams of Hyderabad, lasting all the way, as a Hindu royal line, till 1948. See Cohen, *Kingship and Colonialism*, 33–34.

25. Kodad, *Ramaraya*, 3.
26. Subrahmanyam, 'Vijayanagar,' 97, and Sinopoli, 'From the Lion Throne,' 380.
27. S. Krishnaswami Aiyangar quoted in Stein, *Vijayanagara*, 5.
28. Filliozat, *Vijayanagar Empire*, 1.
29. Thangasamy, *Vijayanagar Empire*, 29.
30. Ibid., 13.
31. Rao, *Mysore Gazetteer*, 1415.
32. Sharma, 18, and Sewell, *Forgotten Empire*, 23. Their names were Hakka, Kampa, Bukka, Marappa and Muddappa.
33. Subrahmanyam, 'Vijayanagar,' 83.
34. Wagoner, 'Sultan among Hindu Kings,' 874.
35. Thangasamy, *Vijayanagar Empire*, 15.
36. Stein, *Vijayanagara*, 19.
37. Eaton, *Social History*, 38–39.
38. Thangasamy, *Vijayanagar Empire*, 14.
39. Subrahmanyam, 'Vijayanagar,' 86.
40. Eaton, *Social History*, 42.
41. Ibid., 43.
42. Rao, *Mysore Gazetteer*, 1452.
43. Eaton, *Social History*, 42–43, Subrahmanyam, 'Vijayanagar,' 90, Sinopoli, 'From the Lion Throne,' 381, and Wagoner, 'Sultan among Hindu Kings,' 862. The female equivalent of the male suratrana appears to be surathani, judging from the story of the Muslim princess worshipped at the Srirangam temple and the Melkote Thirunarayanapuram temple by that name. She is also known alternatively as Tulukka Nachiyar (Tughluq Princess), her story being that she fell in love with the deity when his processional idol was in the custody of her father, the Sultan, so that upon its return to the south, she followed it and either died here (Srirangam version) or merged with the image (Melkote version), earning a place of respect in temple traditions. See Davis, 'Muslim Princess in the Temples,' 137–56.
44. Eaton, *Social History*, 43, 101.
45. Wagoner, 'Sultan among Hindu Kings,' 862.
46. Eaton, *Social History*, 43.
47. Anooshahr, 'Elephant and the Sovereign,' 1–30. Such adoptions of titles, symbols, and more were a two-way street. Ali Anooshahr has shown how, after the Ghaznavid encounter with India – remembered for the

destruction of the Somnath temple in 1024 – the elephant, which was a
symbol of kingship among Hindus, was adopted by this Turkic dynasty,
with Sultan Mahmud often appearing atop magnificent beasts acquired
from India, appropriating a tradition Hindu in its origins. And this when
in Islam, strictly speaking, the elephant was seen as an animal of Satan.
Similarly in a battle he fought in present-day Turkmenistan, the Sultan
not only deployed elephants but also had his military men sound Indian
instruments, including the *shankh* or conch, again so strongly associated
with Hindu ritual. Mahmud (and before him his father also), furthermore,
struck bilingual Arabic–Sanskrit coins, in which the Sanskrit side identified
the Prophet Muhammad as an 'avatar', describing him as 'Narapati' or Lord
of Men in a familiar Indian vocabulary. See Flood, *Objects of Translation*,
3. Meanwhile, the *Rajatarangini* of twelfth-century Kashmir refers to
Harsha (r. 1089–1111) as a 'Rajaturuska', i.e. Turk-king 'on account of his
fondness for Turkic dress and women and occasional bouts of violent image
destruction'.

48. There is also a connection to the Ramayana, and Hampi is believed in some
traditions to be the land of Hanuman.

49. Sewell, *Forgotten Empire*, 19.

50. Rao, *Mysore Gazetteer*, 1430. In another version, it was Vidyaranya himself
who established the city and then granted it to the Sangama brothers. The
Rayavacakamu states that the city was built on fresh ground, while the
Vidyaranya Kriti puts forth that the city was built on the ruins of a once-
great but forgotten city, also called Vijayanagar. There is also a story that
has Vidyaranya causing gold to rain from the heavens, providing the new
capital its initial financial basis.

51. Sinopoli, 'From the Lion Throne,' 372.

52. Ibid., 369.

53. In a similar way, Bukka's son Kampana restored a royal temple of the
Hoysalas in Tamil Kannanur, which had been converted into a mosque,
once again into a temple in 1372, which was both a way of rejecting the
Turks and highlighting Vijayanagar's claim to legitimate and just rule.

54. Rao, *Mysore Gazetteer*, 1421.

55. Saletore, *Social and Political Life*, 8.

56. Davis, 'Muslim Princess in the Temples,' 118. When he wins, the
Madhuravijayam tells us, the world is again at peace: 'With the Persians
destroyed, the south shone again. It shone like the luster of forests when

a forest fire has been put out. It shone like the bowl of the sky when an eclipse has just ended. It shone like the Yamuna River after Krishna killed the serpent-demon Kaliya.' See ibid., 119.

57. Stein, *Vijayanagara*, 1. Many centuries later, when Tanjore was under Maratha rulers, they too sought a link to ancient dynasties. Serfoji II, the last prominent ruler, even when his power was limited to Tanjore fort and its immediate environs, proudly styled himself Choladesadhipati, or Overlord of the Chola Country.

58. Ibid., 65–66. This also has precedent. In Leslie Orr's 1995 study, referred to by Davis, a study of all 644 inscriptions of the Srirangam temple, for example, showed that kings do not appear as frequent donors till the mid-thirteenth century. 'Only in the period of conflict and dynastic transition, with Pandyas and Hoysalas contesting control over the old [Chola] core territories, did Sri Rangam emerge as a significant site for royal donation and legitimation.' See Davis, 'Muslim Princess in the Temples,' 278. It should also be added that Brahmins, with all the advantages of their caste, were favoured by Vijayanagar rulers as officials. See Mahalingam, *Administration and Social Life*, 241–42.

59. Kamath, *Krishnadevaraya of Vijayanagar*, 5. Legitimacy was also certainly derived from the role of the new rulers as restorers of a classical, Brahminical Hinduism, meant evidently to appeal to a priestly class that was integral to giving recognition to the royal house. In the *Madhuravijayam*, aka *Kamparaya Charitam*, a daughter-in-law of the first Raya of Vijayanagar evoked images of the destruction wreaked upon that temple town. Describing the state of the shrine, she writes: 'White-ants have destroyed the doors; the doorframe of the sanctum sanctorum is broken due to the wild growth of trees, plants and creepers . . . the temple premises that formerly echoed the soft beating of the *mridangas* are now full of wild wallowing jackals . . . The place once filled with the odour of the sacrificial smoke and the melodious chant of Vedic mantras is now full of the foul smell of meat and the shouting noise of the Turushkas . . . The coconut palms that bore the weight of their bunches of coconuts are now cut and used as stakes and hung with mercilessly beheaded skulls . . . The royal roads filled with the pleasant sound of the anklet bells of beautiful maidens that traversed them are filled with the unbearable wailing shouts of Brahmins being carried in chains and these shouts pierce the ears like spikes . . . The beautiful lines of salabhanjikas (images of maids) that adore the tall towers of the beautiful

buildings in the city that were covered with silken screens are now covered with layers of cobwebs. The holy river is filled with the blood of cows.' But while Vijayanagar's princess laments the sufferings of the city, the enemy is still not painted in religious colours. The irony lies in the fact that in the poem there are two enemies, one of whom are the Turks and the other fellow Hindus – the Sambuvarayas – who, in the wake of Malik Kafur's destruction, had established themselves in Kanchi. The Sambuvarayas are treated as the branches of a tree, while the Turks are the metaphorical trunk – their faiths do not appear. See Rao, 'From Fear to Hostility,' 72. Accounts of destruction that upsets the correct order of things appear, in fact, in clashes between Hindu kings also – in 1007 when Rajaraja Chola's army seized the area around Bijapur, a local inscription tells, they went about 'ravaging the whole country, perpetuating murders of women, children, and Brahmins, seizing women, and overthrowing the order of caste'. See Davis, 'Muslim Princess in the Temples,' 82. Enemies, regardless of faith, then, were painted as barbaric destroyers of a previous paradise, compared to demons or *asuras* who battled *devas* or gods. It is also interesting to note, as Davis does (ibid., 121). that the Telugu Vijayanagar ruler was also an outsider in Madurai and therefore, 'To make himself less of a foreigner in Tamil country, it would help to make the Turks more so.' Vijayanagar, by restoring a 'classical' order by expelling meat-eating, wine-drinking 'demons' also, thus, builds up its own legitimacy in new territory. And yet, the fact that there remained tensions, still, is clear from the account of Roberto Nobili, an Italian Jesuit, who worked in Madurai in the early seventeenth century – he suggested in his accounts that the Nayaka successors of Vijayanagar there were not altogether seen as legitimate since they were Telugus who had only arrived in this Tamil region some decades before. See Zupanov, *Disputed Mission*, 112.

60. Rao, *Mysore Gazetteer*, 1483. This was an extension of the Idangai–Valangai feud that existed between different groups from the time of the Chola kings, and the Jains were now confirmed as members of the right-hand castes. These groups could also revolt against the state – one inscription reads as follows: 'We, the people belonging to the Valangai 98 [castes] and Idangai 98 of Valudilampattu-*uchavadi*, assembled . . . in full strength and let the following be engraved on the wall of said temple. In this *mandalam*, even if the *uchavadi pradhani* [the local Vijayanagar governor], Vanniyar [military people] and *jivitakkarar*

[holders of official tenure] coerce us, or the Brahmana and Vellala *kaniyalar* [holders of *kani* right] try to oppress us in collusion with the *irajagarattar* [government officers], we shall never submit to such oppression.' See Karashima, *Towards a New Formation*, 142. These groups included merchants, weavers, blacksmiths, carpenters, craftsmen, potters and others from the lower echelons of society at the time.

61. Stoker, *Polemics and Patronage*, 153. Stoker says that the *Vyasa Vijaya* conveys 'a story of Vyasatirtha's confrontation at Kanchi with Shaivas, who refused to let Vyasatirtha enter the temple to Ranganatha on the grounds that Jambukesvara, a form of Siva, was also there. Vyasatirtha arranged to run throughout the jurisdiction holding his breath. The territory he covered would subsequently belong to Ranganatha and what remained would belong to Jambukesvara.' These stories carry in them hints of intra-Hindu competition within specific shrines, as well as for royal patronage. The rulers themselves appear to have tilted from Shaivism at the time of the founding of the kingdom, to favouring Vaishnavism by the time of Devaraya I in the early fifteenth century. There was, however, no formal affiliation nor are there signs of discrimination, though there appears to be caste rivalry and we see in the songs of the saint Purandaradasa, for instance, reflections of this.

62. Subrahmanyam, 'Vijayanagar,' 91.

63. Chekuri, '"Share" in the "World Empire",' 41–50, 62. Thus, between 1371 and 1530, the Tamil lands of the empire were divided among, as per one assessment, fifty-eight nayakas, all of whom derived legitimacy from the authority of the Raya. See Palat, 'Popular Revolts and the State,' 136–37. Noboru Karashima's surveys show altogether 500 nayaka inscriptions in what is today Tamil Nadu, indicating that there may have been even more. See Karashima, *Concordance of Nayakas*, 12, which also contains a comprehensive, alphabetical listing of Vijayanagar Nayakas by name. This system also led to a break from the past, especially in Tamil areas, where earlier changes of dynasties did not lead to a replacement of local institutions on the ground. The amaranayakas, however, changed this and saw such local institutions as 'stumbling blocks' to the power of the centre wielded through them – those old institutions were replaced by forming direct alliances with certain elites and certain temples, on new terms and in a new understanding. See Hall, 'Structural Change and Societal Integration,' 3. It should also be noted that the concept of nayakas did exist in Warangal

from the time of the Kakatiyas – the Vijayanagar amaranayakas were, in
that sense, a new manifestation of an older institution.

64. Rao, *Mysore Gazetteer*, 1534.

65. Ibid., 1540.

66. Ibid., 1556.

67. Ibid., 1554.

68. Which is why, to some, the term 'empire' applied to it can be a little
misleading – we stick to it in this book in the sense that it was a large,
diverse entity with 'little kings', and masses of population from different
linguistic and cultural backgrounds, held ultimately under one common
political umbrella. There was thus the centre, provincial chiefs (the future
Nayaka kings), and concentric devolutions of power under them. Indeed,
the bhakti saint Kanakadasa's father, a chieftain of the Kuruba caste, is also
supposed to have been a Vijayanagar revenue collector, holding power in
this loose chain of command. Kanakadasa inherited his father's position,
and it was on one of his official visits to Vijayanagar that he came across
the saint Vyasatirtha and commenced his journey on the path of bhakti,
according to legend. He was, in fact, before transforming into Kanakadasa,
known as Kanaka Nayaka. Furthermore, Burton Stein has shown how even
in the day of so powerful a monarch as Krishnadeva Raya, the chieftains of
Canara carried out their affairs, petty wars, and political business without
reference to the capital or their overlord, retaining autonomy.

69. Sinopoli, 'From the Lion Throne,' 370.

70. John Haywood quoted in Stoker, *Polemics and Patronage*, 143.

71. Eaton, *Social History*, 85–86. See Palat, 'Popular Revolts and the State,' an
excellent essay on agrarian revolts in the Tamil provinces of Vijayanagar,
and Stoker, 'Polemics and Patronage,' that discusses monastic orders and
the Vijayanagar empire's attempt to weld together its diverse provinces
through the patronage of these *matha*s.

72. Rao, *Mysore Gazetteer*, 1530. See Mahalingam, *Administration and Social
Life*.

73. Eaton, *Social History*, 85. See Karashima, *Towards a New Formation*, which
discusses how, in the fifteenth century, Vijayanagar amaranayakas seem
to have acted as all initial invading forces do, with brutality and force,
leading to discontent among the people. By the sixteenth century, however,
inscriptional evidence demonstrates a settling down of the new order, and
greater peace in the functioning of the amaranayaka system.

74. Mahalingam, *Administration and Social Life*, 65.

75. Guha, 'The Frontiers of Memory,' 273.

76. Nuniz quoted in Filliozat, *Vijayanagar Empire*, 83.

77. Thangasamy, *Vijayanagar Empire*, 41–42.

78. Abdur Razzak quoted in Alam and Subrahmanyam, *Indo-Persian Travels*, 70.

79. Abdur Razzak quoted in Rao, *Mysore Gazetteer*, 1588–89.

80. Abdur Razzak quoted in Khan, *Deccan Policy*, 40.

81. Abdur Razzak quoted in Sharma, *History of the Vijayanagar Empire: Beginnings*, 62–63. The poet Srinatha, however, was quite disappointed by the quality of the food served in Vijayanagar's hotels, if one of his compositions is to be believed.

82. Abdur Razzak quoted in Sewell, *Forgotten Empire*, 92. Razzak was even impressed by sights outside the capital, during his journey into Vijayanagar. Some three leagues outside Mangalore, for instance, this man who in Calicut, Kerala, had denounced local customs and practices, was fascinated by a Hindu temple, its chief image made of gold. 'It had two red rubies for eyes, so cunningly made that you would say it could see. What craft and artisanship!' he cried. See Alam and Subrahmanyam, *Indo-Persian Travels*, 68.

83. Eaton, *Social History*, 102.

84. Wagoner, 'Sultan among Hindu Kings,' 865–66.

85. Eaton, *Social History*, 86.

86. Sinopoli, 'From the Lion Throne,' 385–87. This influence of 'foreign' clothing is not unusual. In the thirteenth century, in Buddhist Ladakh, for instance, Turkish qabas were appropriated as court dress by royalty and the elites. See Flood, *Objects of Translation*, 66.

87. Ibid., 373.

88. Abdur Razzak quoted in Alam and Subrahmanyam, *Indo-Persian Travels*, 73. The ambassador seems to have had some dealings with local prostitutes. 'Each of them is richly arrayed with pearls and jewels, and elegant clothes on their bodies,' Razzak noted. 'They are very young in age, and perfect in beauty. And before them stand one or two slave-girls, praising pleasure, with the doors of joy open, and the instruments of music ready and laid out. Whoever comes there and wishes to do so, enjoys himself. The people there take care of the guests' belongings, and if anything is lost, they compensate him.'

89. Eaton, *Social History*, 101.

90. Sinopoli, 'From the Lion Throne,' 383.

91. Another indication we get of contemporary links with Persia and elsewhere is from the *Haravilasam* of Srinatha, a poet patronized by Devaraya II. Referring to a merchant-sponsor of his called Tipayya Setti of Nellore, Srinatha tells how the latter was an importer of horses from Hormuz ('Hurumanji'), elephants from Sri Lanka, and even goods from Goa, the Punjab in the north and China in the far east. These goods, thereafter, were supplied not only to the Vijayanagar court but also to Orissa and the Bahmani Sultans. See Ayyangar, *Sources of Vijayanagar History*, 4, 57.

92. Eaton, *Social History*, 102. The ruler by whom Devaraya II was so fascinated was Shahrukh of Persia, Timur's son.

93. Stein, *Vijayanagara*, 70.

94. Alam and Subrahmanyam, *Indo-Persian Travels*, 79–82.

95. Abdur Razzak, Devaraya II's contemporary, names the culprit as a brother, while much later Nuniz notes the assassin to be the king's nephew.

96. Abdur Razzak quoted in Sewell, *Forgotten Empire*, 73.

97. Ibid.

98. Ibid.

99. Nuniz quoted in Rao, *Mysore Gazetteer*, 1575–76.

100. Abdur Razzak quoted in Sewell, *Forgotten Empire*, 74.

101. Nuniz quoted in Rao, *Mysore Gazetteer*, 1575–76.

102. Ibid.

103. The first of what is believed to be several joint invasions appears in a Sanskrit work known as the *Gangadasapratapa Vilasam*, and in that instance appears to have been repulsed, though the flexing of muscles by the king of Orissa and the Bahmani Sultan graduated into gains even as Vijayanagar's power eroded.

104. Subrahmanyam, 'Vijayanagar,' 102.

105. Sharma, *History of the Vijayanagar Empire: Beginnings*, 87. The author states that contrary to popular belief, Saluva was a military title and not the name of a family.

106. The Customs Department employee Devaraya II's sister married was his uncle. One of his ancestors, Saluva Mangu, is supposed to have been part of the famous conquest of Madurai by Vijayanagar in the late fourteenth century, and was a major patron of the great temple in Srirangam, according to the *Saluva Abhyudayam*.

107. Subrahmanyam, 'Vijayanagar,' 104.

108. Stein, *Vijayanagara*, 30.

109. The unfortunate father, Virupaksha II, was himself a usurper. See Ayyangar, *Sources of Vijayanagar History*, 68–69.

110. Thangasamy, *Vijayanagar Empire*, 47.

111. Ibid.

112. Perera, *Sexuality in Ancient India*, 148. This is the *Ratiratnapradipika*. Saluva Narasimha himself, incidentally, was a composer and is supposed to have authored the *Rama Abhyudayam*, a retelling of the Ramayana.

113. Subrahmanyam, 'Vijayanagar,' 105.

114. There is an interesting story about Saluva Narasimha who once met the poet-saint Annamacharya around the time of his usurpation of power. He asked the saint to write a few verses in his honour, to which Annamacharya replied: 'My tongue has no knowledge of praising a man like yourself; it is skilled only in praising Lord Hari.'

115. Subrahmanyam, *Courtly Encounters*, 13.

116. Caesaro Federici quoted in Sewell, *Forgotten Empire*, 208.

IV. Rebel Sultans

1. Sherwani, *Bahmanis of the Deccan*, 386.

2. In the case of the Barid Shahs, the title was taken in 1542 by the third of the line.

3. Yazdani, *Bidar, Its History*, 12.

4. Sherwani, *Bahmanis of the Deccan*, 293. The chieftain was one Sabaji who appears to have controlled the area around Jalna.

5. Thomaz, 'Iranian Diaspora,' 10. Ferishta also refers to this Ottoman story but Turkish records show no son of Murad II called Yusuf, though he did have a brother by that name. Cousens, *Bijapur*, 80–81. Cousens describes how Yusuf's mother purchased a slave 'who was remarkably like her son' and had this boy killed and buried, while the actual Yusuf escaped with the merchant who'd sold her the decoy slave Yusuf. In due course the prince had a vision telling him his destiny awaited him in India, and so he left his homeland and came to the Deccan. Subrahmanyam, *Three Ways to be Alien*, 35. Additionally, Subrahmanyam provides Dom Fernando de Castro's account where Yusuf was merely a big merchant's servant who, having made a major loss on a deal in India, chose to stay back in the country, entering

Bahmani service and rising thereafter to prominence.

6. Nayeem in *External Relations of the Bijapur Kingdom* states that he was 'Yusuf Beg Turkman of the Aq-Quyunlu tribe of Diyarbykir in eastern Anatolia' and that his father was the 'Wali of Sawa' in Iran. After 'wandering in Iran' as a young man, Yusuf eventually came to India.

7. Eraly, *The Mughal Throne*, 144.

8. Joshi, 'Adil Shahis,' 291. Before he became Gawan's protégé, Yusuf benefited from the affection and patronage of a senior nobleman, the Nizam-ul-Mulk, who fell in battle in the late 1460s.

9. Nayeem, *External Relations*, 44.

10. Ali, *African Dispersal*, 49.

11. Sherwani, *Bahmanis of the Deccan*, 392.

12. Thomaz, 'Iranian Diaspora,' 23.

13. Taylor, *History of India*, 181, 209.

14. Wagoner, *Tidings of the King*, 62. Reference is to the *Rayavacakamu*.

15. Joshi, 'Adil Shahis,' 293.

16. Ibid., 296.

17. Ibid., 297.

18. Ibid., 296.

19. With Yusuf's resources and the strength of his armies – and given that he had not yet formally thrown off the suzerainty of the titular Sultan in Bidar – there was little Qasim Barid could do to stop him. In 1495, in fact, Yusuf succeeded in a major diplomatic coup by having the Bahmani crown prince betrothed to his own daughter, the endearingly named Bibi Sitti. See Sherwani, *Bahmanis of the Deccan*, 377. Two other daughters, Mariam and Khadija, also made political marriages into the Nizam Shah's and Imad Shah's houses, but with Bibi Sitti, Yusuf's intention was to assert a degree of equality with the royal line. He might have reconsidered the match, though, had he known that his son-in-law would go down in history as that pathetic wretch who sold the Bahmani crown jewels for coins. Or, worse still, that after her husband died, Bibi Sitti would end up in the arms of none other than the cunning Qasim Barid's son (ibid., 416–17). It must have been another unhappy experience for the lady, who had to jostle for space with not only his earlier Maratha wife, but also reconcile with her husband's other affairs. For Qasim Barid's son had even less respect for the Bahmanis than did his father, and when one of the subsequent namesake Sultans expressed outrage after he seduced his wife, Barid simply had him

poisoned. By this time, the very title of Sultan was a travesty, its holder supplied food and clothing, but every other decision concerning even his most mundane domestic affairs directed by agents of the Baridis. No wonder that the last of the Bahmanis disappeared to Mecca in the 1530s with what dignity he could salvage, preferring never to return.

20. Anwar, 'The Safavids,' 257, and Nayeem, *External Relations*, 22. It would be some more years before they started using the title.

21. Nayeem, *External Relations*, 58.

22. Joshi, 'Adil Shahis,' 298.

23. Nayeem, *External Relations*, 48.

24. Joshi, 'Adil Shahis,' 299.

25. Nayeem, *External Relations*, 33.

26. Joshi, 'Adil Shahis,' 300.

27. Nayeem, *External Relations*, 28.

28. Ibid., 20.

29. Eaton, *Social History*, 91, 102.

30. Mathew, *History of the Portuguese*, 193. Amusingly, in order to demonstrate defiant confidence in the face of crisis, the Portuguese made a great show of their grand 'banquet' even though it was rats and leather broth that they were really eating! See Moxham, *Theft of India*.

31. Joshi, 'Adil Shahis,' 303.

32. Shastry, 'Commercial Policy,' 632. And by 1576, after more unsuccessful attempts to displace the Europeans with the aid of Indian and foreign allies, the Adil Shahs would accept the *cartaz* system whereby ships paid a certain fee to obtain from Goa a licence to sail, which guaranteed safety in an Arabian Sea increasingly controlled by the Portuguese.

33. Joshi, 'Adil Shahis,' 305–06. The assassin was, incidentally, a man named Yusuf, while the regent was known as Kamal Khan.

34. Ibid., 395. In the battle that resulted as a consequence, the regent's son besieged Bijapur. And in one of the most curious instances of death in the history of the Deccan, at one point during the bloody proceedings, the man took shelter under a parapet and there met his end – the young Ismail was sitting just above and, recognizing his enemy below, smashed him to pulp by simply having a large rock dropped on him (ibid., 306–07). When the Barid Shah, incandescent at the frustration of his grand scheme, attacked the state, flaunting the (theoretically) august presence of the Bahmani Sultan with him, not only did Ismail's men defeat the invaders, but they

also took temporary custody of the poor sovereign while his keeper rode away to safety. Sixteen years later, Ismail would have his revenge, when one night during the campaign, while the Barid Shah lay drunk in his camp, Ismail's men made a surprise attack and carried the man (with his bed) to their prince. Bidar fort, which the Barid Shah's sons had refused to surrender, was finally handed over once it was made clear that for every minute the boys dawdled, their father came closer and closer to the foot of a large and angry elephant. It was another matter, of course, that once set free the Barid Shah cunningly recovered all that he had lost – where his armies let him down, the man knew how to use his brains.

35. Ibid., 310, 319.
36. Ibid., 314–15.
37. Mallu Adil Shah wasn't even permitted to be properly remembered. When Chand Muhammad and Kamal Muhammad produced their famous painting *The House of Bijapur*, which features all the Adil Shahs seated together on a single carpet, the only ruler left out was this ill-fated son of Ismail Adil Shah.
38. Subrahmanyam, *Three Ways to be Alien*, 58.
39. Ibid., 28.
40. Joshi, 'Adil Shahis,' 321. Joshi places these events in the 1540s and the rival is named as a brother called Abdullah, but from Subrahmanyam's sources, the account of Miyan Ali appears to be more authentic.
41. Subrahmanyam notes that the change of heart came on account of a change of leadership in Goa – when the new viceroy arrived, he refused to act on his predecessor's promise to the Adil Shah.
42. Luis Frois quoted in Subrahmanyam, *Three Ways to be Alien*, 29.
43. Ibid.
44. Ibid., 32.
45. Ibid., 69. A similar story can be found in Kerala. The naval commanders of the Zamorin of Calicut in the sixteenth century were four Muslim men, all styled Kunjali Marakkar, who constituted a short-lived dynasty of sorts, becoming a thorn in the Portuguese's back for many years. In 1600 Kunjali IV, the last of the line, was captured and taken to Goa, where he was beheaded and quartered, but a cousin of his had converted to Christianity a little before, taking the name Dom Pedro Rodrigues and marrying a Portuguese woman. Eventually, however, Dom Pedro wriggled out of Portuguese control, seized his birth family's naval traditions and harassed

Portuguese vessels at sea for nearly two decades, before disappearing from history. He is said to have given up the Christian faith and taken the name Ali Marakkar after escaping from Goa.

46. Eaton, *Social History*, 91.

47. Joshi, 'Adil Shahis,' 325.

48. Eaton, 'Sufis of Bijapur,' 80.

49. Ibid., 82.

50. Dale, *Islamic Society*, 6. Reference is to Zayn al-Din's *Tuhfat al-Mujahidin*, composed around 1584. The author dedicated his work to Ali Adil Shah 'because that ruler was known for his devotion to the *jihad*'.

51. Reference is to Ibrahim Adil Shah II. However, Ali too was a not insignificant patron of the arts, though he was pragmatic about who he supported. Rafi al-Din Shirazi notes: 'The emperor was generous . . . unrestrained, and unceremonious. He never adorned or decorated himself, nor his own palace, and he was of a Sufi temperament. From every place in the country the hermits, whether Muslim or Hindu, now went to converse with him and he weighed each with the touchstone of proof. If he found ecstasy in him he honoured him and took care of him and sometimes went to converse with him. And having the favor of honoring (him) he gave him leave. He never fettered anyone with land or property.' Similarly, 'The sultan was very fond of books and reading. He had collected numerous books relating to all types of subjects, so much so that his library had become completely full.'

52. Cousens quoted in Gray, 'Deccani Paintings,' 74.

53. Ibid., 75.

54. Hutton, *Art of the Court*, 10. Though not constructed in this period, the magnificent dome of the Gol Gumbaz tomb so struck British architects that its method of construction became the staple design for domes in the Indo-Saracenic buildings of the colonial age, scattering a little bit of Bijapur across the Indian terrain.

55. Eaton, 'Sufis of Bijapur,' 88.

56. He was titled 'Sarang Khan' by the Sultan. See Sherwani, 'Reign of Sultan Humayun,' 693–94.

57. Briggs, *Rise of the Mahomedan Power*, 197.

58. Ibid., 192.

59. Ibid., 213.

60. Shyam, 'Nizam Shahis,' 235. Her name was Amna.

61. Ibid.

62. Nayeem, *External Relations*, 60.

63. Harris, *First Firangis*, 30.

64. Ibid., 32, 40.

65. Rotzer, 'Deccani Guns,' 129–31. This gun later seems to have passed into Adil Shahi hands. Ironically, in Europe such heavy guns had ceased being deployed a hundred years earlier.

66. Harris, *First Firangis*, 41–46.

67. Ibid., 32.

68. Shyam, *Kingdom of Ahmadnagar*, 105–06. One, for instance, who married the Imad Shah's daughter, disappeared into his territory, though after Husain issued warnings to Imad Shah, that brother was expelled from Berar. Three others sought shelter with their mother's sibling, Ibrahim, in Bijapur. This uncle happened to be none other than that eccentric, hot-tempered Adil Shah who massacred dozens of noblemen and got all his doctors to scurry in fear – he now decided to take up the cause of one of his nephews, if in return he was handed over the district of Solapur. Alarmed by this combination, Husain rehabilitated his relations with the Imad Shah. The first ambassador he deputed annoyed that ruler by sleeping with his favourite mistress, but a second Brahmin envoy successfully closed the deal. Shyam, *Kingdom of Ahmadnagar*, 105–06.

69. Ibid., 109.

70. Part of this may have been because the then Qutb Shah had spent years in exile in Vijayanagar and owed its ruler his life.

71. Kodad, *Ramaraya*, 7.

72. Eaton, *Social History*, 91. Ramaraya's father was Aravidu Bukka who was closely associated with Saluva Narasimha before switching over to the founders of Krishnadeva's dynasty. Another ancestor, Somadeva Raja, in Muhammad Shah I Bahmani's day is supposed to have conquered seven forts in a single campaign, even, according to a literary source, taking the Sultan himself prisoner and extracting a promise that the Muslim ruler would name his son after him (Somadeva). See Ayyangar, *Sources of Vijayanagar History*, 79.

73. Kodad, *Ramaraya*, preface.

74. The *Achutyaraya Abhyudayam* suggests that this ruler's reign began with promise and that he was an efficient military man, who early on defeated the Adil Shah in battle. The troubles with his reign, then, evidently began

with the ascent of his brothers-in-law to influence. And after his death, it was ironic that his wife, Varadambika, sought the same Adil Shah's aid to protect their son.

75. This was when Ramaraya championed the cause of Krishnadeva's only remaining son, who too, however, soon died.

76. Kodad, *Ramaraya*, 3. See Reddy, *Vijayanagar and Its Lessons*, 36.

77. Ibid., 43.

78. Ibid., 36. Inscriptional evidence also shows that a number of prominent Vijayanagar amaranayakas were members of the Aravidu family – Cynthia Talbot traces thirteen nobles who belonged to this clan, some of them traceable as Ramaraya's first cousins, and others as a little more distant in their exact relationship. Adding members of another branch of the family, we come up to seven more, to which can further be added, to explain Ramaraya's influence, two amaranayakas who were drawn into this group through marriage, making a total of twenty-one nobles, closely related to the man who controlled actual power. See Talbot, 'Nayakas of Vijayanagara Andhra,' 259.

79. Subrahmanyam, 'Vijayanagar,' 25.

80. Eaton also notes that, as Ramaraya's power grew more secure, he began a quest to establish his own dynastic identity, tracing back his lineage to the Chalukyas. He was titled in several ways that linked him to the Chalukyas of Kalyana, a city that for generations lay in the northern Deccan in the hands of its Sultans.

81. Joshi, 'Adil Shahis,' 325–26.

82. Eaton, *Social History*, 96. Ferishta again notes, however, that just like with Firoz Shah Bahmani and his Vijayanagar father-in-law, this time too when the Adil Shah departed Ramaraya did not escort him out a sufficient distance. It was a slight, and the Adil Shah would not forget it.

83. The Imad Shah was also his father-in-law.

84. Shyam, *Kingdom of Ahmadnagar*, 111.

85. Ibid.

86. Eaton, *Social History*, 96.

87. Shyam, *Kingdom of Ahmadnagar*, 113.

88. Eaton, *Social History*, 97.

89. Shyam, 'Nizam Shahis,' 246.

90. Ferishta quoted in ibid.

91. Eaton, *Social History*, 98.

92. The Portuguese also note this turning point, though Husain appears as the chief architect of the league against Vijayanagar. Diego do Couto notes that after 'Rama Rajo' had 'entered the kingdoms of the Nizamoxa and destroyed and devastated them, and carried great riches away from them', Husain was 'so afflicted' that he 'invited the (other) Moorish kings of the Deccan, the Idalxa, Cutibuxa, and Verido so that they could all set out together against Rama Rajo, and destroy him, and divide his kingdoms amongst them'.

93. Subrahmanyam, 'Vijayanagar,' 127.

94. Shyam, 'Nizam Shahis,' 246.

95. Joshi, 'Adil Shahis,' 329.

96. Subrahmanyam, *Courtly Encounters*, 58–59. This comes across in Portuguese records which credit Persian ambassadors with conveying the Shah's suggestion as to how to deal with Vijayanagar.

97. Shyam, 'Nizam Shahis,' 246.

98. Joshi, 'Adil Shahis,' 330.

99. Shyam, *Kingdom of Ahmadnagar*, 126.

100. Joshi, 'Adil Shahis,' 331. The Imad Shahi state was under a regency at this time and was therefore not as fully involved in these military affairs.

101. While in 1520 the Adil Shah placed all his guns in a single line and lived to regret that decision – since the process of reloading meant that suddenly none of the guns was functional, as stated earlier – now in 1565 the guns were placed in three rows, so that when one line was being reloaded, there was another steadily firing. Where the Sultans had 600 cannon, Ramaraya had 1000 at his command, besides 2000 elephants, but with this strategy it was the Sultans who prevailed. It is also said he had 3000 Portuguese mercenaries in his service as gunners, though this number might be an exaggeration.

102. Joshi, 'Adil Shahis,' 332.

103. Shyam, *Kingdom of Ahmadnagar*, 137.

104. Joshi, 'Adil Shahis,' 332.

105. Shyam, 'Nizam Shahis,' 247.

106. Eaton and Wagoner, 'Warfare on the Deccan,' 39–40.

107. Eaton, *Social History*, 98. One account has it that Husain asked after Ramaraya's health and after a polite (or perhaps sarcastic) exchange, had him killed.

108. Subrahmanyam, *Courtly Encounters*, 55.

109. Row, *History of Vijayanagar*, 13.

110. Ramaraya's brother Tirumala first retained Sadasiva as titular monarch. But by 1571 he took the imperial title for himself, having also bypassed the claim made by Ramaraya's son. This is known as the Aravidu dynasty. In 1566–67 Tirumala had also briefly tried to reoccupy Vijayanagar but the city was so devastated that he eventually had to give it up altogether. Meanwhile, with the authority of the Rayas weakened, the amaranayakas who ruled the provinces began to rebel. And by the early seventeenth century we come to what is known as the Nayaka period of South Indian history where families that were once Vijayanagar's governors came to reign as sovereigns from Madurai, Gingee, Tanjore, Mysore and Ikkeri. See Rao, Shulman and Subrahmanyam, *Symbols of Substance*, for a detailed historical analysis of these Nayaka states.

111. Sewell quoted in Reddy, *Vijayanagar and Its Lessons*, 38.

112. Ferishta quoted in Thangasamy, *Vijayanagar Empire*, 87.

113. Ghulam Ali Astarabari quoted in Subrahmanyam, *Courtly Encounters*, 52. It does seem possible that Ibrahim Qutb Shah (who had been Ramaraya's guest for seven years when fleeing his brother, Jamshir) and to some extent Ali Adil Shah (who was his adopted 'son') were hesitant about beheading the Vijayanagar ruler. Art in Aftabi's *Tarif-i Husain Shah* also features, as Subrahmanyam notes, the Qutb Shah attempting to stop Husain Nizam Shah from carrying on the execution of Ramaraya. See ibid., 98.

114. Sewell, *Forgotten Empire*, 208

115. Vijayanagar, though the empire fell, continued in the form of successor states as mentioned above, much like the Bahmani Sultanate, for another century. As late as 1642, thus, we find a great-grandson of Ramaraya's seeking aid from the Adil Shah in Bijapur during his wars against the Tirumala Nayak of Madurai, who in turn was supported by the Qutb Shah in Golconda. In 1648 Vellore came into Golconda's hands, while the next year Gingee was annexed by Bijapur, and this last of Ramaraya's family died without a kingdom of his own. The process took some time – in 1608 we find the Nayakas of Tanjore and Madurai sending tribute to the Aravidu Raya, but not the Nayaka of Gingee, against whom an army then had to be sent. Similarly, Manuel Barradas, around the same time, wrote of how when the Raya's ambassador came to collect tribute from Tanjore, the Nayaka treated him with great honour and regard. In other words, the Nayaka kingdoms broke off slowly, constantly testing the authority of the Rayas over them, after the fall of the capital in Vijayanagar. We see a parallel of this in the

eighteenth century in the Mughal empire as well – when Nadir Shah sacked Delhi and shattered the prestige of the emperor in 1739, feudatories in Bengal, Awadh, and elsewhere slowly began to break away, becoming less than regular in transmitting money to the imperial centre, and eventually ceasing such payment of tribute altogether.

V. Saraswati's Son

1. Sherwani, *Bahmanis of the Deccan*, 417–18. Neither of which province was in his possession to give away, as it happened.
2. Anwar, *Mughals and the Deccan*, 41.
3. Sinha, *Mediaeval History*, 75–76. Sinha makes the point that Kalimullah was Yusuf Adil Shah's grandson from his daughter, Bibi Sitti.
4. Ibid.
5. Pearson, 'Shivaji and the Decline,' 89.
6. Rathore, "Floating Political Rhetoric," 252.
7. Khan, *Deccan Policy*, 30–33. Alam and Subrahmanyam in *Writing the Mughal World*, 193, also note that the Portuguese might have been involved in the death of Akbar's son Prince Murad in 1599.
8. Alam and Subrahmanyam, 'Deccan Frontier,' 370.
9. McInerney, 'Mughals in the Deccan,' 281.
10. Joshi, *Reign of Ibrahim*, 295–96.
11. Anwar, 'The Safavids,' 56.
12. At first, Akbar had wanted to lead the campaign himself, eventually placing Daniyal in charge along with Prince Murad (who, however, resented the chain of command because Daniyal was younger than him).
13. Gouchani and Wannell, 'The Inscriptions of Ibrahim Rauza Tomb,' 276.
14. Joshi, 'Adil Shahis,' 336. These eunuchs were servants of a dead sister of his who was married to the Imad Shah, and had been sent to Bijapur by the latter.
15. Sherwani, *Muhammad-Quli Qutb Shah*, 82.
16. Ali, *Malik Ambar*, 42. It is likely, however, that the paintings were made after her time, though her mother certainly did appear in pictures when she was alive, and there is no reason to doubt that Chand Bibi too was therefore painted while she was alive.
17. Gribble, *History of the Deccan*, vol. 1, 214–15.
18. Briggs, *History of the Rise*, 144–45.

19. Ibid., 148.

20. Ibid., 155. See Joshi, 'Adil Shahis,' 338–39.

21. Joshi, 'Adil Shahis,' 340.

22. Briggs, *History of the Rise*, 159.

23. Ibid., 167.

24. Joshi, *Reign of Ibrahim*, 284.

25. Ibid., 291–92. The fort was Satara fort.

26. Ibid., 294. The brother's name was Ismail, and they were both sons of Prince Tahmasp.

27. Joshi, 'Adil Shahis,' 335.

28. In fact, in 1576 Akbar's earliest contact with one of the Deccan states was when he wrote to Ali Adil Shah asking him to send up Shirazi – the latter sent his polite regrets.

29. Eaton, 'History of the Deccan,' 6.

30. Hutton, *Art of the Court*, 53, 61.

31. Ibid., 61.

32. Flatt, 'Authorship and Significance,' 240.

33. Ibid., 242. The author explains, 'It is hoped these scraps of discourse may be beautiful in the vision of the intelligent ones and good and laudable in the eyes of the buyers … However, after this it should not remain concealed that the original aim of writing these lines and the overall intention of these lines is the aforesaid one. It is an account of created beings from the elements, the heavenly bodies, plants, minerals, animals, an enumeration of angels on top of the sky, the rosaries of their names, the revelation of the benefits that are the necessary essence of the stars of every sky, and so on.'

34. Joshi, 'Adil Shahis,' 396. The librarian was Waman Pandit bin Anant, and he was the grandfather of the famous poet of the same name, Waman Pandit. See Joshi, 'Ali Adil Shah I,' 97–107.

35. Overton, 'Vida de Jacques,' 248.

36. Briggs, *History of the Rise*, 169.

37. Joshi, 'Adil Shahis,' 397.

38. Eaton, 'Sufis of Bijapur,' 110.

39. Ibid., 111.

40. Francois Pyrard quoted in ibid., 110.

41. Hutton, *Art of the Court*, 98. He is described in one painting as 'Khedive of the world, the king of his age, enthroned under an auspicious sign, the

fortunate king, light of the heart and of the eyes of the happy, the benefactor of the soul of the generous', while another line goes: 'He is Khalil, the oystershell of the heavens contains nothing like thee, Faridun and Jam have no son like thee, Solomon.'

42. Joshi, 'Adil Shahis,' 398. Or, more accurately, 'Saraspati'.

43. Eaton, 'Sufis of Bijapur,' 108. A later ruler would rename the place Muhammadpur, apparently, but the people of the city stuck resolutely to Bijapur. See Cousens, *Bijapur*, 86.

44. Quoted in Eaton, 'Sufis of Bijapur,' 110.

45. Haidar, 'Kitab-i-Nauras.'

46. Ibid., 26.

47. Ibid., 34–37.

48. Ibid., 34.

49. Hutton and Tucker, 'Dutch Artist in Bijapur,' 212.

50. Eaton, 'Sufis of Bijapur,' 100.

51. Ibid., 90.

52. Ibid., 108.

53. Joshi, 'Adil Shahis,' 397.

54. Sardar, 'Bahmanis and Their Artistic Legacy,' 96.

55. Eaton, 'Sufis of Bijapur,' 109.

56. Eaton, 'History of the Deccan,' 6.

57. Eaton, 'Sufis of Bijapur,' 99.

58. The actual construction work began in Ali Adil Shah's reign.

59. Hutton, *Art of the Court*, 26–28, 36.

60. Ibid., 107.

61. Eaton, 'Sufis of Bijapur,' 99.

62. It is, however, possible that the ambassador was keen on arousing the emperor's avarice and such descriptions of the Deccan could have helped persuade the latter of the advantage the empire could derive if the Deccan were subdued.

63. See Bayly's *Rulers, Townsmen and Bazaars* for parallels later in North India with successor states of the Mughals, and also Jon Wilson's *India Conquered* for more on this 'public display of power' through which kingship was built as well as reinforced. This also led to economic expansion – demand for luxury goods attracted merchants, courtesans and others to urban centres, leading to a cultural and financial boom. As a British official later noted in the context of the Marathas and the Mughals: 'The Moghuls,

magnificent and ostentatious, required every article of luxury—towns and cities grew out of this spirit. The Brahmins and Marattas, less refined and more parsimonious are averse from and ignorant of these costly modes of expense. Hence those towns and cities, deprived of their cause of existence are mouldering fast into ruin and the wealthier inhabitants have sunk under or fled from, the rapacity of their new masters.' Hindu temples and institutions that sprung around it also played a similar economic purpose, with forward and backward linkages, tanks and works of irrigation, markets, etc. Furthermore, in Mughal India, after the invasion by Nadir Shah demolished the financial backbone of the court in Delhi, demand for goods from provinces like Bengal fell, causing decline in the towns and cities that were till then engaged in the trade. In other words, high-end consumption was essential for the economic sustenance of Indian cities. See Bayly, *Rulers, Townsmen and Bazaars*, 75, 78.

64. Hutton and Tucker, 'Dutch Artist in Bijapur,' 205–32.
65. Ibid.
66. Hutton, *Art of the Court*, 71. Emphasis by the author.
67. Overton, 'Vida de Jacques,' 234.
68. Ibid., 235.
69. Ibid., 234–35, 239–40.
70. Eaton, 'Sufis of Bijapur,' 131.
71. Ibid., 127–28.
72. Alam and Subrahmanyam, 'Deccan Frontier,' 379.
73. Nayeem, *External Relations*, 42.
74. Ibid., 59–60.
75. Subrahmanyam, *Courtly Encounters*, 58–59.
76. Nayeem, *External Relations*, 63.
77. Shyam, 'Imad Shahs,' 283.
78. Ibid., 286–87.
79. Khan, *Deccan Policy*, 52.
80. Joshi, 'Adil Shahis,' 340.
81. Shyam, 'Nizam Shahis,' 254.
82. Gribble, *History of the Deccan*, vol. 1, 222.
83. Chandra, *Medieval India*, part 2, 191. Reference is to Fahim Khan, who retained his influence, however, and would wield power even over Burhan Nizam Shah who died in 1595.
84. Gribble, *History of the Deccan*, vol. 1, 220.

85. Shyam, 'Nizam Shahis,' 248. Her record was not a happy one, in that she seemed to keep her son permanently waiting to inherit his powers, causing a group of nobles to finally come together and topple her 'petticoat government'. Her son, later, even had her form painted over in miniatures, leaving her as nothing more than a 'large smudge', to borrow from Sanjay Subrahmanyam (a practice not altogether restricted to India – in a surviving painting of the Roman emperor Caracalla with his parents and brother, the brother was also turned into a smudge after his treacherous assassination in 211 CE). In the *Tarif-i Husain Shah Padshah-i Dakan* by Aftabi, Khunza features in some detail. As Subrahmanyam notes, 'Not only her face with its shapely moles, but her breasts like "fresh pomegranates"... and various other physical attributes are set out in loving detail in verse after verse.' Husain Nizam Shah, who is credited here as ruling as far as China, is painted as very much in love with his wife. See Subrahmanyam, *Courtly Encounters*, 91–92.

86. Shyam, 'Nizam Shahis,' 254.

87. Shyam, *Kingdom of Ahmadnagar*, 202.

88. Ibid., 205.

89. Ibid., 206.

90. Not without reason: this Nizam Shah, Burhan II, had stayed at the Mughal court but refused military assistance, and took Ahmadnagar's throne without Akbar's help, freeing him from obligation while also winning him loyalties at home. He did have an interesting reign, however, during which time he was under the influence of a eunuch called Fahim Khan. He also clashed, Sanjay Subrahmanyam notes, with the Portuguese, after the latter seized gold belonging to him from a ship that sank off the coast of Chaul – the Nizam Shah was defeated in 1594.

91. Subrahmanyam, 'Life and Actions,' 68.

92. Alam and Subrahmanyam, 'Deccan Frontier,' 355–56.

93. Gribble, *History of the Deccan*, vol. 1, 232–33. The candidate Chand Bibi supported was Burhan's grandson through his son Ibrahim, who had an Ethiopian mother.

94. Shyam, 'Nizam Shahis,' 258.

95. Syed Ali Tabatabai quoted in Sherwani, *Muhammad-Quli Qutb Shah*, 127.

96. This particular invasion was not led by Daniyal but by Akbar's other son, Murad, who was the governor of Gujarat.

97. This was in 1472 at the siege of Belgaum, where the local ruler inside the

fort, a Vijayanagar ally, unfamiliar with mining technology, did nothing but quietly watch as the Bahmanis dug their trenches, only to shrink in horror when his fortifications crumbled soon afterwards. See Khan, *Gunpowder and Firearms*, 31–32.

98. Gribble, *History of the Deccan*, vol. 1, 234.

99. Anwar, *Mughals and the Deccan*, 72.

100. Gribble, *History of the Deccan*, vol. 1, 237.

101. Quoted in Eaton, *Social History*, 113.

102. Shyam, 'Nizam Shahis,' 259.

103. Joshi, *Reign of Ibrahim*, 297.

104. Gribble, *History of the Deccan*, vol. 1, 237.

105. Shyam, 'Nizam Shahis,' 260. As T.C.A. Raghavan notes, however, Mughal infighting also had much to do with this ad hoc conquest of Ahmadnagar. When Akbar appointed Prince Daniyal in charge, for instance, Prince Murad (who was older) resented the decision. The seniormost general, the KhanKhanan Abdur Rahim, may have also delayed matters not only at this time but also in the future to protect his own interests. See Raghavan, *Attendant Lords*, 170–95.

106. Quoted in Ali, *Malik Ambar*, 48.

107. Gribble, *History of the Deccan*, vol. 1, 241.

108. Shyam, 'Nizam Shahis,' 260.

109. Khan, *Deccan Policy*, 87.

110. Ibrahim Adil Shah quoted in Gribble, *History of the Deccan*, vol. 1, 250.

111. Alam and Subrahmanyam, *Indo-Persian Travels*, 64. This was not unusual. When Shahrukh of Persia sent Abdur Razzak as his envoy to Calicut where ruled the Hindu Zamorin in 1442, already well regarded on account of the friendly treatment he gave to Muslim merchants in his port capital, the envoy in his memoirs initially refers to the Zamorin only as the Wali or governor of Calicut, not as a sovereign prince.

112. Joshi, 'Adil Shahis,' 344.

113. Alam and Subrahmanyam, 'Deccan Frontier,' 382.

114. Joshi, 'Adil Shahis,' 344.

115. Alam and Subrahmanyam, 'Deccan Frontier,' 382–83.

116. Haidar, 'Art of the Deccan Courts,' 19.

117. Overton, 'Vida de Jacques,' 242.

118. Alam and Subrahmanyam, 'Deccan Frontier,' 384.

119. Gribble, *History of the Deccan*, vol. 1, 245.

120. Gokhale, 'Tobacco in Seventeenth-Century India,' 486–87.
121. Akbar quoted in Gribble, *History of the Deccan*, vol. 1, 249.

VI. The Ethiopian Kingmaker

1. Pieter van den Broecke quoted in Ali, *Malik Ambar*, 119.
2. Eaton, *Social History*, 122.
3. Sherwani, *Bahmanis of the Deccan*, 334, and Eaton, *Social History*, 111.
4. Joshi, 'Adil Shahis,' 307. This was the regent Kamal Khan.
5. Joshi, *Reign of Ibrahim*, 287. His name was Ikhlas Khan.
6. Ibid., 289. This was Dilawar Khan, whom Ibrahim eventually blinded.
7. Alavi, *Studies in the History*, 7. This was the son of the Mughal nominee to the Nizam Shahi throne, and his name was Ibrahim Nizam Shah who reigned between 1595 and 1596. His son was the candidate Chand Bibi subsequently favoured. See Gebremariam, 'The Habshis,' 94.
8. Raghavan, *Attendant Lords*, 175.
9. Eraly, *Mughal Throne*, 487.
10. Ibn Batuta quoted in Ali, *Malik Ambar*, 11. In his account he also mentions a habshi called Bard who was 'tall and corpulent, and used to eat a whole sheep at a meal', following which he drank, reportedly, over a pound of ghee.
11. Francisco Alvares quoted in Eaton, *Social History*, 105.
12. Zakaria, *Razia, Queen of India*, 93, 98.
13. Khalidi, *Muslims in the Deccan*, 79.
14. Ibid., 79, 81.
15. Khalidi, *Muslims in the Deccan*, 80, 83. In the eighteenth century, the French Muslim (born M. Raymond, and known later as Haji Mustafa) said of the habshis: 'Habissinian men and women bear the highest price for their unshaken integrity and their exemplary fidelity . . . there are some secret reasons that render the women especially so highly valuable, although they are by no means comparable to Indians in beauty: they have long unhandsome faces betwixt the tawny and olive, and hair just hanging in ringlets as far as the shoulder, and never farther: But then they make up for this by three qualifications that set them above all the women of the two continents, save perhaps the Negroes: to wit, a mobility and versatility of body that amazes a philosopher; and an animal warmth and personal

elasticity that surpasses all belief; hence eight hundred Mohurs have been offered in India for an Habissinian virgin of sixteen, and refused.'

16. Ali, *Malik Ambar*, 18.
17. Ibid., 21.
18. Ibid., 25.
19. Eaton, *Social History*, 106.
20. Kumar, 'Service, Status, and Military Slavery,' 83.
21. Quoted in Eaton, *Social History*, 110.
22. Ali, *Malik Ambar*, 8.
23. Ibid., 44.
24. Eaton, *Social History*, 112.
25. Ibid., 115.
26. Ali, *Malik Ambar*, 54–55.
27. Ibid., 87.
28. Chowdhuri, *Malik Ambar*, 69.
29. Ibid., 45.
30. Shyam, 'Nizam Shahis,' 262.
31. Eaton, *Social History*, 118. The rival was one Raju Polad.
32. Ali, *Malik Ambar*, 40.
33. Eaton, *Social History*, 120.
34. Ibid., 121.
35. Quoted in Ali, *Malik Ambar*, 60.
36. Eaton, *Social History*, 121.
37. Shyam, *Kingdom of Ahmadnagar*, 242.
38. Van den Broecke quoted in Ali, *Malik Ambar*, 66.
39. Ibid., 70.
40. Green, *Indian Sufism*, 4.
41. Eaton, *Social History*, 123.
42. Ibid., 123, 128.
43. Pieter Gillis van Ravesteyn quoted in Ali, *Malik Ambar*, 95.
44. Asad Beg quoted in ibid., 68–69.
45. Ibid., 71, and Shyam, 'Nizam Shahis,' 266.
46. Jehangir quoted in Gribble, *History of the Deccan*, vol. 1, 254.
47. Ali, *Malik Ambar*, 89. These later attempts were by Adil Shahi agents.
48. Shyam, 'Nizam Shahis,' 266.
49. Chowdhuri, *Malik Ambar*, 110.

50. Gribble, *History of the Deccan*, vol. 1, 255.

51. Fuzuni Astarabadi quoted in Ali, *Malik Ambar*, 86.

52. Ali, *Malik Ambar*, 70.

53. Alam and Subrahmanyam, *Writing the Mughal World*, 179. Meanwhile the Mughals, as Faizi's accounts show, saw Ibrahim only as the *hakim* or governor of Bijapur!

54. Ali, *Malik Ambar*, 87.

55. Alam and Subrahmanyam, *Writing the Mughal World*, 379.

56. Ibrahim Adil Shah quoted in Overton, 'Vida de Jacques,' 236.

57. Khan, *Deccan Policy*, 136. The Qutb Shah had also at the same time come to terms with the Mughals and sent them presents.

58. Ali, *Malik Ambar*, 89.

59. Shyam, 'Nizam Shahis,' 269.

60. Ali, *Malik Ambar*, 91.

61. Ibid.

62. Ibid.

63. Hutton, *Art of the Court*, 72.

64. Shyam, 'Nizam Shahis,' 269.

65. Gribble, *History of the Deccan*, vol. 1, 252. It is interesting that even at the time, observers noted that the Mughal emperor did not actually control all the territory he claimed as his own. Francisco Pelsaert, a Dutch merchant, noted, for example, that the 'whole country is enclosed and broken up by many mountains and the people who live in, or beyond the mountains know nothing of any king or of Jahangir; they recognize only their rajahs who are very numerous. Jahangir, whose name implies that he grasps the whole world, must therefore be regarded as ruling no more than half the dominions which he claims.' See Moreland and Geyl, *Jahangir's India*, 58.

66. Ali, *Malik Ambar*, 102.

67. Harris, *First Firangis*, 106.

68. Quoted in Gribble, *History of the Deccan*, vol. 1, 257.

69. Shahji, Shivaji's father, too raised a Nizam Shahi child to the throne, and this boy also was packed off to Gwalior.

70. Shyam, 'Nizam Shahis,' 270–75. Interestingly, in the early 1620s when Shahjahan rebelled against his father, he had sought aid from Malik Ambar to carry out his war. Ambar, the first time, did not respond, though he does appear to later have extended some help to the future emperor.

71. Overton, 'Vida de Jacques,' 245.

72. Ibid., 242.

73. Flood, *Objects of Translation*, 127.

74. De Coutre tells that by the end Ibrahim 'found himself without a treasure and poor, he became a tyrant and killed his own legitimate sons, and his oldest wife, and he never used to leave his court, and only very infrequently even went out from his palace'.

75. *Cambridge History of India*, 265.

76. Gribble, *History of the Deccan*, vol. 1, 264.

77. *Cambridge History of India*, 196.

78. Khan, *Deccan Policy*, 239.

79. Anwar, 'The Safavids,' 123.

80. Khan, *Deccan Policy*, 247.

81. Ikhlas Khan was originally known as Malik Raihan and grew up with Muhammad Adil Shah – when the latter came to the throne, his star also rose, and he was granted the title of Ikhlas Khan. He remained prominent until, soon after Muhammad's death and the succession of his heir, he was executed, closing his story in tragedy.

82. *Cambridge History of India*, 208.

83. Moreland, 'From Akbar to Aurangzeb,' 6.

84. Pearson, 'Shivaji and the Decline,' 89.

85. Joshi, 'Adil Shahis,' 372.

86. Ibid., 371. It was of course a pretext to invade – when finally Bijapur fell, Aurangzeb found that there were not less than sixteen male heirs to its throne descended from Yusuf Adil Shah still living in Bijapur.

87. Thevenot quoted in Khan, *Deccan Policy*, 252.

88. Joshi, 'Adil Shahis,' 374.

89. *Cambridge History of India*, 212.

90. Eraly, *Mughal Throne*, 485.

91. Jai Singh quoted in ibid. The rebels were, of course, led by Shivaji.

92. *Cambridge History of India*, 254.

93. Joshi, 'Adil Shahis,' 380–81.

94. Eraly, *Mughal Throne*, 486.

95. Eraly, *Mughal World*, 166.

96. *Cambridge History of India*, 255. Under Aurangzeb too, the city would prosper. As Thevenot described it: 'There are several other pretty fair Mosques in this town, and it is not destitute of publick places, Caravanseras and Bagnios. The buildings are, for the most part, built

of Free-stone, and pretty high; before the Doors there are a great many Trees growing in the Streets and the Gardens are pleasant and well cultivated, affording refreshment of Fruit, Grapes, and Grass-plats . . . This is a Trading Town and well Peopled, with excellent Ground about it.'

97.   Ibid., 255.

98.   Eraly, *Mughal Throne*, 487.

99.   *Cambridge History of India*, 256.

100. Eraly, *Mughal Throne*, 488.

101. Ibid., 489.

102. *Cambridge History of India*, 286.

103. Stuart Cary Welch quoted in Hutton, 'Memory and Monarchy,' 22.

104. Eraly, *Mughal Throne*, 489.

105. Sir James Mackintosh quoted in Eaton, 'Sufis of Bijapur,' 302.

VII. House of Sheep

1.   See Minorsky, 'Qara-Qoyunlu,' for more on the origins of the dynasty. See also Sherwani, *Muhammad-Quli Qutb Shah*.

2.   Minorsky, 'Qara-Qoyunlu,' 70.

3.   Sherwani, 'Qutb Shahis,' 413.

4.   Rocco, *Golconda and the Qutb*, 4–15.

5.   Sherwani, *Muhammad-Quli Qutb Shah*, 5.

6.   Rocco, *Golconda and the Qutb*, 5.

7.   Sherwani, *Bahmanis of the Deccan*, 414.

8.   Sardar, 'Circular Cities,' 3. This reinforcement of the city would continue under later rulers as well. According to the *Tarikh-i Muhammad Qutb Shah*, in 1559 Ibrahim Qutb Shah 'reflected on the awkward situation in which he would have been placed if [Vijayanagar] had besieged him in his capital, which was incapable of defense, [therefore] he resolved to rebuild the fort of Golconda with stone and mortar'.

9.   Eaton, *Social History*, 156, and Sherwani, *Muhammad-Quli Qutb Shah*, 3.

10.   See Benjamin B. Cohen's *Kingship and Colonialism in India's Deccan* for a good study on these Samasthan states. Some of these families had strong links with the Qutb Shahs – the rulers of Wanaparthi, for example, bore the hereditary title of Bahiri (Eagle), conferred upon them by Abdullah Qutb Shah in the seventeenth century, and the family under Rani Janamma

stood by their overlords in Golconda against Aurangzeb, until after the latter's victory they were absorbed into the new Mughal order.

11. Rao, *Krishnadeva Raya*, 16–17.

12. Briggs, *History of the Rise*, 353. As given by Ferishta, the forts were 'Rajconda, Kovilconda, Dewurconda, Pangul, Gunpoora, Jirconda, Yelgundel, Mulungoo, Etgeer, Meduk, Bhowungeer, Belumconda, Wurungole, Cumamett, Indraconda, Ramgeer, Condapilly, Ellore, Chitcole'.

13. Rocco, *Golconda and the Qutb*, 6.

14. Sherwani, 'Qutb Shahis,' 422. Sherwani mistakenly states that the dynasty was Shia until 1687. It was in practice but officially, after 1636, the state was no longer a Shiite entity.

15. Rocco, *Golconda and the Qutb*, 7, and Sherwani, 'Qutb Shahis,' 422. Sherwani also points out that the story of an assassination may well have been invented to tarnish the image of Sultan-Quli's successor, Jamshid.

16. Sarma, 'Rama Raya's Policy,' 143, and Eaton, *Social History*, 79.

17. Sherwani, *Muhammad-Quli Qutb Shah*, 7.

18. Rocco, *Golconda and the Qutb*, 8.

19. Sherwani, *Muhammad-Quli Qutb Shah*, 7.

20. Rocco, *Golconda and the Qutb*, 9.

21. Sherwani, 'Qutb Shahis,' 429, 433.

22. Sardar, 'Circular Cities,' 17.

23. Sherwani, *Muhammad-Quli Qutb Shah*, 9.

24. Ibid.

25. Sardar, 'Circular Cities,' 17.

26. Sherwani, *Muhammad-Quli Qutb Shah*, 69.

27. Ibid., 44.

28. Eaton, *Social History*, 145.

29. Rocco, *Golconda and the Qutb*, 11.

30. Ibid., 13.

31. Seshan, *Trade and Politics*, 8–10. Ordinarily, the fact that ships could not anchor in a port and had to send material out in small boats from miles away could work against that place. It took the Danes, for instance, decades to get their settlement in Tranquebar, afflicted by the same problem, off the ground economically, and often goods dispatched in small boats towards the beach capsized and large quantities of cargo were thus lost. The success of Masulipatam, despite such weaknesses, stands out.

32. William Methwold quoted in Moreland, *Relations of Golconda*, 35.

33. Seshan, *Trade and Politics*, 8–10.

34. Singh, 'Golconda Chintz,' 302. Such was the value attached to the painters of chintz that after Golconda was destroyed by the Mughals in 1694, the directors of the East India Company wrote to their subordinates in India to try and ensure that 'the fine painters' could be persuaded to move to Madras and carry on work under Company patronage.

35. Seshan, *Trade and Politics*, 60.

36. Ansari, 'Economic Condition,' 230.

37. Sardar, 'Bahmanis and Their Artistic Legacy,' 200.

38. Sharma, 'Diamond Mines of the Deccan,' 236. Incidentally, the famous poet-saint Purandaradasa was the son of a diamond merchant in Vijayanagar.

39. Eaton, *Social History*, 157. The city still exists.

40. Weinstein, 'Variations on a Persian Theme,' 180.

41. Ibid., 185.

42. Ibid., 182.

43. Sherwani, *Muhammad-Quli Qutb Shah*, 14.

44. Sherwani, 'Qutb Shahis,' 457.

45. Alam and Subrahmanyam, 'Deccan Frontier,' 373.

46. Sherwani, 'Qutb Shahis,' 457–59. Europeans do refer to Bhagnagar, except they, like Tavernier, connect the word to 'bagh' or garden, i.e. city of gardens.

47. Tavernier quoted in Phillips, *Tavernier's Travels*, 123.

48. Sherwani, *Muhammad-Quli Qutb Shah*, 14–15.

49. Ibid., 16–20.

50. Ibid., 23.

51. Methwold quoted in Moreland, *Relations of Golconda*, 8–9. Methwold, at some point, appears to have got drunk in Cambay where he inscribed in a pleasure garden: 'The English and Dutch were here, and drank toddy for want of beer.'

52. Ibid., 9–10.

53. Bayly, *Rulers, Townsmen and Bazaars*, 200. This method of financial management would feature more prominently in India in the next century. In the princely state of Awadh in the 1770s, for instance, up to 60 per cent of the total revenue of the Nawab was controlled by two men alone – the eunuch Almas Ali Khan and a Hindu called Bhawani Singh.

54. Thevenot quoted in Ansari, 'Economic Condition,' 229. The British too profited from similar arrangements – in 1717, the emperor Farukhsiyar granted them the right to trade freely in Bengal, fixing customs at 3000

rupees per annum, no matter what their gains or losses. At least one source suggests that this arrangement was partly arrived at after a British doctor helped cure the emperor of venereal disease. See Moorhouse, *India Britannica*, 36.

55. Moreland, *Relations of Golconda*, 30.

56. In the Deccan itself, more broadly, we find mention of a diamond mine as early as 1425 in the reign of Ahmad Shah Bahmani.

57. Moreland, *Relations of Golconda*, 32.

58. Phillips, *Tavernier's Travels*, 330, 355. In terms of the numbers of workers, we must be somewhat wary, like with other sources of this period. '60,000' might really mean 'many thousands' rather than an accurate enumeration of the exact number of workers.

59. Another version states that the Koh-i-Noor was lost as early as the time of Malik Kafur's invasions when the Kakatiyas surrendered it to the Sultan of Delhi.

60. Schorer quoted in Moreland, *Relations of Golconda*, 56.

61. Sherwani, *Muhammad-Quli Qutb Shah*, 44.

62. Ramanujan, Rao and Shulman, *When God Is a Customer*, 3. The Qutb Shah at the time was Abdullah Qutb Shah.

63. Kruijtzer, 'Madanna, Akkanna,' 243–44.

64. Sherwani, *Muhammad-Quli Qutb Shah*, 63.

65. Moreland, *Relations of Golconda*, 59.

66. Subrahmanyam, *Three Ways to be Alien*, 20. The French were quite ungrateful to the poor Armenian, who was arrested, punished and harassed for years mainly due to their own prejudice and lack of trust.

67. Hansen, *Peacock Throne*, 21.

68. Subrahmanyam, 'Portuguese Response,' 129, and Subrahmanyam, *Portuguese Empire*, 267. At the close of the 1590s the Qutb Shah did agree to a Portuguese Resident in Masulipatam, but the post lapsed after the tenure of a single officer – the arrival of the Dutch in 1605 meant the Qutb Shah prevailed upon them to side with him against Portuguese pressure.

69. Schorer quoted in Moreland, *Relations of Golconda*, 77.

70. Nikitin quoted in Fisher, *Visions of Mughal India*, 20.

71. Ansari, 'Economic Condition,' 232.

72. Thomas Bowrey quoted in Gokhale, 'Tobacco in Seventeenth-Century India,' 468. On the eve of the annexation of Golconda by the Mughals, the traveller Mirza Muhammad Mufid Mustaufi ibn Najm-ud-Din Mahmud

Bafiqi Yazdi also recalled seeing some human curiosities in Hyderabad. 'In the early days of [1674],' he writes, 'two women were brought [to Hyderabad] from a village of Karnatak, who had beards like men. Their entire bodies were covered with hair, and their breasts were a cubit large, so that when they walked they were obliged to carry them wrapped up around their waist in their clothes. In Hyderabad, in those very days, a man appeared who could tear a goat with his teeth, drink its blood and then skin the animal, swallow its flesh and chew its bones. Every day, a large goat was provided for him.' See Alam and Subrahmanyam, *Indo-Persian Travels*, 211.

73. Sherwani, *Muhammad-Quli Qutb Shah*, 116. Ferishta states she was sent off to Persia but this has been shown to be incorrect.
74. Sardar, 'Circular Cities,' 16.
75. Rocco, *Golconda and the Qutb*, 16.
76. Kruitjzer, 'Fighting on the Wall,' 148.
77. Bernier quoted in Eraly, *Mughal Throne*, 489.
78. Tavernier quoted in Rocco, *Golconda and the Qutb*, 19–20.
79. *Cambridge History of India*, 269.
80. Khan, *Deccan Policy*, 204.
81. Rocco, *Golconda and the Qutb*, 19.
82. Bayly and Subrahmanyam, 'Portfolio Capitalists,' 410.
83. Seshan, *Trade and Politics*, 64.
84. Subrahmanyam, 'Iranians Abroad,' 347.
85. Quoted in Bayly and Subrahmanyam, 'Portfolio Capitalists,' 411.
86. Seshan, *Trade and Politics*, 59, and Subrahmanyam, 'Iranians Abroad,' 347. This was not unusual as such – even senior members of the Mughal court were permitted to own ships and invest in the international trade, not to speak of ladies of the harem. Emperor Jehangir's mother, a Rajput princess styled Mariam uz-Zamani, was the owner of one of the greatest ships of her time, the *Rahimi*, till it was captured and destroyed by the Portuguese in 1613. See Findly, 'Capture of Maryam,' 227–38.
87. Rocco, *Golconda and the Qutb*, 23.
88. Khan, *Deccan Policy*, 204.
89. Aurangzeb quoted in ibid., 211.
90. It appears that the Qutb Shah's approach was to lobby Aurangzeb's rival Dara Shukoh, who in turn prevailed over the emperor. Prince Dara's interest

in preserving Golconda was mainly to prevent Aurangzeb from acquiring too much strength in the south.

91. Rocco, *Golconda and the Qutb*, 24.

92. Khan, *Deccan Policy*, 216–17.

93. There are some who suggest that Shahjahan might have encouraged this delay out of his own avarice.

94. Hansen, *Peacock Throne*, 174.

95. Rocco, *Golconda and the Qutb*, 24.

96. *Cambridge History of India*, 270.

97. Hansen, *Peacock Throne*, 174, and Rocco, *Golconda and the Qutb*, 25. See Khan, *Deccan Policy*, 223.

98. Khan, *Deccan Policy*, 220. In 1639 some female relations of the Qutb Shah had personally travelled to Safavid Persia to pay homage to the Shah.

99. Abdullah Qutb Shah to Shah Abbas II in Sarkar, 'A Letter of Abdullah,' 607–09.

100. Phillips, *Tavernier's Travels*, 132.

101. Sherwani, 'Qutb Shahis,' 483.

102. Sarkar, *Anecdotes of Aurangzib*, 17.

103. Eraly, *Mughal Throne*, 490.

104. Rocco, *Golconda and the Qutb*, 26.

105. Kruijtzer, 'Madanna, Akkanna,' 240. Though popularly held to be Telugu Brahmins, the scale of their donations to the Tuljapur temple in Maratha country and their future alliance with the Marathas suggest they may well have been from that part of the Deccan and not the south.

106. Akkanna quoted in ibid., 232.

107. Ibid., 252.

108. Sherwani, 'Qutb Shahis,' 484.

109. Kruijtzer, 'Madanna, Akkanna,' 258–59.

110. Seshan, *Trade and Politics*, 33.

111. Eraly, *Mughal Throne*, 490.

112. Havart quoted in Kruijtzer, 'Madanna, Akkanna,' 248.

113. Seshan, *Trade and Politics*, 34.

114. Ibid.

115. Nayeem, *External Relations*, 278–79. Shivaji's letter to Maloji Ghorpade in March 1677.

116. Quoted in Kruijtzer, 'Madanna, Akkanna,' 259.

117. Ibid., 247.

118. Ibid., 245.

119. Eraly, *Mughal Throne*, 490–91.

120. *Cambridge History of India*, 286, and Eraly, *Mughal Throne*, 491.

121. *Cambridge History of India*, 287.

122. Kruijtzer, 'Madanna, Akkanna,' 241.

123. Ibid., 250.

124. Eraly, *Mughal Throne*, 491.

125. Ibid.

126. Ibid., 492.

127. Nimat Khan quoted in Ansari, *Chronicles of the Seige* [sic], 3.

128. *Cambridge History of India*, 288.

129. Eraly, *Mughal Throne*, 493.

130. Ansari, *Chronicles of the Seige* [sic], 5.

131. Ibid., 14.

132. Ibid., 7.

133. Sarkar, *Anecdotes of Aurangzib*, 16.

134. *Cambridge History of India*, 288. Hyderabad, however, to this day remains the city with the largest concentration of Shias in the Deccan.

135. Abul Hasan quoted in Eraly, *Mughal Throne*, 493.

136. Ibid., 494.

137. Ansari, *Chronicles of the Seige* [sic], 21.

138. Ibid., 27–28.

139. *Cambridge History of India*, 289.

Epilogue

1.   Wagoner, *Tidings of the King*, 55.

2.   Ibid., 52.

3.   Ibid., 54.

4.   Sathianathaier, *Tamilaham in the 17th Century*, 1.

5.   Chekuri, '"Share" in the "World Empire",' 54. It is likely, though Ain al-Mulk is not named clearly, that in the 'Battle of Talikota', he was one of the two Muslim generals to betray Ramaraya and go over to the Sultans.

6.   Alam and Subrahmanyam, *Indo-Persian Travels*, 79–82.

7.   Joshi, *Ali Adil Shah I*, 10. This exile of a North Indian prince in the far south is not unusual, and as late as the early nineteenth century, we have the case

of a Mughal prince, Mirza Ali Bakht Azfari, a descendant of Aurangzeb (and, incidentally, of Jai Singh), who lived under the protection of the Nawabs of Arcot, including in what is present-day Chennai ('Chinnapattan Mandraj').

8. Sohoni, 'Vernacular as a Space,' 264–65.

9. Zelliot, 'Medieval Encounter,' 171. It is also believed by some that Eknath's guru, Janardhan, was a member of the Sijra-i-kadri Sufi order, which may or may not be altogether true, though it is clear that like Eknath he did have intellectual engagements with Muslims. He was also, evidently, the commandant of the Daulatabad fort for the Nizam Shah. Eknath himself is a fascinating example of the cultural synthesis of this period. In the 300 *bharuds* he composed in his lifetime, we see not only this Hindu–Muslim dialogue, but also one between a Brahmin and an 'untouchable' Mahar. Characters, in whose voice Eknath speaks, range from madmen and prostitutes, to Muslim fakirs and even a habshi who 'ends each second line in his accounting of the ten incarnations of Vishnu with the word Muhammad'. In Eknath's hagiographies, when God appears to test him, it is often in the guise of a Muslim.

10. Wagoner, *Tidings of the King*, 61–63. In the *Rayavacakamu*, one character even goes on to exclaim: 'You should realise that those three Lion-Thrones [Ashvapati in the north, Gajapati of Orissa, and Narapati of Vijayanagar] exist as emanations of the gods Brahma, Vishnu, and Maheshvara.'

11. Rao, David and Subrahmanyam, *Symbols of Substance*, 1–7. It should be noted, furthermore, that the *Rayavacakamu* was not alone in such texts emerging at this time. Thus, Venkatadhvarin's *Visva-Gunadarsana-Campu* of the same early seventeenth-century period makes note of Muslims in these words: 'Equipped with horses swifter than wind / intent on cutting off the practice of dharma at the root / terrifying Yavanas are on the move / against temples of Siva and of Vishnu on his serpent couch.' But like the *Rayavacakamu*, this too sees redeeming qualities when one of its characters states, 'do observe that the Turushkas, Yavanas and others have an unparalleled claim to the virtue of heroism'. This work also takes note of Europeans in Madras in a fascinating way (they are 'evil people' who 'treat Brahmins with contempt, as if they were no better than blades of grass'), and is also revealing in its demarcation of the south through regional divisions of Maharashtra, Andhra, Karnataka, and of course the Tamil lands.

12. Quoted in Deshpande, *Creative Pasts*, 9.

13. Ibid., 43–44. Indeed, when he called on the Ghorpades of Mudhol to join him, this is the reply he received: 'Until today we have spent time under the service of the Adil Shahi and Bahmani Badshahs and achieved great honour. We do not think it appropriate to desert them when they don't have a capable leader . . . bringing down the Adil Shahi will not be possible for us in this life.' Furthermore, it was added, 'Your father and you also earned many honours from them . . . returning this favour [by turning against the Adil Shah] does not show your lineage in good light. Conduct yourself so your father's exploits are not dishonoured.' Gordon, *New Cambridge History*, 58. Even Shivaji's father, who had had his fair share of rebelling against authority, did not side with his son in this matter, and wrote to Bijapur to ask that his son's actions should not be construed as a test of his own loyalty. 'Be it known to this loyal subject,' came the royal reply, 'that the improper conduct and acts of Shivaji are evident to His Majesty . . . [and that] the faults of Shivaji will not be laid on you.'

14. Sitapathi, *Farmans and Sanads*, viii.

15. Gordon, *New Cambridge History*, 44.

16. Ibid., 45–55, and Eaton, *Social History*, 123.

17. Contemporary sources as well as later accounts state that Shahji's marriage with Jijabai was an unhappy one, partly because her family, which considered itself superior to Shahji's, was not pleased with the union.

18. Gordon, *New Cambridge History*, 58.

19. Pearson, 'Shivaji and the Decline,' 91.

20. Khafi Khan quoted in Bhave, *From the Death*, 39.

21. Guha, 'Transitions and Translations,' 278.

22. Laine, 'Dharma of Islam,' 305. Laine suggests here that Maloji was buried and that this is a tomb, but what appears more likely is that this spot was marked – in the architectural style of the time – as the spot where Maloji was *cremated*. See Michell and Johar, 'Maratha Complex,' 69–88.

23. Laine, 'Dharma of Islam,' 305.

24. Sardesai, *New History*, 53.

25. Gordon, *New Cambridge History*, 66.

26. Ibid., 59.

27. Guha, 'Transitions and Translations,' 27. Some influence of the Bhakti saints can also be seen here. Tukaram, for instance, as Guha notes, describes one marker of the Kali Age – the worst, in Hindu mythology – as the use even by Brahmins of the *avindhvani*, i.e. the language of 'those who have

unpierced ears', that is Muslims. The *Rajyavyavaharakosha* was essentially a thesaurus offering Sanskrit words for about 1500 Persian words that were generally used in courts and for diplomatic correspondence.

28. Ibid., 29.

29. Ibid., 27.

30. Deshpande, *Creative Pasts*, 42. The process was complicated, however, and the divorce from the past was not immediate or stark – in some Maratha sources, Shivaji is described as a Maratha Padshah, just as Vijayanagar's kings once called themselves Hindu Sultans.

31. Gordon, *New Cambridge History*, 33–36. Thus, for instance, many lines could claim generations of continued military and economic service under the rule of Muslim kings – the Shindes of Kanerkhed, the Manes of Mhasvad, the Nimbalkars of Nimbalak, the Ghatges of Malavdi and the Jadhavs of Sindhkhed, to which house Shivaji's mother belonged. Even the celebrated future queen Tarabai's family served the Adil Shahs, accepting from that ruler robes of honour in return for declarations of fealty. See Eaton, *Social History*, 128, 188. See also Fukazawa, *Study of the Local Administration* for a sense of how local affairs were managed by Marathas. See also reference earlier to the regional identities manifesting in the Tamil composer Venkatadhvarin's *Visva-Gunadarsana-Campu* in the seventeenth century.

32. Gordon, *New Cambridge History*, 61.

33. Sardesai, *New History*, 103.

34. Ibid., 93.

35. Gordon, *New Cambridge History*, 62.

36. Eaton, 'Sufis of Bijapur,' 197.

37. Laine, 'Dharma of Islam,' 307.

38. Sardesai, *New History*, 129. Interestingly, among the men put to death on the losing side were numerous Marathas, while one of Shivaji's comrades in planning the whole episode and executing it successfully was a Muslim called Siddi Ibrahim. See Gordon, *New Cambridge History*, 66, 68.

39. Quoted in Gokhale, *Surat in the Seventeenth Century*, 24.

40. Bernier, *Travels in the Mogul Empire*, 211. About a decade after Shivaji's first raid on Surat, the English in that city received orders from London that every civil servant should also receive military training so that should the need arise for them to defend themselves and English possessions from such attacks, they would be able to do so.

41. Quoted in Sardesai, *New History*, 150.

42. Tavernier quoted in Pearson, 'Shivaji and the Decline,' 92.

43. Sardesai, *New History*, 144.

44. Pearson, 'Shivaji and the Decline,' 93. This included a letter sent to the Mughals where the Maratha flaunted his successes. 'You know very well,' he wrote, 'what results have been achieved by the famous generals and the able counsellors sent by the Emperor during the last three years for seizing my country and my forts. How is it that you don't realize that this is an impossible task? . . . My home here is not like the towns of Kalyani and [Bidar] which would be easily assaulted and taken. My country has lofty hill-ranges two hundred leagues in length and forty in breadth and is protected by sixty strong forts newly built. Your great Amir-ul-Umra Shaista Khan [the uncle] labored hard for three years and went away in disgrace after suffering a terrible disaster. It is my duty to guard my land, and I will do it. Thank God, no invader of my beloved country has yet bloomed forth.' See Sardesai, *New History*, 150.

45. Kulkarni, 'A Note on Mirza,' 274.

46. Gordon, *New Cambridge History*, 73–74.

47. Eraly, *Emperors of the Peacock Throne*, 537.

48. Kulkarni, 'A Note on Mirza,' 279.

49. Ibid.

50. Quoted in Gordon, *New Cambridge History*, 76.

51. Pearson, 'Shivaji and the Decline,' 95.

52. Truschke, *Aurangzeb*, 60. In subsequent years, Shivaji would demonstrate a pronounced disdain for the idea of merging into the Mughal order. As Bhushan Tripathi, a poet at his court, wrote in 1673, 'A governorship from Delhi is like an enticing prostitute. Seeing her beauty, who doesn't long to possess her? Her manner is to conquer the world by the power of trickery. Whomever she approaches she immediately renders penniless. Bhushan says, spending time in her company brings no reward.'

53. Pearson, 'Shivaji and the Decline,' 95.

54. Sardesai, *New History*, 174.

55. Gordon, *New Cambridge History*, 78. Such dramatic escapes are not unusual. In 1849 the Rajah of Wanaparthi, subordinate to the Nizam of Hyderabad, was imprisoned for debt. He obtained permission to go out of jail to a temple to perform an annual death ceremony for his father, where the guards stood outside, listening to the tinkling of the bell inside. After a few hours had passed with sporadic tinkling but no sign of the ceremony ending,

they discovered that the rajah and his companions had escaped through a small, quickly dug tunnel under the temple wall, met by horses on the other side which took them back to Wanaparthi. The tinkling came from a cat, around the neck of which a bell had been tied! See Cohen, *Kingship and Colonialism*, 62–63.

56. Pearson, 'Shivaji and the Decline,' 96. A later account by Ghulan Ali Azad Bilgrami in the eighteenth century attempted to explain Maratha intransigence in terms of their culinary choices. The Marathas, he argued, put 'hot chillies into everything they eat. That is why their nature has become dry and hot'! Quoted in Rao, *Eighteenth Century Deccan*, 227.

57. Shastry, 'Commercial Policy,' 632.

58. Bernier quoted in Pearson, 'Shivaji and the Decline,' 98.

59. This coronation was itself an example in what can be called the 'invention of tradition'. The Marathas, as a landowning class, were dominant, and there were aristocratic houses among them. But they were classed by Brahmins in the Sudra *varna* of the Hindu social order. Shivaji, however, sought superior Kshatriya status, for which reason this elaborate coronation ceremony was organized at considerable expense, culminating with the acquisition of the sacred thread and his remarriage to his wives under a whole new set of rituals. Gaga Bhat (aka Visveshwar Pandit), a leading Benares-based Marathi Brahmin, helped put together a genealogy connecting Shivaji to the Sisodia Rajputs, and confirming his claim as a Kshatriya. (Interestingly, in accounts of Ali Ibrahim Khan and Murtaza Hussain Bilgrami in the eighteenth century, this claim is extended – Shivaji was descended from the last Zoroastrian king of Persia, whose family fled to Rajasthan before some members came down to Maharashtra!) This claim to Rajput heritage, however, was not entirely new – Shivaji's father had also made this claim a generation before, and when Shivaji was in Agra, some Rajputs themselves recognized him as a 'good genuine Rajput' (see Gordon, *New Cambridge History*, 88). It is also noteworthy that generations later when a descendant of Shivaji, Maharajah Shahu of Kolhapur, allowed a turn of policy that reduced Brahmin influence at his court and in his government in the early twentieth century, Brahmins retaliated by refusing to acknowledge him as a Kshatriya. The debate, in other words, was never settled. This was an issue that concerned other groups as well – it was in Shivaji's lifetime, for example, that Gaga Bhat also helped confirm that Saraswat Brahmins were indeed Brahmins, and he also allowed what is called the Chandraseniya

Kayastha Prabhu community their claim to Kshatriya status. This, when the Brahmin Peshwas became real rulers of the Maratha Swaraj in the eighteenth century, was rejected, though, and the Prabhus had to provide in writing that they were not, in fact, Kshatriyas, and had no right to wear the sacred thread. See Deshpande, 'Ksatriyas in the Kali Age,' 95–120.

60. Richards, 'Imperial Crisis,' 55–58.

61. Pearson, 'Shivaji and the Decline,' 98.

62. There were several factions jostling for power among the Marathas. Shivaji's younger son, Rajaram, died in 1700 'spitting blood', after living nearly a decade in Gingee (where the Mughal general sent to besiege him was regularly bribed into inaction for eight whole years). His two widows formed camps and put forth their respective sons for the throne. Meanwhile, the dead Sambhaji's son grew up in Mughal captivity and was also eventually released to add another claim to this saga, so that three grandsons of Shivaji competed with each other for primacy.

63. Manucci quoted in Eraly, *Mughal World*, 304. This is not an exaggeration at all. As late as 1782, when the Nawab of Awadh marched an army of 20,000 soldiers, they had with them another 150,000 camp followers. See Bayly, *Rulers, Townsmen and Bazaars*, 65.

64. It was also the cavalry-oriented armies of Golconda and Bijapur that, due to their relative advantage, were ultimately able to subdue the Nayaka successor states of Vijayanagar, which, in turn, were heavily infantry based. For a long time these rulers too followed that old technique of guerrilla warfare from forest terrains. See Rao, Shulman and Subrahmanyam, *Symbols of Substance*, 240–41.

65. Eraly, *Emperors of the Peacock Throne*, 497.

66. Ibid., 502.

67. It was the periodic revenue remitted from Bengal, though reduced to a third of what it was in Shahjahan's time, that kept even the imperial household going.

68. Deshpande, *Creative Pasts*, 11.

69. Bayly notes that from 'the beginning the Marathas had a plebian character'. One Mughal account notes how 'most of the men in the Maratha army are unendowed with illustrious birth, and husbandmen, carpenters and shopkeepers abound among their soldiery'. As Bayly adds, a leading general like Tukoji Rao Holkar, for instance, was 'only a generation away from a grazing and nomadic background'. In other words, the Marathas also

provided upward mobility to large groups of people in a changing world.

70. Bayly, *Indian Society*, 8.

71. Kulkarni, *The Marathas*. Gangaram's *Maharashtra Purana* from the eighteenth century describes in graphic (and perhaps exaggerated) detail the horrors inflicted by the Marathas in Bengal. As Kulkarni writes, 'Barring the exaggerated part of it, one could hardly deny the anti-Maratha feeling generated' by some of the actions of the great Maratha warlords and their armies that invaded other areas of India. Bayly, *Rulers, Townsmen and Bazaars*, 93. This could lead to economic loss as well. The region of Rewari, for instance, was assessed as capable of providing revenue worth three lakh rupees in the time of emperors Akbar and Aurangzeb. By 1803, however, it was recorded that it was only capable of generating Rs 140,000 due to Maratha 'depredations' that caused much of the population to migrate out of the area.

Bibliography

Books

Alam, Muzaffar, and Sanjay Subrahmanyam. *Indo-Persian Travels in the Age of Discoveries*. Cambridge: Cambridge University Press, 2007.

Alam, Muzaffar, and Sanjay Subrahmanyam. *Writing the Mughal World: Studies on Culture and Politics*. New York: Columbia University Press, 2012.

Alavi, Rafi Ahmad. *Studies in the History of Medieval Deccan*. New Delhi: Idarah-i Adabiyat-i Delli, 2009.

Ali, Omar H. *Malik Ambar: Power and Slavery Across the Indian Ocean*. New York: Oxford University Press, 2016.

Ali, Shanti Sadiq. *The African Dispersal in the Deccan: From Medieval to Modern Times*. Hyderabad: Orient Longman, 1996.

Allen, Charles. *Coromandel: A Personal History of South India*. London: Little Brown, 2017.

Ansari, N.H. *Chronicles of the Seige* [sic] *of Golconda Fort: An Abridged Translation of the Waqa'i of Nimat Khan Ali*. New Delhi: Idarah-i Abadiyat-i Delli, 1975.

Anwar, M. Siraj. *Mughals and the Deccan: Political Relations with Ahmadnagar Kingdom*. Delhi: BR Publishing Corporation, 2007.

Appadurai, Arjun. *Worship and Conflict Under Colonial Rule: A South Indian Case*. Cambridge: Cambridge University Press, 1981.

Ayyangar, S. Krishnaswami, ed. *Sources of Vijayanagar History: Selected and Edited for the University*. Madras: University of Madras, 1919.

Barendse, Rene J. *The Arabian Seas: The Indian Ocean World of the Seventeenth Century*. Armonk: M.E. Sharpe, 2002.

Bayly, C.A. *Indian Society and the Making of the British Empire*. Cambridge: Cambridge University Press, 1988.

Bayly, C.A. *Rulers, Townsmen and Bazaars: North Indian Society in the Age of British Expansion, 1770–1870*. 3rd ed. New Delhi: Oxford University Press, 2012.

Beal, Samuel, trans. *Travels of Fah-Hian and Sung-Yun, Buddhist Pilgrims from China to India (400 AD and 518 AD)*. London: Trubner and Co., 1869.

Bernier, François. *Travels in the Mogul Empire*, trans. Irving Brock. Vol. 1. London: William Pickering, 1826.

Bhave, Y.G. *From the Death of Shivaji to the Death of Aurangzeb: The Critical Years*. New Delhi: Northern Book Centre, 2000.

Briggs, John, trans. *History of the Rise of the Mahomedan Power in India*. Vol. 3. London: Longman, Rees, Orme, Brown & Green, 1829.

Chandra, Satish. *Medieval India: From Sultanat to the Mughals, Delhi Sultanat, Part One*. New Delhi: Har Anand, 2004.

Chandra, Satish. *Medieval India: From Sultanat to the Mughals, Mughal Empire, Part Two*. New Delhi: Har Anand, 2005.

Chandra, Satish. 'The Jagirdari Crisis: A Fresh Look.' In *The Decline of the Mughal Empire*, edited by Meena Bhargava, 13–22. New Delhi: Oxford University Press, 2014.

Chattopadhyaya, B.D. 'Other, or the Others? Varieties of Difference in Indian Society at the Turn of the First Millennium and their Historiographical Implications.' In *The World in the Year 1000*, edited by James Heitzman and Wolfgang Schenkluhn, 303–24. Maryland: University Press of America, 2004.

Chowdhuri, Jogindra Nath. *Malik Ambar: A Biography Based on Original Sources*. Dacca: The Author, 1934.

Cohen, Benjamin B. *Kingship and Colonialism in India's Deccan, 1850–1948*. New York: Palgrave Macmillan, 2007.

Cousens, Henry. *Bijapur: The Old Capital of the Adil Shahi Kings*. Poona: Orphanage Press, 1889.

Dale, Stephen F. *Islamic Society on the South Asian Frontier: The Mappilas of Malabar, 1498–1922*. Oxford: Clarendon Press, 1980.

Davis, Richard H. *Lives of Indian Images*. Princeton: Princeton University Press, 1997.

Deshpande, Prachi. *Creative Pasts: Historical Memory and Identity in Western India, 1700–1960*. New York: Columbia University Press, 2007.

Dowson, John, and H.M. Elliot. *The History of India As Told by its Own Historians*. Vol. 3. London: Trubner & Co., 1871.

Eaton, Richard M. 'A History of the Deccan.' In *Sultans of Deccan India: Opulence and Fantasy, 1500–1700*, edited by Navina Najat Haidar and Marika Sardar, 3–14. New York: The Metropolitan Museum of Art, 2015.

Eaton, Richard M. *A Social History of the Deccan, 1300–1761: Eight Indian Lives*. Cambridge: Cambridge University Press, 2005.

Eaton, Richard M. 'Muhammad bin Tughluq and the Temples of the Deccan.' In *Sultans of the South: Art of India's Deccan Courts, 1323–1687*, edited by Navina Najat Haidar and Marika Sardar. New York: The Metropolitan Museum of Art, 2011.

Eaton, Richard M. *Temple Desecration and Muslim States in Medieval India*. Gurgaon: Hope India, 2004.

Eaton, Richard M. 'The Sufis of Bijapur, 1300–1700.' 1972. (thesis submitted to the University of Wisconsin).

Ekambaram, C.N. *Krishna Deva Raya: His Life and Times*. Madras: The Guardian Press, 1910.

Eraly, Abraham. *Emperors of the Peacock Throne: The Saga of the Great Mughals*. New Delhi: Penguin, 2000.

Eraly, Abraham. *The Mughal Throne: The Saga of India's Great Emperors*. London: Weidenfeld & Nicolson, 2003.

Eraly, Abraham. *The Mughal World: Life in India's Last Golden Age*. New Delhi: Penguin, 2007.

Filliozat, Vasundhara, ed. *The Vijayanagar Empire: As Seen by Domingos Paes and Fernao Nuniz*, trans. Robert Sewell. Delhi: National Book Trust of India, 1977.

Fisher, Michael H., ed. *Visions of Mughal India: An Anthology of European Travel Writing*. London: IB Tauris, 2007.

Flood, Finbarr B. *Objects of Translation: Material Cultural and Medieval 'Hindu-Muslim' Encounter*. Princeton: Princeton University Press, 2009.

Fukazawa, Hiroshi. *A Study of the Local Administration of the Adilshahi Sultanate (AD 1489–1686)* (reprinted from *The Hitotsubhashi Journal of Economics* 3, no. 2 [June 1963]).

Fukazawa, Hiroshi. *The Medieval Deccan: Peasants, Social Systems and States: Sixteenth to Eighteenth Centuries*. Bombay: Oxford University Press, 1991.

Gokhale, B.G. *Surat in the Seventeenth Century: A Study in Urban History of Pre-Modern India*. Bombay: Popular Prakashan, 1979.

Gordon, Stewart. *The New Cambridge History of India: The Marathas, 1600–1818*. Cambridge: Cambridge University Press, 1993.

Gouchani, Abdullah, and Bruce Wannell. 'The Inscriptions of Ibrahim Rauza Tomb.' In *Sultans of the South: Art of India's Deccan Courts, 1323–1687*, edited by Navina Najat Haidar and Marika Sardar. New York: The Metropolitan Museum of Art, 2011.

Green, Nile. *Indian Sufism Since the Seventeenth Century: Saints, Books and Empires in the Muslim Deccan*. Abingdon: Routledge, 2006.

Gribble, J.D.B. *A History of the Deccan*. Vol. 1. London: Luzac & Co., 1896.

Gribble, J.D.B. *A History of the Deccan*. Vol. 2. London: Luzac & Co., 1924.

Haidar, Navina Najat. 'The Art of the Deccan Courts.' In *Sultans of Deccan India: Opulence and Fantasy, 1500–1700*, edited by Navina Najat Haidar and Marika Sardar, 15–28. New York: The Metropolitan Museum of Art, 2015.

Haidar, Navina Najat. 'The Kitab-i-Nauras: Key to Bijapur's Golden Age.' In *Sultans of the South: Art of India's Deccan Courts, 1323–1687*, edited by Navina Najat Haidar and Marika Sardar. New York: The Metropolitan Museum of Art, 2011.

Hall, Kenneth. 'Structural Change and Societal Integration in Early South India: An Introductory Essay.' In *Structure and Society in Early South India: Essays in Honour of Noboru Karashima*, edited by Kenneth Hall, 1–27. New Delhi: Oxford University Press, 2001.

Hansen, Waldemar. *The Peacock Throne: The Drama of Mogul India*. Delhi: Motilal Banarsidass, 1996.

Harris, Jonathan Gil. *The First Firangis: Remarkable Stories of Heroes, Healers, Charlatans, Courtesans & other Foreigners who Became Indian*. New Delhi: Aleph Book Company, 2015.

Heesterman, J.C. 'Was there an Indian Reaction? Western Expansion in Indian Perspective.' In *Expansion and Reaction: Essays on European Expansion and Reaction in Asia and Africa*, edited by H.L. Wesseling, 31–58. Leiden: Leiden University Press, 1978.

Husaini, S.A.Q. 'The Sultanate of Ma'bar.' In *History of the Medieval Deccan*, edited by H.K. Sherwani and P.M. Joshi, 1: 59–75. Hyderabad: Government of Andhra Pradesh, 1973.

Hutton, Deborah. *Art of the Court of Bijapur*. Bloomington: Indiana University Press, 2006.

Hutton, Deborah, and Rebecca Tucker. 'A Dutch Artist in Bijapur.' In *The Visual World of Muslim India: The Art, Culture and Society of the Deccan in the Early Modern Era*, edited by Laura E. Parodi, 205–32. London: IB Tauris, 2014.

Joshi, P.M. *Ali Adil Shah I of Bijapur and his Royal Librarian* (reprinted from the Sardhasatabdi Commemoration Volume. Bombay: Asiatic Society, 1804–1954).

Joshi, P.M. 'The Adil Shahis and the Baridis.' In *History of the Medieval Deccan*, edited by H.K. Sherwani and P.M. Joshi, 291–412. Hyderabad: Government of Andhra Pradesh, 1973.

Joshi, P.M. *The Reign of Ibrahim Adil Shah II of Bijapur* (reprinted from the Munshi Diamond Jubilee Commemoration Volume. Part I. Bharatiya Vidya Bhavan, 1948).

Joshi, P.M., and Mahdi Husain. 'Khaljis and Tughluqs in the Deccan.' In *History of the Medieval Deccan*, edited by H.K. Sherwani and P.M. Joshi, 1: 29–55. Hyderabad: Government of Andhra Pradesh, 1973.

Kamath, Suryanath U. *Krishnadevaraya of Vijayanagar and His Times*. Bangalore: IBH Prakashana, 2009.

Karashima, Noboru. *A Concordance of Nayakas: The Vijayanagar Inscriptions in South India*. New Delhi: Oxford University Press, 2002.

Karashima, Noboru. *Towards a New Formation: South Indian Society Under Vijayanagar Rule*. New Delhi: Oxford University Press, 1992.

Khalidi, Omar. *Muslims in the Deccan: A Historical Survey*. New Delhi: Global Media Publications.

Khan, Iqtidar Alam. *Gunpowder and Firearms: Warfare in Medieval India*. New Delhi: Oxford University Press, 2004.

Khan, Yar Muhammad. *The Deccan Policy of the Mughuls*. Lahore: United Book Corporation, 1971.

Kitab-i-Nauras by Ibrahim Adil Shah II. New Delhi: Bharatiya Kala Kendra, 1956.

Kodad, S.B. *Ramaraya: The De-Facto Ruler of Vijayanagar*. New Delhi: Sri Ramachandra Publications, 1986.

Kulkarni, A.R. *The Marathas*. Pune: Diamond Publications, 2008.

Kumar, Sunil. 'Service, Status, and Military Slavery in the Delhi Sultanate: Thirteenth and Fourteenth Centuries.' In *Slavery and South Asian History*, edited by Indrani Chatterjee and Richard M. Eaton, 83–114. Bloomington: Indiana University Press, 2006.

Kruijtzer, Gijs. 'The Fighting on the Wall: Animal Symbolism of the Deccan in a Eurasian Perspective.' In *The Visual World of Muslim India: The Art, Culture and Society of the Deccan in the Early Modern Era*, edited by Laura E. Parodi, 143–75. London: IB Tauris, 2014.

Lovell, Archibald, trans. *The Travels of Monsieur de Thevenot into the Levant*. Vol. 3. London: H. Clark, 1687.

Mahalingam, T.V. *Administration and Social Life Under Vijayanagar*. Madras: University of Madras, 1940.

Mathew, K.M. *History of the Portuguese Navigation in India (1497–1600)*. Delhi: Mittal, 1988.

McInerney, Terence. 'The Mughals in the Deccan.' In *Sultans of Deccan India: Opulence and Fantasy, 1500–1700*, edited by Navina Najat Haidar and Marika Sardar, 281–84. New York: The Metropolitan Museum of Art, 2015.

Michell, George. 'Migrations and Cultural Transmissions in the Deccan.' In *The Visual World of Muslim India: The Art, Culture and Society of the Deccan in the Early Modern Era*, edited by Laura E. Parodi, 79–95. London: IB Tauris, 2014.

Michell, George, and Mark Zebrowski. *Architecture and Art of the Deccan Sultanates*. Cambridge: Cambridge University Press, 1999.

Michell, George, and Richard Eaton. *Firuzabad: Palace City of the Deccan*. Oxford: Oxford University Press, 1992.

Moorhouse, Geoffrey. *India Britannica*. London: William Collins Sons & Co. Ltd, 1983.

Moreland, W.H. 'From Akbar to Aurangzeb: A Study in Indian Economic History.' In *The Decline of the Mughal Empire*, edited by Meena Bhargava, 1–2. New Delhi: Oxford University Press, 2014.

Moreland, W.H. *Relations of Golconda in the Early Seventeenth Century*. London: The Hakluyt Society, 1931.

Moreland, W.H., and P. Geyl, trans. *Jahangir's India: The Remonstrantie of Francisco Pelsaert*. Cambridge: W. Heffer & Sons Ltd, 1925.

Moxham, Roy. *The Theft of India: The European Conquests of India, 1498–1765*. Noida: HarperCollins India, 2016.

Nayeem, M.A. *External Relations of the Bijapur Kingdom (1489–1686)*. Hyderabad: Bright Publishers, 1974.

Nayeem, M.A., Aniruddha Ray and K.S. Mathew, eds. *Studies in History of the Deccan: Medieval and Modern*. Delhi: Pragati Publications, 2002.

Overton, Keelan. 'Vida de Jacques de Coutre.' In *The Visual World of Muslim India: The Art, Culture and Society of the Deccan in the Early Modern Era*, edited by Laura E. Parodi, 233–64. London: IB Tauris, 2014.

Pearson, Michael. 'Shivaji and the Decline of the Mughal Empire.' In *The Decline of the Mughal Empire*, edited by Meena Bhargava, 84–106. New Delhi: Oxford University Press, 2014.

Perera, L.P.N. *Sexuality in Ancient India: A Study Based on Pali Vinyapitika*. Sri Lanka: University of Kelaniya, 1993.

Phillips, John, trans. *Tavernier's Travels in India*. Calcutta: N. Roy, Bangabasi Press, 1905 (reprinted from the 1677 original).

Raghavan, T.C.A. *Attendant Lords: Bairam Khan and Abdur Rahim, Courtiers and Poets in Mughal India*. Noida: HarperCollins India, 2017.

Ramanujan, A.K., V. Narayana Rao and David Shulman, eds. *When God is a Customer: Telugu Courtesan Songs by Ksetrayya and Others*. Berkeley: University of California Press, 1994.

Rao, C. Hayavadana. *Mysore Gazetteer*. Vol. 2. Part 3. Bangalore: Government of Mysore, 1930.

Rao, K.G. Gopala Krishna. *Sri Krishnadevaraya: Monarch of Vijayanagara*. Bangalore: Bharatiya Vidya Bhavan, 2010.

Rao, M. Rama. *Krishnadeva Raya*. Delhi: National Book Trust of India, 1971.

Rao, P. Setu Madhava. *Eighteenth Century Deccan*. Bombay: Popular Prakashan, 1963.

Rao, V. Narayana, David Shulman and Sanjay Subrahmanyam. *Symbols of Substance: Court and State in Nayaka Period Tamilnadu*. New Delhi: Oxford University Press, 1992.

Rathore, Manya. "'Floating Political Rhetoric"in the Indian Ocean.' In *The Indian Ocean in the Making of Early Modern India*, edited by Pius Malekandathil, 249–62. Abingdon: Routledge, 2017.

Rau, G. Hari Sarvottama. *The Neglected Emperor Poet: A Critical Essay on Krishnadeva Raya's Amuktamalyada*. Madras: Jyotishmati Press, 1912.

Reddy, D. Ramalinga. *Vijayanagar and Its Lessons for Modern India*. Madras: University of Madras, 1967.

Richards, John F. 'The Imperial Crisis in the Deccan.' In *The Decline of the Mughal Empire*, edited by Meena Bhargava, 53–83. New Delhi: Oxford University Press, 2014.

Rocco, Sha. *Golconda and the Qutb Shahs*. Hyderabad: Government Central Press, 1929.

Rotzer, Klaus. 'Deccani Guns.' In *The Visual World of Muslim India: The Art, Culture and Society of the Deccan in the Early Modern Era*, edited by Laura E. Parodi, 123–42. London: IB Tauris, 2014.

Row, Suryanarain. *A History of Vijayanagar: The Never to be Forgotten Empire*. Madras: Addison & Co., 1910.

Saletore, B.A. *Social and Political Life in the Vijayanagara Empire*. Vol. 1. Madras: BG Paul & Co., 1934.

Sardar, Marika. 'The Bahmanis and Their Artistic Legacy.' In *Sultans of Deccan India: Opulence and Fantasy, 1500–1700*, edited by Navina Najat Haidar and Marika Sardar, 29–33. New York: The Metropolitan Museum of Art, 2015.

Sardesai, Govind Sakharam. *New History of the Marathas: Shivaji and his Line*. Vol. 1. Bombay: Phoenix Publications, 1946.

Sarkar, Jadunath. *Anecdotes of Aurangzib and Historical Essays*. Calcutta: MC Sarkar & Sons, 1917.

Sathianathaier, R. *Tamilaham in the 17th Century*. Madras: University of Madras, 1956.

Seshan, Radhika. *Trade and Politics on the Coromandel Coast*. Delhi: Primus Books, 2012.

Sewell, Robert. *A Forgotten Empire (Vijayanagar): A Contribution to the History of India*. London: Swan Sonnenschein & Co. Ltd, 1900.

Sharma, M.H. Rama. *The History of the Vijayanagar Empire: Beginnings and Expansion*. Bombay: Popular Prakashan, 1978.

Sharma, M.H. Rama. *The History of the Vijayanagar Empire: The Last Phase*. Bombay: Popular Prakashan, 1980.

Sherwani, H.K. 'The Bahmanis.' In *History of the Medieval Deccan*, edited by H.K. Sherwani and P.M. Joshi, 1: 143–222. Hyderabad: Government of Andhra Pradesh, 1973.

Sherwani, H.K. *The Bahmanis of the Deccan: An Objective Study*. Hyderabad: Saood Manzil Himayatnagar, 1953.

Sherwani, H.K. *Muhammad-Quli Qutb Shah: Founder of Haidarabad*. London: Asia Publishing House, 1967.

Sherwani, H.K. 'The Qutb Shahis of Golkonda-Hydarabad.' In *History of the Medieval Deccan*, edited by H.K. Sherwani and P.M. Joshi, 1: 413–90. Hyderabad: Government of Andhra Pradesh, 1973.

Shyam, Radhey. 'The Imad Shahs.' In *History of the Medieval Deccan*, edited by H.K. Sherwani and P.M. Joshi, 1: 277–87. Hyderabad: Government of Andhra Pradesh, 1973.

Shyam, Radhey. *The Kingdom of Ahmadnagar*. Delhi: Motilal Banarsidass, 1966.

Shyam, Radhey. 'The Nizam Shahis.' In *History of the Medieval Deccan*, edited by H.K. Sherwani and P.M. Joshi, 1: 225–76. Hyderabad: Government of Andhra Pradesh, 1973.

Siddiqi, Muhammad Suleman. *The Bahmani Sufis*. Delhi: Idarah-i Abadiyat-i Delli, 2009.

Sinha, S.K. *Mediaeval History of the Deccan*. Hyderabad: Government of Andhra Pradesh, 1964.

Sitapathi, P. *Farmans and Sanads of the Deccan Sultans (1408–1687)*. Hyderabad: Andhra Pradesh State Archives, 1980.

Smith, David. *Hinduism and Modernity*. Malden: Blackwell Publishing, 2003.

Stein, Burton. *Vijayanagara*. Cambridge: Cambridge University Press, 1989.

Stoker, Valerie. *Polemics and Patronage in the City of Victory: Vyasatirtha, Hindu Sectarianism, and the Sixteenth-Century Vijayanagara Court*. Oakland: University of California Press, 2016.

Subrahmanyam, R. 'Vijayanagar.' In *History of the Medieval Deccan*, edited by H.K. Sherwani and P.M. Joshi, 1: 79–139. Hyderabad: Government of Andhra Pradesh, 1973.

Subrahmanyam, Sanjay. 'Europeans in the Deccan.' In *Sultans of Deccan India: Opulence and Fantasy, 1500–1700*, edited by Navina Najat Haidar and Marika Sardar, 309–12. New York: The Metropolitan Museum of Art, 2015.

Subrahmanyam, Sanjay. *Courtly Encounters: Translating Courtliness and Violence in Early Modern Eurasia*. Cambridge: Harvard University Press, 2012.

Subrahmanyam, Sanjay. *The Portuguese Empire in Asia, 1500–1700: A Political and Economic History*. 2nd ed. Chichester: John Wiley & Sons, 2012.

Subrahmanyam, Sanjay. *Three Ways to be Alien: Travails & Encounters in the Early Modern World*. Waltham: Brandeis University Press, 2011.

Talbot, Cynthia. 'The Nayakas of Vijayanagara Andhra: A Preliminary Prosopography.' In *Structure and Society in Early South India: Essays in Honour of Noboru Karashima*, edited by Kenneth Hall, 251–75. New Delhi: Oxford University Press, 2001.

Taylor, Meadows. *The History of India: From the Earliest Period to the Present*. London: Longmans, Green & Co., 1870.

Thangasamy, S.A. *Vijayanagar Empire: A Brief History*. Madurai: Pannai Pathipagam, 1978.

The Cambridge History of India, Vol. 4, The Mughul Period. S. Chand & Co., 1971.

Truschke, Audrey. *Aurangzeb: The Man and the Myth*. Karachi: Oxford University Press, 2017.

Vanita, Ruth, and Saleem Kidwai, eds. 'Khaljis in Love.' In *Same-Sex Love in India*. New York: Palgrave, 2001.

Vanita, Ruth, and Saleem Kidwai, eds. *Same-Sex Love in India*. New York: Palgrave, 2001.

Wagoner, Phillip B. *Tidings of the King: A Translation and Ethnohistorical Analysis of the Rayavacakamu*. Honolulu: University of Hawaii Press, 1993.

Waring, Edward Scott. *A History of the Mahrattas: To Which is Prefixed an Historical Sketch of the Decan Containing a Short Account of the Rise and Fall of the Mooslim Sovereignties Prior to the Era of Mahratta Independence*. London: John Richardson, Royal Exchange, 1810.

Watson, Adam. *The War of the Goldsmith's Daughter*. London: Chatto & Windus, 1964.

Weinstein, Laura. 'Variations on a Persian Theme.' In *The Visual World of Muslim India: The Art, Culture and Society of the Deccan in the Early Modern Era*, edited by Laura E. Parodi, 179–204. London: IB Tauris, 2014.

Wheeler, J. Talboys. *The History of India Under Mussulman Rule*. London: Trubner & Co., 1876.

Yazdani, Ghulam. *Bidar: Its History and Monuments*. Delhi: Motilal Banarsidass Publishers, 1995.

Zakaria, Rafiq. *Razia, Queen of India*. Karachi: Oxford University Press, 1966.

Zelliot, Eleanor. 'Medieval Encounter between Hindu and Muslim: Eknath's Drama-Poem *Hindu Turk Samvad*.' In *Images of Man: Religion and Historical Process in South Asia*, edited by Fred W. Clothey, 171–95. Madras: New Era Publications, 1982.

Zupanov, Ines G. *Disputed Mission: Jesuit Experiments and Brahmanical Knowledge in Seventeenth-Century India*. New Delhi: Oxford University Press, 1999.

Journal Articles

Alam, Muzaffar, and Sanjay Subrahmanyam. 'The Deccan Frontier and Mughal Expansion, ca. 1600: Contemporary Perspectives.' In *Journal of the Economic and Social History of the Orient* 47, no. 3 (2007): 357–89.

Ali, Daud. 'Between Market and Court: The Careers of Two Courtier-Merchants in the Twelfth Century Deccan.' In *Journal of the Economic and Social History of the Orient* 53, no. 1/2 (2010): 185–211.

Ali, M. Athar, 'The Passing of Empire.' In *Modern Asian Studies* 9, no. 3 (1975): 385–96.

Ali, Mir Mahmood. 'Contributions of the Bahmani Kings to Indian Civilisation.' In *Proceedings of the Indian History Congress* 5 (1941): 593–96.

Anooshahr, Ali. 'The Elephant and the Sovereign.' In *Journal of the Royal Asiatic Society* (March 2018): 1–30.

Ansari, Muhammad Azhar. 'The Economic Condition of Golconda in the 17th Century (From European Sources).' In *Proceedings of the Indian History Congress* 27 (1965): 229–37.

Anwar, M. Siraj. 'The Safavids and Mughal Relations with the Deccan States.' In *Proceedings of the Indian History Congress* 52 (1991): 255–62.

Bayly, C.A., and Sanjay Subrahmanyam. 'Portfolio Capitalists and the Political Economy of Early Modern India.' In *The Indian Economic and Social History Review* 25, no. 4 (1988): 411–24.

Chekuri, Christopher. 'A "Share" in the "World Empire": Nayamkara as Sovereignty in Practice at Vijayanagara, 1480–1580.' In *Social Scientist* 40, no. 1/2 (2012): 41–67.

Davis, Richard H. 'A Muslim Princess in the Temples of Visnu.' In *International Journal of Hindu Studies* 8, no. 1/3 (2004): 137–56.

Deshpande, Madhav M. 'Ksatriyas in the Kali Age.' In *Indo-Iranian Journal* 53, no. 2 (2010): 95–120.

Eaton, Richard M. '"Kiss My Foot", said the King.' In *Modern Asian Studies* 43, no. 1 (2009): 289–313.

Eaton, Richard M., and Philip B. Wagoner. 'Warfare on the Deccan Plateau, 1450–1600: A Military Revolution in Early Modern India?' In *Journal of World History* 25, no. 1 (2014): 5–50.

Findly, Ellison B. 'The Capture of Maryam-uz-Zamani's Ship: Mughal Women and European Traders.' In *Journal of the American Oriental Society* 108, no. 2 (1988): 227–38.

Firouzeh, Peyvand. 'Sacred Kingship in the Garden of Poetry: Ahmad Shah Bahmani's Tomb in Bidar.' In *South Asian Studies* 31, no. 2 (2015): 187–214.

Flatt, Emma J. 'Practicing Friendship: Epistolary Constructions of Social Intimacy in the Bahmani Sultanate.' In *Studies in History* 33, no. 1 (2017): 61–81.

Flatt, Emma J. 'The Authorship and Significance of the Nujum al-ulum: A Sixteenth-Century Astrological Encyclopedia from Bijapur.' In *Journal of the American Oriental Society* 131, no. 2 (2011): 223–44.

Gokhale, B.G. 'Tobacco in Seventeenth-Century India.' In *Agricultural History* 48, no. 4 (1974): 481–92.

Gray, Basil. 'Deccani Paintings: The School of Bijapur.' In *The Burlington Magazine for Connoisseurs* 73, no. 42 (1938): 74–77.

Guha, Sumit. 'The Frontiers of Memory: What the Marathas Remembered of Vijayanagara.' In *Modern Asian Studies* 43, no. 1 (2009): 269–88.

Guha, Sumit. 'Transitions and Translations.' In *Comparative Studies of South Asia, Africa and the Middle East* 24, no. 2 (2004): 23–31.

Haig, Wolseley. 'The Religion of Ahmed Shah Bahmani.' In *Journal of the Royal Asiatic Society of Great Britain and Ireland*, no. 1 (1924): 73–80.

Hutton, Deborah. 'Memory and Monarchy: A Seventeenth-Century Painting from Bijapur and its Afterlives.' In *South Asian Studies* 32, no. 1 (2016): 22–41.

Khan, Mir Ahmad Ali. 'The Condition of Education under the Bahmanis.' In *Proceedings of the Indian History Congress* 5 (1941): 586–93.

Kruijtzer, Gijs. 'Madanna, Akkanna and the Brahmin Revolution.' In *Journal of the Economic and Social History of the Orient* 45, no. 2 (2002): 231–67.

Kulkarni, G.T. 'A Note on Mirza Rajah Jai Singh's Purander and Bijapur Campaigns.' In *Proceedings of the Indian History Congress* 71 (2010–11): 274–83.

Kulkarni, G.T. 'A Note on Taxation under the Bahmanis based on an Unpublished Bahmani "Farman" (1514 AD).' In *Proceedings of the Indian History Congress* 59 (1998): 287–92.

Kulkarni, G.T. 'Deccan (Maharastra) under the Muslim Rulers from Khaljis to Shivaji.' In *Bulletin of the Deccan College Research Institute* 51/52 (1991–92): 501–10.

Laine, James W. 'The Dharma of Islam and the Din of Hinduism.' In *International Journal of Hindu Studies* 3, no. 3 (1999): 299–318.

Mangalam, S.J., and M.R. Kantak. 'A Grant of Muhammad Adil Shah II to the Temple of Vithoba.' In *Bulletin of the Deccan College Research Institute* 46 (1987): 59–63.

Mengesha, Astair Gebremariam. 'The Habshis.' In *International Journal of Ethiopian Studies* 1, no. 1 (2003): 91–102.

Michell, George, and Sugandha Johar. 'The Maratha Complex at Ellora.' In *South Asian Studies* 28, no. 1 (2012): 69–88.

Minorsky, V. 'The Qara-Qoyunlu and the Qutb-Shahs.' In *Bulletin of the School of Oriental and African Studies* 17, no. 1 (1955): 50–73.

Moosvi, Shireen, 'The Mughal Empire and the Deccan: Economic Factors and Consequences.' In *Proceedings of the Indian History Congress*, 43 (1982): 365–82.

Palat, Ravi Arvind. 'Popular Revolts and the State in Medieval South India: A Study of the Vijayanagara Empire (1360–1565).' In *Bijdragen tot de Taal-, Land-, en Volkenkunde* 142, no. 1 (1986): 128–44.

Rao, Ajay K. 'From Fear to Hostility: Responses to the Conquests of Madurai.' *South Asian Studies* 32, no. 1 (2016): 68–79.

Sardar, Marika. 'The Circular Cities of the Deccan.' In *The Visual World of Muslim India: The Art, Culture and Society of the Deccan in the Early Modern Era*, edited by Laura E. Parodi, 3–30. London: IB Tauris, 2014.

Sarkar, Jagadish Narayan. 'A Letter of Abdullah Qutb Shah to Shah Abbas II.' In *Proceedings of the Indian History Congress* 5 (1941): 607–09.

Sarma, P. Sree Rama. 'Rama Raya's Policy.' In *Proceedings of the Indian History Congress* 36 (1975): 142–56.

Shaikh, C.H. 'Literary Personages of Ahmadnagar.' In *Bulletin of the Deccan College Research Institute* 2, no. 3/4 (1941): 383–96.

Sharma, Ramesh Chandra. 'The Diamond Mines of the Deccan during the Second Half of the Seventeenth Century.' In *Proceedings of the Indian History Congress* 44 (1983): 234–50.

Shastry, B.S. 'Commercial Policy of the Portuguese vis-à-vis the Adil Shahis of Bijapur in the Seventeenth Century AD.' In *Proceedings of the Indian History Congress* 48 (1987): 632–40.

Shivarudraswamy, S.N. 'Hindu–Muslim Relations under the Vijayanagara Empire.' In *Proceedings of the Indian History Congress* 66 (2005–06): 394–98.

Sherwani, H.K. 'The Reign of Sultan Humayun Shah Bahmani and His Character.' In *Proceedings of the Indian History Congress* 3 (1939): 688–700.

Siddiqi, A.M. 'Mohammad Shah II Bahmani: The Pioneer of the Medieval Culture of the Deccan.' *Proceedings of the Indian History Congress* 5 (1941): 582–86.

Singh, Seema. 'Golconda Chintz.' In *Proceedings of the Indian History Congress* 49 (1988): 301–05.

Sinopoli, Carla M. 'From the Lion Throne: Political and Social Dynamics of the Vijayanagara Empire.' In *Journal of the Economic and Social History of the Orient* 43, no. 3 (2000): 364–98.

Sohoni, Pushkar. 'From Defended Settlements to Fortified Strongholds: Responses to Gunpowder in the Early Modern Deccan.' In *South Asian Studies* 31, no. 1 (2015): 111–26.

Sohoni, Pushkar. 'Vernacular as a Space: Writing in the Deccan.' In *South Asian History and Culture* 7, no. 3 (2016): 258–70.

Subrahmanyam, Sanjay. 'Iranians Abroad: Intra-Asian Elite Migration and Early Modern State Formation.' In *Journal of Asian Studies* 51, no. 2 (1992): 340–63.

Subrahmanyam, Sanjay. 'Persians, Pilgrims and Portuguese.' In *Modern Asian Studies* 22, no. 3 (1988): 503–30.

Subrahmanyam, Sanjay. 'The Life and Actions of Mathias de Albuquerque (1547–1609): A Portuguese Source for Deccan History.' In *Portuguese Studies* 11 (1995): 62–77.

Subrahmanyam, Sanjay. 'The Portuguese Response to the Rise of Masulipatam.' In *The Great Circle* 8, no. 2 (1986): 127–31.

Talbot, Cynthia. 'Inscribing the Self: Hindu–Muslim Identities in Pre-Colonial India.' In *Comparative Studies in Society and History* 37, no. 4 (1995): 692–722.

Thomaz, Luis Filipe F.R. 'Iranian Diaspora and the Deccan Sultanates in India: A Study of Sixteenth Century Portuguese Sources.' In *Studies in History* 30, no. 1 (2014): 1–42.

Wagoner, Phillip B. 'Money Use in the Deccan.' *Indian Economic and Social History Review* 54, no. 4 (2014): 457–80.

Wagoner, Phillip B. '"Sultan among Hindu Kings": Dress, Titles and the Islamicization of Hindu Culture at Vijayanagara.' In *Journal of Asian Studies* 55, no. 4 (1996): 851–80.

Acknowledgements

This book is a tribute to the Deccan, a place much neglected in retellings of India's past. Whether it does justice to its ambition, however, is quite another discussion.

For me, the Deccan was the scene of my boyhood years. Pune, where I was raised, lives still in awe of Shivaji, though every now and then, almost by accident, tantalizing glimpses appear of a time before that celebrated king. The names of obscure Sultans were woven through my school textbooks – a Nizam Shah here, an Adil Shah there – all, however, in supporting roles on a stage dominated by another. Some fragments remained with me from my childhood, and then travel, much later, resurrected others. A few months in Goa four years ago, for instance, led again to an encounter with the Adil Shahs whose palace stands reincarnated there as a popular cultural centre. A train to the south during a holiday, similarly, halted at a hot, dry place called Gulbarga, where too, I remembered, lay buried heroes from a forgotten universe. The stories were all around me, and over time I became their admiring collector.

The decision to write a short, readable account – a modest overview of this majestic chapter of Indian history – took form, however, only in 2016. In October that year I made a visit to Hyderabad and spent a day amidst the ruins of the fort of Golconda. My then colleague Aalim Javeri acted as my tour guide as we trekked up the hillside, and his mother, Begum Scheherazade Javeri, told me much about the tombs of the Qutb Shahs. They all survive in dilapidated splendour, but I began, at last, to think of putting pen to paper.

What you have read, it must be said, stands on the shoulders of the works of many generations of scholars. From H.K. Sherwani and P.M. Joshi to Richard Eaton and Sanjay Subrahmanyam, it is to the depth of their scholarship and the painstaking detail of their research that I owe my chief debt as the writer of this volume. If there are strengths to this book, they come from the excellent sources that appear in my bibliography. But where there are weaknesses – as there necessarily must be – these deserve to be laid at my door alone. It was my decision to structure this book in the way that it appears, covering some centuries but not others, including certain characters at the cost of their brothers.

There were some tricky bends I had to negotiate with my material. There is, for instance, only the Portuguese translation of a letter that reveals how the king of Vijayanagar sought a bride from faraway Lisbon. Uncorroborated elsewhere, the letter is an old one, and in accepting its contents I trusted the judgement of reputable scholars who saw no reason to raise questions. Ferishta, similarly, is a useful chronicler of information, but comes with biases, and not a little selective exaggeration. Once again, where the wisdom of senior historians accepts him, I do the same; where he has been challenged, I too attempt to follow suit. It is a dangerous thing, Mary Beard once wrote, to fancy ourselves better historians than those who came before, and I am content to trust in the judgement of the more gifted.

When this book was at last written, a number of people offered me help and guidance. Varun Rana in Delhi combed through the first draft of my manuscript and gave me both his opinion and a boost of friendly confidence. Dr Pushkar Sohoni of IISER, Pune, an excellent scholar of the Deccan, was most encouraging and made time between his own projects to go through my work. Anirudh Kanisetti, a bright, gifted researcher at the Takshashila Institute in Bengaluru, was incisive and discerning in his comments, reading through hundreds of pages between his travels. And in Thiruvananthapuram, Prof. P. Vijayakumar, one of the most informed minds I have had the privilege of knowing, gave me valuable observations and several suggestions.

Thanks are also due to Sunil Khilnani, William Dalrymple, Muzaffar Alam, Navina Najat Haidar and Rudrangshu Mukherjee for their words of praise – their endorsement means a great deal. At Juggernaut, Chiki Sarkar and Nandini Mehta were, as ever, sharp in their comments and reviews, while Cincy Jose and Shyama Warner deserve my thanks for their patience and careful attention. Gavin Morris helped create a beautiful cover for this book, capturing perfectly the world of the Rebel Sultans. But most of all it is to Parth Phiroze Mehrotra, friend and editor, that I am grateful to for his support and calming wisdom.

Before I conclude this note, I must also express my immense gratitude for the help and encouragement I have received from Gitanjali and Sandeep Maini in Bengaluru. Friends, and now sponsors of my research, this book would not have been possible without the generosity of the Maini Foundation. I hope they will find in its pages an endeavour they are proud to have supported.

And finally, I reserve my most important line of thanks for three special people – MS, Pushpa, and Indrani – to whom I remain forever dedicated.

Manu S. Pillai
London, April 2018

Index

A Note on the Author

Manu S. Pillai is an Indian writer whose book *The Ivory Throne* won the Sahitya Akademi Yuva Puraskar in 2017. Currently studying for a PhD at King's College London, he is also the author of *The Courtesan, the Mahatma & the Italian Brahmin*, a collection of essays compiled from his column in *Mint Lounge* (2016–2019). His writing has appeared in *The Hindu, Hindustan Times, Times of India, New Statesman* and other publications. *Rebel Sultans* is his second book.

juggernaut

THE APP FOR INDIAN READERS

Fresh, original books tailored for mobile and for India. Starting at ₹10.

juggernaut.in

1

CRAFTED
FOR MOBILE
READING

Thought you would never read a book
on mobile? Let us prove you wrong.

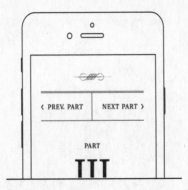

Beautiful Typography

The quality of print transferred
to your mobile. Forget ugly PDFs.

Customizable Reading

Read in the font size, spacing
and background of your liking.

AN EXTENSIVE LIBRARY

Including fresh, new, original Juggernaut books from the likes of Sunny Leone, Praveen Swami, Husain Haqqani, Umera Ahmed, Rujuta Diwekar and lots more. Plus, books from partner publishers and loads of free classics. Whichever genre you like, there's a book waiting for you.

DON'T JUST READ; INTERACT

We're changing the reading experience from passive to active.

Ask authors questions

Get all your answers from the horse's mouth.
Juggernaut authors actually reply to every
question they can.

Rate and review

Let everyone know of your favourite reads or
critique the finer points of a book – you will be
heard in a community of like-minded readers.

Gift books to friends

For a book-lover, there's no nicer gift than
a book personally picked. You can even
do it anonymously if you like.

Enjoy new book formats

Discover serials released in parts over
time, picture books including comics,
and story-bundles at discounted rates.
And coming soon, audiobooks.

juggernaut.in

4

LOWEST PRICES & ONE-TAP BUYING

Books start at ₹10 with regular discounts and free previews.

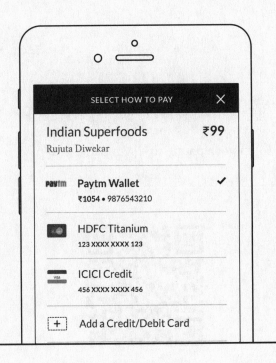

Paytm Wallet, Cards & Apple Payments

On Android, just add a Paytm Wallet once and buy any book with one tap. On iOS, pay with one tap with your iTunes-linked debit/credit card.

Click the QR Code with a QR scanner app
or type the link into the Internet browser
on your phone to download the app.

For our complete catalogue, visit www.juggernaut.in
To submit your book, send a synopsis and two
sample chapters to books@juggernaut.in
For all other queries, write to contact@juggernaut.in